GETTING DEALS DONE

FATHERS AND SONS
MELVIN AND MARIO
DENZEL AND JOHN DAVID
JULIUS AND CHRIS
WILL, TREY, AND JADEN
FRED AND LAMONT
CLIFF AND THEO
JAMES, J.J., AND MICHAEL
OLU DARA AND NAS
STEPH AND CANON
FURIOUS AND TRE
CARL AND EDDIE
GEORGE AND LIONEL
JOHN AND MILES
ME AND MINE

GETTING DEALS DONE

The Memoirs of a Super-Achiever in an Era of Apex Capitalism

Patrick A. Howell

Repeater

Published by Repeater Books

An imprint of Watkins Media Ltd

Unit 11 Shepperton House

89-93 Shepperton Road

London

N1 3DF

United Kingdom

www.repeaterbooks.com

A Repeater Books paperback original 2026

1

Distributed in the United States by Random House, Inc., New York.

Frontispiece photograph by Brevin Blach, and artwork by Milton Bowens.

ISBN: 9781915672919

Ebook ISBN: 9781915672902

Printed and bound by CPI Group (UK) Ltd, Croydon, CR0 4YY

FSC www.fsc.org MIX Paper | Supporting responsible forestry FSC® C013604

"Your task is not to seek for love, but merely to seek and find all the barriers within yourself that you have built against it."

—Rumi

This work is a memoir first — told through the lens of capital markets, ancestry, and the lived experience of race in America and the diaspora.

In God We Trust. In Cash We Pay.

Table of Contents

Dedications

"Daddy"
—Dr. Bing P. Howell

Dr. Reverend Mark E. Whitlock of the ***African Methodist Episcopalian*** Church and **Dr. Thomas Parham**, architect of the **100 Black Men of America** Passport Program — *Superheroes* aren't people idolized in the movies or social media. Heroes are folks *you know* in your community.

Leslie K. Brown, thank you for being my first mentor and an exceptional exemplar — never dreamed I would learn so much high- heel shopping in Manhattan! Also, big sis, thank you for your introduction to **Sabrina Lamb** and her incredible disruptor **World of Money**.

John J. Kennedy, rest in continued prosperity, & thank you Sir for all the ancestral keys to the doors of opportunity from Historic Pasadena — your sartorial resplendence, a massive heart and keen intelligence that always moved us forward in BIG steps.

Roona Moore, thank you for the leadership and friendship at Wells Fargo Treasury Management. Knowing your Chris is well. My kind regards.

Lion in Winter **Tony** "*The Truth*" **Thompson**, thank you Godfather for demonstrating the power of perseverance, redemption, and abundance. Thank you for the incredible friendship — continued blessings — you bad! I mean, *good.*

Mary Borg, you are the very best at what you do. Thank you for the guidance, leadership and being a cool exemplar at Bank of the West

Cecil J. Howell, a.k.a. QoolBreeze, a.k.a. the Goodfather, a.k.a. Man of Deen, thanks brother — you know what for…

Thank you, **Mommy**, love you, sweetie.

Hanna, life partner, love you sweetie — and you know I know you are a cutie pie

God Almighty, father, thank you for that Spirit Force — I am your imminent remarkable Noble Man

Introduction: Capital Formation

Aiming for Greatness and Doing Some Good, One Deal at a Time

Patrick and I have been friends and colleagues for over three decades, bonding over shared experiences, perspectives, a love of family, and our passion for capital market formation. We've witnessed firsthand the successes and failures of many, the roller coaster of the capital markets and the American economy, and lived lives far richer than many. Why? Because we both embody the spirit of Patrick's book, *Getting Deals Done*. We are enthusiastic doers, embracing and learning from both triumphs and setbacks, but always moving forward.

A true test of friendship is the ability to respect differing opinions. With us, it's never been a question. We value each other's perspectives, whether we agree or agree to disagree, knowing we both represent what our country stands for: unity, respect for freedom of speech, and the pursuit of success in the best country for those with aspirations. We share a capitalist heart, guided by Benjamin Franklin's mantra of "doing well by doing good."

Our goals in the capital markets extend beyond personal gain. Specifically, we strive:

- To create a better future for our children, as our parents did.
- To learn from mentors and pay it forward.
- To lead by example and action.
- To earn without exploiting others and empower those who follow us.
- To acquire more resources, so that we can help others more.

Our journey began in the dynamic landscape of Southern California. When I started in the financial markets in the '90s, I was often the only Asian American at financial conferences across the U.S. In Southern California. There is an imaginary line between Los Angeles and Orange County referred to as "The Orange Curtain." At its center is Newport Beach, the epicenter and last bastion of the country club GOP in California. This is where the money is, and it's where both Patrick and I launched our capital markets careers. When we first crossed paths in those rooms, Patrick was often the only Black man. We both understood the challenges of being outliers, but also recognized the power of the "green" equalizer: money.

Newport Beach is the heart of Orange County by design. Positioned on the "Pacific Riviera" with unparalleled beauty, the financial hub revolves around Newport Center Drive, where all the players have offices. At its core is Fashion Island, where power lunches are the norm for a world-class community of investors and financiers with PIMCO at its zenith. Newport is predominantly white, including the capital market players. We both stood out as anomalies and had to overcome obstacles to be accepted. As I noted earlier, I was usually the only Asian American — and *always* the only one willing to speak.

We used different tactics to become players in the financial world, but we shared similar traits: charisma, confidence, knowledge, respect for mentors, and a readiness to fight our way in with a smile. Patrick is a master networker, a "super connector" and "force multiplier" and has been since before those terms existed, forging connections with influential figures even in the pre-LinkedIn era. While my comfort zone has been in building relationships with high-profile athletes, Patrick's prowess in the financial and political world is unmatched.

Like Patrick's, my experience in capital formation markets is unique. I've been involved in every stage of the business lifecycle, from a napkin-sketch idea to IPO (initial public offering) to M&A (merger and acquisition). I've been party to every perspective: the entrepreneur's sweat and tears, the investor's capital deployment, and the facilitator's role as an advisor, consultant, and broker. We are dealmakers. What's your deal? We've been there and done that, thriving under the high-stakes pressure of our industry.

As I write this, I've relocated to the East Coast, building on existing relationships and forging new ones in the vibrant Raleigh-Durham-Cary region of North Carolina. After leaving my career in professional sports, I became the U.S. point man for a German VC fund. Eventually, I became CEO of one of our tech portfolio companies, taking it public at age 28 with the help of investment banker Grant Bettingen, a major player at the time. Grant often collaborated with industry veterans like Gary E. Bryant, one of Patrick's mentors.

In the early 2000s, I launched ProFormance Capital, a boutique investment bank focused on emerging growth companies, doubling as a family office. I created a first-of-its-kind investment showcase series featuring our portfolio companies and clients at Crevier Auto Museum in Costa Mesa. We produced high-end events with cars, cigars, hors d'oeuvres, wineries, microbreweries, and news crew profiles. Our events foreshadowed the rise of experiential marketing in finance. Attendees were capital sources, broker-dealers, accredited and institutional investors, key business leadership, and market makers. Patrick and I delight in job creation, economic development, serving as conduits for prosperity and abundance, and leading in the business community while being socially moderate and sensible.

This is where I first met Patrick — at one of my events. He was the first Black attendee we ever had. Actually, he was the first minority to attend besides myself, friends, staff, and interns. Patrick introduced himself, and we quickly sensed a camaraderie. From then on, we would see each other often, and we were frequently the only Black and Asian men present. Despite growing up in diverse areas, we understood the subtle nuances of race and power dynamics in the business world, recognizing that true equality often comes down to financial success.

Sometime later, I received an invitation to attend an investor conference at the Balboa Bay Club, a hub for Newport's old-school wealth. Patrick was running the event, and his acumen had grown significantly. It was evident. It was the first of many events he produced, blending all he absorbed from family, friends, colleagues, professors, and mentors like Gary E. Bryant and Grant Bettingen. He made it his own, hosting a series of events at high-end venues like the Pacific Hotel, Island Hotel, The Four Seasons, Beverly Wilshire, and upscale bistros along the Pacific Coast Riviera. His events exposed nearly 300 companies to billions in funding opportunities across various industries.

We share similar goals, ambitions, and a moral code, and we relate to the challenges of being outliers in our respective communities. I am proud of my Chinese American heritage, a fourth-generation American on my father's side. In many ways, Patrick and I are pioneers and trailblazers, carving a path for others like us in the financial world. We certainly aren't the first or the only ones, but I know we both have played important roles in fostering more diversity in markets and capital formation and creating an inclusive environment.

In 2017, I co-founded DPOUSA, a direct funding platform ahead of its time, and assembled the DPOUSA Special Council, a group of 50 leaders from diverse backgrounds. With Patrick's instrumental support, we continued to promote progress. While some ventures have come and gone, we remain steadfast in our pursuit of new heights for ourselves, our families, our teams, and all the stakeholders in our lives.

Patrick's story, as told in *Getting Deals Done*, is a testament to the power of perseverance, mentorship, and an unwavering belief in the American dream. It is a story that will inspire anyone who has ever dared to dream big, challenge the status quo, and create a new reality.

Brian has over 30 years of professional experience, including as CEO and COO of publicly traded and privately held companies. Brian is the COO of Small Business Development Group, Inc., the parent company of Stony Hill Advisors. https://www.stonyhilladvisors.com/brian-jue

Brian J. Jue

Preface

When I contemplate my ancestors and all that they have left to me, I do not know what to do. *Truly*, it is a humbling and overwhelming experience of *gratitude* — I cannot put it into words, and I'm good with the verbs, even better with transitions, and practiced at the values and ideas that spirit language. Fundamentally, however, *I am exalted*. When I contemplate the Transatlantic Slave Trade, I recognize the face of *Love*. Somehow, we survived one of the most brutal, dysmorphic, inhumane acts of terrorism in the history of mankind. And that's nearly *inconceivable* when you consider the existence and atrocities of spirits such as Adolf Hitler, Mobutu, King Leopold II, Idi Amin or Augusto Pinochet and the resurrection of those spirits in the modern era into the very political discourse of our current zeitgeist. *Evil* is alive and well. That is our light and our resilience in the face of *true* terror and even starker evil. I am overwhelmed with a sense of imperial and immaculate *power*. These are the burdens we bear from our ancestors in the modern age: the *weight of responsibility*, the weight of knowing and doing better, of *being our best. That's why those sacrifices were made.* I understand the power of prayers, the powers of our homeland, the power of our people *(humankind)*, the power of my spirit, and I understand the power of intuition, instinct and intention. I understand my God and His Spirit Force. We are not here because *they*, evil incarnated, wanted us here. We *are where we are because* we *survived… because our spirit found a way to thrive despite the unimaginable. We are here because we are Blessed and Chosen.*

We should not be where we are based upon what happened when Africa's children were spread out around the globe in the Transatlantic Slave Trade, murdered, raped and bereft of our culture, traditions and language and subjected to centuries of systemic disenfranchisement, exploitation and terrorism. However, our *spirit* remains powerfully intact from the cultures of our very first civilizations. *'That's pretty good'* I'll think to ourself!

I contemplate the Springer family, who had come from a generation out of Barbados and St. Lucia, along with a whole generation of Caribbean and Black souls from the Caribbean diaspora to — as we have throughout the eras of mankind — build a great wonder of the world: *the Panama Canal Zone.* Just as our ancestors from the ancient kingdoms of Benin engineered the current world of commerce, trade, capital and economic formation; just as we constructed those kingdoms of Ghana, Mali and Songhay from the dust of the News Kingdom, and the greatest empire in the history of mankind: the Egyptian Empire. Even as we — super achievers and apex- capitalists — built the American empire with our bare hands; with blood, sweat and tears; body, soul and mind.

As the winds of the Nile River whisper to all of us, we are a race of kingdom designers and builders; just as Benjamin Banneker and our West African counterparts in the Americas designed and built the White House and the apparatus by which the USA has governed the world, we also opened up the trade routes in the Americas and around the world with our work of sheer industry, prosperity, vision and genius. I think about the generation of super achievers — nurses, leaders, blue- collar workers, home makers, farmers, educators — that came from my maternal great- grandparents, and how I am their dream and the dreams I have for my son, his friends and those to come.

I *remember* Cecil and Dorothy Reynolds, my grandparents on my mother's side, and how a churchgoing woman and manager of a post exchange in the Panama Canal Zone got us to where we are. I am so grateful and so enamored with my grandparents: Cecil Reynolds was the manager of a restaurant for the American military in the Canal Zone. With his 6th- grade education, he secured the highest social and financial position that could be attained by non-white, non-Americans for his family. My grandmother, Dorothy Reynolds, had three years at the University of Panama under her belt but left school to start her family and make a home for my mother and her brother and sister. He sent all three of his children to university in the United States, paid for their college educations, and would only stop supporting them financially when they were married. All of their children and grandchildren and our children have thrived financially, educationally and spiritually. That's my stock; that's my bloodline and pedigree.

When I think of John and Magnolia Howell, my grandparents on my father's side, and how a Caribbean homemaker and butcher managed to create the generation of an attorney, airline manager, businessman, professors and successful fathers, husbands, homemakers and mothers, I am, again, overwhelmed. *And somehow their DNA is my own?* Again, I recognize the authority and the power with which I make my claims in this world. For I recognize what Love Almighty has done. I recognize that I — in my blood and my bones —

am made of that infinite cosmic permanent power of *Love, Almighty*.

> *"All day I think about it, then at night I say it. Where did I come from, and what am I supposed to be doing? I have no idea. My soul is from elsewhere, I'm sure of that, and I intend to end up there. Who looks out with my eyes?*
>
> *What is the soul? I cannot stop asking. If I could taste one sip of an answer, I could break out of this prison for drunks. I didn't come here of my own accord, and I can't leave that way. Whoever brought me here, will have to take me home."*
>
> — **Rumi**

The first home I remember living in was a one-level, ranch-style green duplex in Land Park, Sacramento. That was somewhere around 1978. The neighborhood was sparsely integrated but we lived across the street from Irene and Clifton West, parents to Dr. Cornel West and his siblings, including Clifton West Jr. and his sister, who used to babysit my brother and me. There was this cool little park around the corner, only three or four blocks — and a twenty -minute walk from our home. We would take family walks when grandmothers, uncles and aunts came in from Trinidad or Panama.

My brother and I attended Pony Express Elementary School and were, for a time, two of only about five or six African Americans throughout our entire elementary school of predominantly white and Asian students. We played tetherball, wall ball, ball bombardment, and read Marvel Comics stealthily stashed in our history, English and math textbooks. And when Daddy would come into our rooms on spot inspections to see if we were studying, we'd flip the text pages over the comic books — adolescent technology in a home ruled by a Trinidadian chieftain. We never learned our history in school, but that was okay because Dr. Howell, my father, and Mrs. Howell, my mother, would teach us at home with a pride as fierce as a butcher's cutlass, supplying a wealth of knowledge that would open our minds, spirits and imagination to our bloodlines.

I remember getting carte blanche from Mommy on the RCA music selections — books of promotional stamps that we would place on order forms and I would — shhhhhhh!!! — order Barry Mani low, Earth Wind and Fire, Helen Ready, the Captain and Tenille, the Gap Band and anything from Stevie Wonder's timeless catalogue. From Scholastic Readers, I ordered the biographies of the champion Muhammad Ali, the emancipator Frederick Douglass and the great educator Mary McCloud Bethune. From Daddy I learned about Prime Minister Dr. Eric Williams, the Trinidadian liberator and Kwame Toure, the Trinidadian Black Panther revolutionary. And my God, if I didn't hear about John George Howell, my grandfather, *a giant*, who, as generations before him accepted a low post to get a high result — made a way out of *no way*. The butcher and homemaker raised 11 children and dozens of us grandchildren to stake a significant claim in this world.

From Mommy, I learned about George Westerman, my great- grand uncle and the great Panamanian diplomat, author and leader whose papers are now filed at the Schomburg Museum in Harlem.

He met with congressman Adam Clayton Powell and President Franklin Delano Roosevelt and was a friend of Ralph Abernathy, the colleague of Martin Luther King. He brought Mahalia Jackson — the American gospel singer and predecessor to the Whitney Houstons and Beyonces — to Panama.

The fifth child of George Benjamin Westerman and Marie Josephine Rosena Bridget, George Washington Westerman Spalding, the great- grandson of a slave, was born in Coolie Town, on the Atlantic Coast of the Republic of Panama. My family traveled from Barbados to Panama in 1905 with so many enterprising Caribbean families to build the Panama Canal, which was completed in 1914 as one of the world's great wonders. At the time in which it was constructed by the United States, the Panama Canal allowed for the free flow of products, trade and commerce throughout the Americas, and from Asia to Europe. The Panama Canal Zone linked the Pacific and Atlantic oceans. Rather than traveling from Europe, Africa or Asia, and having to travel around the isthmus of the Americas around Argentina or Chile, ships would use the Panama Canal Zone to cut across to port cities like San Francisco or San Diego. This essentially created a sea faring shortcut for ships through fifty miles of mountainous and tropical terrain. The Panama Canal is often noted as one of the world's great wonders, as it is the key to commerce in the Western Hemisphere.

Much of who we are is determined by those who ca me before us. They pave the way, lead the way and set standards. I've always taken a supernatural pride in who I am and those who came before me. *It's one of my superpowers — and I have a* few powers *that are classified at Level Alpha 1. Ha!* George Westerman is an ancestor whose works have consistently motivated me as an adult and set the standard for so many of my accomplishments and ambitions. To me, Ancestor George Westerman is the definition of "*ancestry in motion*". He is my definition of success. Sure, there are the great inspirators such as Muhammad Ali, Prince, Tupac and Toni Morrison, but truly, heroes and mentors are those *whom we know.*

Considering the bigger picture of your life can change your path to action. This *"ancestry in motion"* — immersing yourself in the story of your ancestors — can be powerful in helping you create new emotions in tough seasons of your life, or elevate, stabilize and find clarity when success is accomplished. *Ancestry in motion* is a through line across the generations and the valleys and peaks of life and lifetimes, from one to the next.

In my earlier years, I never consciously looked to my great-grand uncle as a source of inspiration. Moreso, it was my parents, both college and university professors who were my exemplars and exceptional motivators. My dad met my great-grand uncle George, who had given him total access to his archives of papers on the Canal Zone. They were enamored with Daddy, a beautiful young man who had studied at the University of Cambridge, University of London, Chapman College, Sacramento State University and the University of California at Los Angeles. Much of that work served as one of the primary sources for his PhD thesis at UCLA: *The Anatomy of Discrimination in the Canal Zone vis a vis Stated United States Policy from 1940 to 1977.*

Then there has been my mother, and if I have an ounce of storytelling capability in me, it all comes from her tirelessly, and with permanent residency in my soul, whispering, talking, telling, sharing since my earliest days about my family and our journey. Those stories and developing relationships with great-granduncle George's descendants including his nephew, my great-uncle George Springer and great-uncle Leroy have always had me believing I could change the world if I followed my heart and did my very best. And I believe that great-uncle

George Chelson Springer took his cues and crafted his own form of a noteworthy and exceptional life from Ancestor George Westerman (in 1938 he was a member of the tennis team representing Panama in the IV Central American and Caribbean Olympiad). That great-uncle George played baseball for a junior college in the Canal Zone and now has a grandson in Major League Baseball, George Springer, who is now right outfield for the Toronto Blue Jays and one of Major League Baseball's greatest sluggers. His dad — known by family and friends as "Champ" — is a partner with a prominent law firm in Connecticut, was a standout football player at UConn and a pillar in his community just as his dad before him.

I've met, worked with and interviewed heads of state, icons and business leaders; worked as a journalist or, in current parlance, *a blogger*; enjoyed the turbulent economic choppy waters of American capitalism as a serial entrepreneur; been pulled under by powerful riptides, but bounced up balancing those waves. I've contributed to and worked on multiple political campaigns at the national and municipal levels, worked with national leaders in business and taken up the mantle of business leadership in my own endeavors just like my great-granduncle George Westerman and great-uncle George did in diplomacy and education the previous century and decades earlier.

Our family business, however, has been education and many of the great and enduring lessons of my life, certainly the first and foremost, I took by my father's bedside while he would prepare lectures for his classes at Cosumnes River Junior College in Elk Grove. From Mommy, a lifelong mentor and teacher, I learned a love of the arts and the abiding disciplines of goodness and righteousness — *Christ Consciousness*, as the

New Age connoisseurs such as Marianne Richardson, Eckhart Tolle or don Miguel Ruiz may refer to it. She eventually became an engineer with Pacific Bell, but before I was born she taught high school Spanish at St. Francis High School, and was an associate Professor at the University of California at Davis. She recently retired from a career of service, education and administration as faculty at Mt. San Antonio Junior College in Southern California, and is writing stories of her beloved parents in her native Spanish, editing her brother's family histories, crocheting blankets for our children and pets, practicing her own divine magic of ancestry in motion and taking piano classes just like my grandmother, who was an accomplished organist for the church.

Certainly, all my great passions — literature, film, music — spring forth from that passion: *her*. She does not support my idealization of her and laughs, *"Please don't hold me to that standard like I do with my mother."* But, like all boys who adore their mothers, she is my archangel — *love incarnated*. And it hasn't always been perfect but it has been powerful and sustaining. From Mommy, I've learned that *true beauty* comes from within and will radiate — even in the darkest seasons — the way back home where brilliance, abundance and beauty are plentiful and everlasting.

But that is prologue and herein, context: Before I lived Napoleon Hill's *Think and Grow Rich* or spent time with a Tony Robbins' genius on motivation and self-determination; before I consumed Toni Morrison's strategic treatise on race and relations and literature, *Playing in the Dark*, or Derrick Bell's *Faces at the Bottom of the Well* or before Alex Haile's masterpiece, *The Autobiography of Malcolm X* and Spike Lee and Denzel Washington's triumphal interpretation; before my spiritual curiosity peaked and the pendulum swung back on Sir

Richard Attenborough's *Mahatma Gandhi*, which was preceded by *Siddhartha* by Herman Hesse; before even Benjamin Graham's *The Intelligent Investor* or my 6th- grade teacher Mr. Spencer's introduction to the business sections stock charts in the *Sacramento Bee*… there was *Daddy*.

Before my first job in retail banking with Wells Fargo as an administrative assistant in San Francisco at the repeal of the Glass Steagall Act in 1999 (deregulating the banks) during the Clinton Administration; then, later as a personal banker with Fleet Boston Financial in Syracuse New York, there was this beautiful Black Caribbean man whispering unseemly ambitions into my very spirit. In between, I worked at 75 Park Place in Manhattan and afterwards at Smith Barney in Syracuse. I did all of this because my dad, "*Daddy*," thought it would be *cool*. That's all he had to do to command my attention, direct my spirit and although I don't think I ever told him that, *he probably knew*. Daddy was discerning like the wise old owl, and the more he looked, the more he saw, and the more he saw, the more he looked, developing a spindle eye. He was a *charismatic intergalactic*.

Yes, there was Dr. Bing Patrick Howell, professor of Political Science and History at Cosumnes River College, Stanford University (co-founder of the Alternative to Western Civilization program, along with Dr. Clayborn Carson) and Roger Williams University. I realize now, as a father myself, that Dr. Bing P. Howell was a character played by my father, a vision of everything I could be in the form of *"Daddy."* He was playing a role, communicating a very material message with his spirit. And I got the message… *with my spirit*. I think that's part of *our systems* and our ways of doing what we have done through the centuries and millennia.

I know he took his lessons from my charismatic, mercurially blue-, auburn-, green- and gray- eyed Grenadian grandmother, Magnolia, the wife of a Trinidadian butcher, whose sweet canary Caribbean lilt still fills my dreams and fuels my visions and ambitions. Her voice is the sound of our ambitions to be *truly great*. I remember most famously from her, *"know thyself," "to thyself be true"* and *"one day you will be truly, truly great."* She was a handsome woman of indomitable will and fearless vision for her children, who with my grandfather, a butcher, and the north star of multitudes of orbits, raised 11 children in Trinidad and Tobago with an uncommon and undeniable stamp of excellence — they are and were a London- educated attorney working outside Trinidad and Tobago's Red House (equivalent of the D.C.s White House counsel), professors at leading American universities, a businessman, airport manager and successful wives and mothers in London, Toronto, The Virgin Islands, Florida, Virginia.... *every last one without exception*. And when people would compliment her with, "Mrs. Howell you are very, very *lucky*." Magnolia would retort in a singsong, without a hint of irony, dry and rye, *"If it is luck?* You should try it some time."

Well, okay now. *Don't mind if I do Grandmother — Love you my sweet Magnolia.*

Now, this is how ancestry moves through our markets.

"Love is cure. Love is power. Love is the magic of changes. Love is the mirror of divine beauty."

— Rumi

PART I

On Fathers and Sons

Chapter 1:
About the Boy Who Frees the Man Who Wants to Fly

"Never say never, because limits, like fears, are often just an illusion."
— Michael Jordan

Deep inhale. I turned forty-six years old this year. That's like a personal monument of sorts (best Rocky Balboa imitation). Dog-ear it, affix a yellow sticky memo note. Engrave it on my own personal statue of me for me. I keep thinking, *"That's fifty minus four years old."* — *please!* I never thought I would be that age. #Oldassdude. *Ha!* Exhale quickly. *But am I an old-ass dude?*

When I was a kid, fifty was *kind of* an old dude. And I really think that back in the 1980 s, fifty- and sixty-year-old dudes were older dudes than they are now. They were tired, right? Slow and defeated. Wrinkly skin? Darkened eyes? Spirits weary and wearing the world on their faces, abdomens bloating and shoulders sulking. I can remember the seventeen-year-old young man I was and I remember wondering who I would become; if I would become one of those grays, erudite though impolite, furrowed brows and sideways smiles — teeth missing. A man not unlike T.S. Eliot's "Prufrock ("I grow old… I grow old… I shall wear the bottoms of my trousers rolled") or his

"Gerontion," a Greek-titled opus meaning "little old man." I'll hear the admonishment, *"Grow up!"* and wonder, *"Why? Why would I ever?* The goal is to get *wiser*, not older." *You* get older. So yeah, wisdom,

My grays, however, have begun to peak, like pixie dust or ashes on my temples and around the corners of my goatee, a median step between youth and a penultimate step just before death. The aches are more pronounced on certain days than others. Most days I am mistaken in my voice, attitude and appearances for a thirty-three-year-old or even twenty-seven-year-old when I am at my best. And all my life, most people have mistaken me for someone they know. I've always wondered what that means. *I think I know though.*

Yes, that pilot fire is still lit and sometimes it blazes for city blocks. *Sometimes?* It rages across continents. That inferno is the seventeen -year-old me who knew everything. Raw uncut passion, pleasure and pure love were poured into me by Dr. and Mrs. Howell. Truth? *That's how I was created. Their love.*

It's a *total* trip because that seventeen-year-old boy and confident, bold, aggressive and righteous young man is still very much a part of me. His voice is strong. And while there is the bold and relentless twenty-five-year-old me (who learned how to apply to endeavors with the tenacity that was taught to me by my father), and while there is the thirty-five- and forty-year-old me, like granite and steel, *or water, formlessness and flow*, who has learned that I can pretty much do whatsoever I set my mind to because, well, *I have*; there is also this part of me that is a father to an eleven-year-old son and loves him so very much and doesn't want him to go through the self-mutilation of those thoughts and those apex Uber Capitalist ways of being. I look for the archangel in him versus the apex-capitalist whose spirit has inhabited my own.

Competition and capital market formation in the United States are not unlike the Roman amphitheaters of gladiatorial sport. As a matter of fact, its spirit is derived from the blood sport of aggression, violence and sheer spectacle. *These systems are about power.* The me that is approaching fifty wants him to be better than that. Freer. *More loving.* Warmer. He wants him to have more than that. So I open up the cornucopia that is me, lay it out flat on the wood of this reality, study it and I realize that there are two binary primers I have always held onto in experiencing myself in everyday life. They are, *YES Radio Raheem*, Love and Hate.

In between? I've had a pretty consistent array of life-defining fears: fear of failure and fear of success. And those feelings of fear were related to other emotions of anxiety, anger, worry, sadness, doubt and even foresight and longing. I had a fear that I would be homeless (and I remember the conversation with a homeless gentleman on Telegraph Avenue at Cal, Berkeley that pretty much crystallized that fear, and then I remember actually not having a home as an undergraduate but bumming with friends, a realization of those fears,). I still occasionally experience that fear in a two-million-dollar home in a beach community suburb. I had a fear that I would never have the life I wanted. I had a fear that the voices that were against me were right. I had a fear that I was somehow not equipped; that I was somehow not worthy of the life I imagined for myself.

I've had a fear of not knowing. I had a fear of being successful and that success not being enough, or not being what I thought it would be. I had a fear that I would never have any money, that I was just a fraud pretending to be me (or that the me I was being was a complete fraud)… I think they call it imposter syndrome.

I have had a fear of unseen enemies trying to take everything away from me (or is that just paranoia?). I have so many fears, my fears have fears (for fears, like ambitions, are children that give birth to other little fellows and strange realities) But in the end, if now were the end — which it is not — none of those fears have ever really been real. I see that clearly like looking back at a sun setting over the horizon. There was never a threat promised by fear that, in the end, was really real. It was life posturing as a delusion in my mind. Delusions are not real. But *damned* if those demons posing as fears didn't seem truly real.

Now, some of those fears — miniscule versions of them — have found their place in my reality, all lumpy and bold and ugly. And the truth is they were invited into being by my own mind. And that Fear always comes with its motley crew of Insecurity, Rage, Depression, Self-Sabotage, Self-Loathing and Loneliness. I've learned to sit still in the space when these fellows come to play. I just become still as a winter solstice and don't move a muscle. I peek at them and see the game that they are running on me. I don't let those fellows define me because I know *they are not real.*

See, I always wonder if they didn't occupy space in my mind, would they have come to be? In fact, we live in a reality that is the summation of our dreams and nightmares, our ambitions and failures as members of the human species. We are the CEOs, the gods, the authors of the realities we inhabit. We are the manifestors on a collective plane that is a prism, a collection of all of our envisionings intersecting. Each of us is a point of intersection, an avatar of our realities, potentials, thoughts, feelings, dreams, visions and memories. Each of us possesses *the power of our lives.* We are masters of our living dreams. We are the architects of our living nightmares.

Life is always changing and in the free flow of the continuum that is our existence, we project what we are and what we will be from within; from within our souls, from within our inner-minds. Our Spirits do the work with our conscious mind and within the continuum of the Spirit Force. It's like the sun giving light and energy, power and growth to the day. That's how our eyes and our visions for ourselves work.

So. What. Do. I. Do? What will I do? What will I do to deal with these Fears, these demons masked as low-frequency emotions? Fear has its motley crew of Shame, Indecision and Loss, who are really just steppingstones. Really, they are intruders coming from the spaces within ourselves that we don't give voice to, give light, or acknowledge in the company of intelligent minds. This is where my gift of self-awareness comes into play. *I don't think of me as me.* I think of me as the me I project myself to be. Then, I think of all the other echoes of me. Then I look at all the other elements that are around me — my friends, my family, my partners, my endeavors and environments and I begin to move pieces around. It helps if I am exercising, if I am prayerful, if I am NOT mindful, if I am developing my spiritual practices from within, if I am engaging the spirits around me to deal with the wars being waged from within, if I meditate on where I have been and where I have yet to go. If, within the province of the inner eye, I apply wisdom. *I master those fears.* I come up with this… *wisdom: Get up Son and Let's Climb…*

Try to be the summation of your greatest ambitions with the wanton abandonment of a child. Do not be the adult who is taught behaviors by others, "the system," "the society of men," but principally, always yourself costumed by those other entities. Be gentle with yourself in your application of learning, use your soft powers but climb mountain tops, *seek to fly to the stars* or bathe cosmic in the pool of light and gasses that is sun, aspire to your highest dream by making a go of a secret, long-held ambition. Or, by challenging a long-held negative belief utilized for survival purposes. Because the only thing consistent in this universe is *Love*.

Hatred is all-encompassing — a delusion of Forever — when you are in it, but fleeting nonetheless. The permanency of hatred occurs when we allow it into our souls without challenging it, without facing the devil disguised as ourselves. So, find your mountain and climb, for you will find freedom not in reaching the summit but in the act of lifting one foot over the other and repeating the process. *The child in you is right.* The boy or girl inside you is omnipotent and has been correct: *you can do anything you set your mind to.*

Now, let go, jump and fly. Go ahead. *It's gonna be alright.*

Now, *fly. Fly, cosmic kings and queens of our eternal midnights,* fly.

Chapter 2:
Red House from Across the Street

FEBRUARY 2005, Downtown Trinidad, Port of Spain today, right now — FOUR BLACK MEN, TWO GENERATIONS, ONE AFTERNOON — LIFETIMES

In a white office building with a shingle reading 'attorney at law', there's a teal-green vintage Land Rover stylin' right up front in Downtown Port of Spain, around the corner from Woodford Square, around the corner from the Red House where parliament meets, on a street called Sackville. A professor, an attorney, a vice president banker and the business owner of a fashion recruiting business in Japan — yes, we live in Asia and the Americas, but today we live where Black men in the Caribbean do: *in that space.*

The two griot generals, Daddy and my uncle, share family memories, telling stories, reading one another, remembering old remedies, singing old soca melodies, piecing out the past and looking to the future just by looking into each other's eyes. Ultimately we are enjoying each other's auras and our time in the world, telling wicked stories, laughing hard, long and loud at stories inclusive of such instruments as cutlass and bull pistles (a bull's hardened sun-dried penis) used for disciplining and whoopings that do not leave marks.

"It's in the blood!" they lymin', *"If Daddy naked!* — just finished showering and he heard someone do something to one of his kids? He's leaving the house — *naked,* ya hear?! With that red paisley handkerchief around his neck — ya?" They stchups sucking their teeth then double over laughing until the laughter spreads like wildfire and tears are cascading as a deluge from riverbanks. I've never seen my father like this before. *Ever.* Well, maybe with us — he's told stories of his days at Chapman and growing up how he refused to salute the queen when she came to their boot-shaped island nation.

But this is different: I've never seen Daddy as a little brother. He's strong headed — and *like I didn't know that before? Ha!* The laughter has them doubling over because this is how they get their start — *this is how they all made it* — wars waged when nobody was looking, when nobody was knowing; heavyweight championship fights where Black men with blood-red, rum-soaked eyes would go stand up for his kids, walking up a winding boulevard with broken sidewalks and bumpy roads in those days of the smoky Trinidadian suns.

A confession, as they do, comes nearly fifty years after the crime, the elder Maillard says bluntly, wiping tears from his eye, "But we were wrong man. *How we used to provoke people.* God, man! We were so wrong, man."

Daddy is crying — tears of pure joy — "You remember that one in the corner shop where they sell dem hot sardines, and we go right there underneath the building and tickle the bee next with a long tree branch and maaan… dem bees man, dem run you down, you have to fast — fast, fast, fast. We have to speed up, on the edge of our toes. But we were bad boy, we were so bad! You're right. We were so, so wrong!"

You can't buy this; you can imitate this. I wish we could stay in this time *forever*. Our certainty, deep-rooted and undeniable, comes from that unbroken chain of ancestors, from the rhythms of our islands, from the grit of our history. The men from across the street? The Black men populating the streets in downtown Port of Spain? They're not just our fathers, our uncles, our griots — *they are us.* We are them. And the hustle, the resilience, the defiance in the face of everything: that's the legacy. It runs so deep that it feels like an instinct. Whether we're holding a book, a bull pistle, or a business plan, it's the same energy. The same need to make it, not just for us, but for everyone who came before and everyone coming after.

Back in 2005, sitting in that office, soaking in their laughter, their memories, *I realized something.* They weren't just talking about past mischiefs or hard-won victories. They were laying down *the blueprint.* They were passing the baton.

And here I am now, years later, in California, nearly a continent from the Red House, from those winding streets, alleys and avenues in Trinidad, but the hustle is the same. The stakes? Just as high. The mission? Aim, focus with purpose. And the lesson from Daddy, the one about PLAY? That one sticks.

Whether I'm negotiating a deal, building a business empire, a business network or just trying to make sense of our red and orange angry world, I know how to play. I know how to flip the script, how to make a way out of no way. I know that we — African, Caribbean folk and African American folk — are built for this. *We don't just survive.* We outthink, we outwork, we out-hustle — *we thrive.* Because that's the thing about being from the Caribbean or African American. You might leave Africa, even by a few generations, but Africa never leaves you.

Ever.

The Trinidadian

Yep, Daddy was a hustler. He was a *Trinidadian.* And that about says it all. So, not Nigerian or Jamaican — "*After you shake hands with a Nigerian or Jamaican, count your fingers to make sure they are still all there,*" and this, in my best broken English African dialect. But the hustle is embedded in the soul of the Trinidadian. They hustle hard. And they *hustle hard high.* I know it because I got that Trinidadian blood coursing through my bloodstream. And I'm a high-frequency hustler too. But I'm a Capricorn, or the GOAT on the cosmology of astrological charts — up and down desert peaks and lush valleys — so I'm always thinking about systems on the macro and how they work and how to operate those systems from the standing position of an individual, a mere man or capitalist denizen.

I'm always showing myself how to become *institutional* in my personal power. How can I operate systems from where I stand? *Because* that's what we are dealing with: *systems designed* to keep me in my place versus moving forward. *Fuck that.* Sometimes I'll fall down and hurt myself pretty badly. *No problemo.* Or, as Depeche Mode sings, "First we stand up, then we fall down, we have to move forward — *before we drown.*" I am backed by ancestors, wisdom and spirits designed to help me accomplish *anything* I set my mind to.

I've mastered the art form of *a winning attitude.* I'm not a politician or a diplomat but I incorporate those didactics into everyday prosaics of doing business. (*By the way,* Leo on my rising and Virgo on my moon, so a lot of cosmic healing in my Black cosmic spirit.)

I'll call the head of a nation for an interview on Wednesday. Or, from nowhere, call a Fortune 500 CEO and speak with calm vim, vigor and charm, confused when I am not transferred to the executive's office or prepared with a svelte request when I am: *make a way for the whole way out of no way.* I'll know where in a deal to negotiate a higher take, typically, after I have performed to excellence. And I know how to get my take on the back end if I get screwed on the front end of a deal. *I know how to leverage a considerable intellect, wisdom, and sense of who I am to get what is fair, what is due.* I know how to turn 10x blessings and their inverse function into a deal. And I understand, well, my axiom of *"I made the deal, I'll break the deal"* just as I do my axiom of *"everybody's got an excellent idea until they get the invoice"* reformulation of Mike Tyson's savage, "*Everyone has an idea until they get punched in the face.*" I understand that the bottom line is love but that doesn't mean you do not earn it by learning it.

Some might call it ambition. Maybe, they might even confuse it with a form of *egotism.* But I think of it as getting what's due to me. Maybe it's some sort of Black ambition and I am a mutant? Ha! I don't care, on any given day, what I am *supposed* to do. What *they say* I can and cannot do. *I don't care what the limitations or rules are (remember, in 1787, Black people were legally considered 3/5ths of a person in the United States of America for taxation and determining congressional districting in America. And before that? We were* **legally** *slaves).* I don't care about no solicitation signs. I don't care about how things are supposed to be done or what the protocol is. *They* change the rules and entire systems, institutions and regulations structures whenever it suits them — I just care that it *gets done.* Or, as one of Daddy's lasting lectures was titled, "The Name of the Game is Play, Patrick. *Do you know how to play that game?*"

"No."

"Play. *P.L.A.Y.* And the objective is to get what you want. Zero sum," he would roar in the sublimated tones and vernacular of an ordinary human, "Either something happened or it did not. Did you get what you wanted? Binary. Zero or one. Win or lose. All or none. *That. Is. All.* Or did you make an excuse? You get done what is in your vested interest, *baby*. Not what's fair. Not what's right. *Not what you wish.* This is America. *So, unfortunately, baby, you won't get what's right or what you think would be nice* — You get what *you give yourself* — *you get only what you negotiate.*"

"What's vested interest?"

"Wow," he said, somewhat playfully and with more than a hint of sarcasm, "if you don't know what your vested interests are, *I feel very sorry for you*. If you don't know what your vested interests are, then who will, Patrick? Wow, *how very, very sad,*" derision coloring his voice, ever the performer at the lectern, "*Patrick,* I feel very sad for you and your kids, my grandchildren." *I didn't like that at all.*

See, Daddy was a West Indian Trinidadian Calypsonian in the form of a political science professor, and that's a very telling, well… *tell sign*. He was God in the form of my earthly father. Pay close attention if you are in business and someone calmly says, "*I'm from the Islands*" or, "I am from the West Indies" or they say they are "Caribbean" or, if they say, "*my parents are from…*" because they are providing you with some very important intelligence about them: who they are and how far they are willing to go to get their agenda accomplished. They may say it very calmly, sanguinely or even gently. Heavens, it may even sound as if they are reciting poetry, or singing a beautiful song.

They are telling you, however, you cannot control their mind, particularly with some racial animus, or accomplish some ulterior agenda, *even if you are an entire system* — and this is *no joke*. They are telling you how far they are willing to go to *get it done*. They are telling you that they operate from their spirit and that there is an unending army of ancestors who are superiorly boosting them with infinite intelligence (instincts), abundance, guidance (feelings) and prayers (secured blessings) from the previous generations and epochs. They are telling you that they are covered in prayers and practiced, believe in, and excel at the magical practice of self-invention. If you ever speak with a Trinidadian or Caribbean and cannot believe what you just heard? What was just said or the absolute ordinary boldness with which it was stated in a sing-song vernacular, well you heard *exactly* what you cannot believe you just heard. Be very *careful* and *believe that.*

You know who else is from Trinidad, that small boot-shaped island in the Caribbean off the coast of Venezuela, right? That little Afro-Indian island is renowned for its Calypso and Socas and its international Carnival season — *you know who else is from there, right?* That's right: *the cosmic intellectual revolutionaries.* Dr. Eric Williams, the first prime minister of the island, widely considered the father of the nation, is our super spirit and our captain of kingdoms inlaid with honor and integrity, not unlike America's Thomas Jeffer son in nation-building combination with George Washington and Alexander Hamilton.

CLR James is a tireless Afro-Trinidadian activist, historian and journalist. He wrote books like *The Black Jacobins,* the widely respected book that talks about Toussaint L'Ouverture and the San Domingo Revolution in Haiti, August 1791. CLR also wrote *State Capitalism and World Revolution* as well as *Nkrumah and the Ghana Revolution.* CLR was Dr. Eric Williams's intellectual mentor. Stokely Carmichael a.k.a. Kwame Ture is also a great Trinidadian-American — he's the one who is recognized as the honorary prime minister of the Black Panther Party, initially as a leader of the Student Nonviolent

Coordinating Committee (SNCC) and in later years instrumental in the global Pan-African movement.

You know who else comes by way of the West Indies, right? Our shining prince, Malcolm X, or el-Hajj Malik el-Shabazz; the Honorable Louis Farrakhan; James Weldon Johnson (the author of the Black National Anthem); Celia Cruz, the world-renowned "Queen of Salsa" music; reggae pioneer Bob Marley; General Colin Powell; pioneering, erudite, and fearless Shirley Chisholm; masterclass visionary Marcus Garvey; handsome crooner Harry Belafonte; the beautiful and fearless Cicely Tyson; the incomparable Roxie Roker and her son, Lennie Kravitz (and his daughter, Zoe); the svelte uncompromised erudite Sidney Poitier; Black Enterpriser and son of a garment worker Earl Graves; billionaire icon and artist Rihanna' the singular Mia Mottley; former attorney general Eric Holder' and the phenomenal vice president Kamala Harris are some other examples of the spirits produced. It is this type of erudite, intellectually distinct, and bold human being who comes from these small Caribbean islands. Do you see the median line that passes through this *breed of humans*? The Caribbean will see his or her vision of reality manifested in real time *or? They will die.*

Every single one of us, without exception, is produced and armed with equal parts brilliant spirituality, the veneer of conservatism inlaid with a militant revolutionary, a healthy self-esteem, a ferocious if not violent intellectual independence and a determination to see that will become part and parcel of the living day — *by hook or by crook.* We understand that you cannot have social justice without economic justice. *And if that's not a fact?* Then I don't know what is, and those *are the facts*.

As someone who derives one half of his blood line from Trinidad, and other parcels from Barbados, Jamaica, Costa

Rica, St. Lucia, Guyana and Grenada, I've come to find this: We are the ones who will either torch your home or buy your entire block, call you anonymously for a meet and greet, then sit down over let's say Starbucks Coffee or, even better, say Better Buzz, and explain over a chai tea or macchiato, in a very folksy, sanguine, intimate and charismatic manner exactly how we did it and *why it had to be done.*

We'll even ask you to buy the coffee and you will gladly oblige. And here's the kicker: You'll be glad we spoke to you so civilly about it, *so delightfully.* And we have no doubt about our ability to pull off the spiritual transaction — we are all practiced and prepared.

If I'm a reforming capitalist, a change catalyst if not a spiritual tsunami from the ancestors and I am in *my* manner of being and communications, it's the erudite Trinidadian composition with basics of Akon, Igbo, Benin, Yoruba and Kemet algorithms from which we all take our calculation, strategy and tactics. Trinidadians in particular have a reputation throughout the Caribbean islands for their entrepreneurship. That's the means by which I compose the sentences which you are reading right now: I hear the staccato of drums and declarative sentences in my inner mind's ears, punctuated with a bass kettle and the merengue and tango of snares; my prose is the harmonic overlay and counterbalance to this percussionary orchestra that is the collective heart of a people beating; *it's in my blood. Sometimes?* I hear the melody of the steel pan in my soul. The ancestors and those to come communicate through the rays of the sun and activate a whole different level of participation in this reality. As I've made clear earlier, I lend my entire mind and body to those spirits who came before me and those to come. Angels also regularly stand in my space and sometimes, I'm ashamed to say it, a demon has had his way with me too.

APRIL 2014

It's Black History Month, idyllic oceanside community in Carlsbad at the Foothills

When Chris is seven, we watch NBA games together in the "Heat Zone" — a man space with three love recliners, Miami Heat memorabilia, steel nunchucks I have owned since Guadalajara, a sling shot we got in Cancun during a family cruise, a framed rookie card of King James in his Cleveland Cavalier gear that my capital market formation buddy Brian Jue gave Chris. I also possess a samurai sword that Preshas Jankins of Angry Squirrel gifted me when I was his banker at Wachovia Banker — Preshas would go on to do stunts for *Black Panther*. There are NBA commercials with Miami's Chris Bosh and Ray Allen talking passionately to a new generation about the sacrifices of those generations who came before. Then, there are the inevitable images of Martin Luther King and Malcolm X, Kareem Abdul Jabbar, Nelson Mandela, and the undisputed Greatest of All Time, Bill Russell, Muhammad Ali.

Chris will know his rich history, and we have raised him to take pride in the struggle against our inevitable successes. His mother and I include YouTube sessions on the Queen of Sheba, Haile Selassie and Emperor Menelik II; and Google searches of Maurice Bishop of Grenada and Dr. Eric Williams of Trinidad and Tobago. I read to him about those ancient kingdoms of Ghana, Songhai and Mali. *He is*, psychologically, *marked for success.* We read from the texts of *Mansa Musa, The Most Famous African Traveler to Mecca, Stolen Legacy* by George G.M. James, *The Isis Papers* by Frances Cress Welsing, *Blacks Before America* by Mark Hyman, and *Mansa Musa and the Empire of Mali* by P. James Oliver — all books that have most certainly been banished from MAGA's "vision" for America — *Ha! Too late suckas!*

Race is real, and the ideology of racism which his grandfather wrote so compellingly about in the 1999 release by Simon and Schuster, yes, baby, they are real. Just as real in the United States of America as the sky is blue and the sun radiates down on our kinky heads, communicating very real and brilliant messages of self-reliance, self-creation and brilliance.

Then one day King says, getting dressed for catholic school, "Daddy, do you know Kevin Hart?"

I got him started on all the comedians, the truth tellers from our traditions of *color political commentary* and he took immediately to it — Kevin Hart was a gateway to *The Bernie Mac Show*, *The Cosby Show*, and Chris Rock's *Everybody Hates Chris*. "He is so funny, Daddy," he cracks up like some sort of miniature man, "He's white! He's white! He don't fight!" I remember my initiation into the conscious constructs of American racism and discrimination around the first grade, and meeting ancestors Muhammad Ali and Frederick Douglass, and I wonder if this is the way it is going to go. Another generation fed this garbage like produced food filled with preservatives and cancer inducing agents.

It's really simple. And I know Kevin Hart is just making jokes — feeding into a common anti-Eminem Caucasoid stereotype, selling tickets on a movie trailer for Ride Along. What's the harm in that counter measure? White people can't dance? They can't sing, they can't run and they can't jump? *They are... corny.* But this is not the point. And generally, who cares? Our counter measure slaps us in the face regularly; magnificent images of Black rappers and Black athletes inundate every form of popular culture, bringing with them the kind of stereotypical bravado that scorches our image, singes our collective self-esteem with distorted mass imagery. I have to search out astronaut Mae Carol Jemison or astrophysicist Neil DeGrasse Tyson to share their exploits with my son. His repeating Hart's stereotype *is... different. Christian* is my crowning jewel, *a young king on the rise.*

I hate hearing the comedian's crass coming from my son's mouth. Chris is a king, and for the last few months after Barack Obama's election, everybody has been talking about a post-racial society. I mean, what does it matter, right? Barack Obama will have to procure a longform birth certificate to satisfy the ascension and race baiting of an albino King Kong, and you know, we are, through the Hollywood Industrial Complex, regularly caricatured as athletes and performers. What's the harm in a little counter-programming? But this is different! Christian, my baby, is my little King, and whether it is a post-racial society or not, it will be and that's where I want him planted, firmly in the world of tomorrow that Martin Luther King would invoke as the prophet he has become to the world. MLK's visions is real.

***

Kings are discerning, and they pay attention to details in a manner that is sanguine, detached. Kings are discriminating without judging, and absolutely judgmental when occasion demands it, sans personal attachment. Kings are exacting in their effect. They are tender hearted towards their people and righteous in dealing with their sworn enemy. They are open to the spiritual ebbs and flows of the times and know what to do and when. They operate outside of time in an absolute construct of eternity. Kings are ordained by God Almighty and His Spirit Force.

You see? In our ancient tribes, we were communities of tribesmen and women, teaching our progeny not only about their gifts but about their responsibilities to a greater humanity. Ubuntu is a Southern African humanist philosophy meaning "I am because we are." We showed them how the greatest technology we have ever possessed is our love and how that love is interrupted by hatred as a ploy to move us from our greatness. Kings can be exacting when dealing with the enemy, they may even be ruthless, but righteous is where he needs to aim himself. A king knows what to do, when. A king operates outside the continuum of time and as ancestor Marcus Garvey directed, the sky is our floor, and eternity the measure. All of the great peace makers, kings, and governors of the peace are structured in a system ordained by the Lord himself.

Yes, our Kings move in a continuum of those Kingdom Builders who came countless millennia before our time. Our Kings and Queens — the Nubians; Clitus Niger, aide to Alexander; Zenobia, the queen of the East; the Land of Punt; Saint Augustine; Egypt's twenty-fifth dynasty; those who first smelted iron; the Black Africans who taught the world how gold works; our kings of Ghana — Boamponsem, Nana Dokua, Nana Kuntunkununku II, Nana Kwaku Boateng, Nana Nkuah Okomdom II so forth and so on; our dynastic magistrates of Songhai and Mali Muḥammad I Askia; Imhotep and the Black Egyptians; the Falashas, the Black Jews; Abubakari and his people's African voyage to the Americas before that mass genocide initiated by Christopher Columbus; of our early Black migrations to the lands with contemporary nomenclature as 'The United States of America'; Bilal, the aide to Mohammad; Ann Zingha, Warrior Queen of Angola; and Aesop, the Black fabulist.

Our greats *move through the diaspora, through us, in us, with us. Our greats* are *us.* I say to my king, a child now, *you were somebody long before we were brought to America in chains*. It's our time — *time of the Kingdom Builders*. These are his — Ato King Haille Christian's — *bedtime* stories before he goes to the cosmos of sleep.

I want the new future for my son. Or, as James Baldwin so wisely observed, *"Our crown has already been bought and paid for. All we have to do is wear it."*

When Chris gets out of the car, I see a population dense with the part of our bloodline outside the kingdom-makers of the original civilizations, filled with governors, children of this system, English and Irish men, German and Scot children, crowding the sidewalks from the austerity of the school and the religious, firm hold of the church with its arcane practices. I remember sitting in the back seat of Daddy's sky-blue Monte Carlo in the '80's and how he would sit still for other Black men being harassed by the system, instructing us to just watch, by speaking forth from his spirit with a steady gaze. I realize now that we have all been survivors of a spiritual war not declared but there, visceral, and claiming the psyches and spiritual well-being of so many, including myself. I realize I am a casualty and I wonder if I can work a way around the system for my King who is so much brighter and regal than I was or will ever be.

I recognize in my face a joyful warrior who has learned to smile and make light of some of the heaviest burdens, recalling World War Three battles in corporate America, with provisions made by ancestor Thurgood Marshall under Title 7 and subsequent EEOC (Equal Employment Opportunity Commission) declarations. I remember the relief I would feel when I realized that a whole generation who comported within their very being the spiritual rot of racism. I recall understanding they would pass from the earth and we would done with their evil. I remember thinking to myself, as a sacred vow, *Next time will be different*, and if it's not? I… *we* would know what to do *and when.* You see, from 1619, our curve has been on the undeniable arc prescribed by our king, MLK.

"Listen," I tell my baby, Christian, feeling the powerful rush of an unbearable pain but even greater determination that when the time is right, we will not only *have survived but thrived*, "always try to be like Jesus, baby, not a Christian." He looks at me quizzically, and I smile at King, cute, smart, and as quick as can be, "*Well, baby* — always be yourself — but realize that Jesus and his father God have been together for billions of years, and the father knows his son, and the son knows his father, so his personality reflects the father's. So, imitate Jesus, the bronze skinned middle eastern man whose father is our Lord." He doesn't think about what I say too much — he is light and easy, his mother and mine's very best. *"King* — some folks might try that, sweetie, but *you know who you are*. That Kevin Hart joke might be funny… but it is also a stereotype. You will encounter the enemy in the form of classmates, teachers and principals, officials, policemen, and judges, but we are wiser than that, *better* than that. *Be* better than that — you are a king for kingdom come, and well, just as all the prophecies have come true, so will this one — Love wins in the end. Know that — *Love alone*."

"*Ok, Daddy.* Bye." he says, grabbing his backpack and giving me a hug before getting out of the car and walking into the gates of that school. There are going to be a lot more conversations before Chris is 18. It seems I somehow genetically inherited the lecture gene from my professor father.

"Okay, baby."

Chapter 3:
When Giants Depart This Realm, *My Eulogy*

Daddy transitioned at the end of Winter when there were plenty of new celestial lights formatting our consciousnesses and our very way of life. The death season of the year aligns perfectly with his transition to the spirit realm. *I almost don't believe it. Was he really mortal?* Just as Spring was about to renew all of us, he departed from this earthly realm. When you are a little boy and the sky and the sun reach out to you in the form of a handsome bearded man who is as tough and determined as he is gentle, so sweet and handsome, you become a little one protected by a real giant in this crazy world. It never occurs to you that the sun and the sky will one day pass from this realm. *They are permanent, right?*

I remember sitting in the back seat of his sky-blue Monte Carlo when we lived in Land Park, Sacramento and 7039 Winnett Way feeling that fierce sensation of *"protector."* I also still feel that gentle incandescent glow, a current sensation of his immense love & life *force.* His energy is unmistakable. It was always there beneath the exterior of bravado, confidence and gallantry that was his Caribbean swagger. And it is here now. *Always.* There aren't a lot of men like Daddy. In fact, there are none. *He is distinct.* His own Trini creation. *We* are *all* creators made in the image of our fathers and mothers.

He raised all of us the best way he knew how and that is to be the very best that we can be. The art form and practice of parenting is one of several disciplines he absolutely mastered in his lifetime. He was a genius strategist and mind, awarded degrees, teaching assignments and designations by some of the most illustrious academic institutions on the planet. He was an avid reader and published author, publishing *The Ideology of Racism* with Simon and Schuster in 1999 as well as his dissertation in previous decades.

He was for the spirit and love. And he was a lover who was willing to protect that love with his fierce and righteous warrior. He was against the system and the disenfranchisement of the spirit. He fought and won epic battles. And we all take not only tremendous inspiration but see the magnificent example he set for us as a father and human being making his way through life. We are all making our way as he did, determined to be the best version of ourselves. Or as he loved in Frank Sinatra's classic, *"I did it my way."*

Some of his earliest accomplishments in life are engraved in the NCAA record books 10 different times during his two-year track and field career where he was amongst the best sprinters in the USA. He was an athletic talent who took that currency and turned it into academic gold as a doctoral candidate in history. Daddy was a visionary and a manifestor before those terms were in parlance vogue of our New Age. He was the spirit of a king in this material world. And this means that he spent time mastering himself as well as spiritual principles.

I would never say he was perfect. *Ever.* But I've learned this: how one mourns the passing of a loved one is a very personal experience as well as it is a transformative experience. Just as how a man lives, loves and is? That's his poem to all of eternity and statement of philosophy to the galaxy; his treatise to the cosmos.

Now, I feel aged; somehow *matured*. And this is *miraculous* if you know me at all. Me? Older? His last words to me were, *"Patrick, I love you, baby."* He knew *precisely* what he was doing. He told my son to listen to his mother and father, *to be guided by our wisdom*. His tactical and strategic deployment of his intentions was another area of mastery in his life. Like an archer, He knows how to have a vision and put real-world energy into its manifestation. He is a magic man, practiced and perfected in his craft.

Spirit man — 'from the brim to the dregs.'

The sun is bright today and there is a preternatural calm everywhere. Backyard chimes singing in a gentle breeze. Spring is casting her spell and singing her song. And we are all enchanted. A perfectly blue sky, not unlike my Magnolia's steely blue and mercurial gray-blue eyes. Darwinian varieties of birds singing, chirping and cawing in a bird watcher's haven. Trees are rustling and shimmering with new photosynthetic green, so today I can know all of these things with startling clarity and permanency.

In a way, Daddy lived his life hard. Passionately and fully. Always told us to be better than him. And, well, *I'm trying.* (I'm confident that the assertion "*try*" vexes him). It's hard to follow in the rather large footsteps of a giant calypso man who came to the land of opportunity only as a determined young man *(really just a teenager,* a kid*)*. And I will keep trying because one of the fifty or so edicts he engraved with blood, sweat and tears on my heart and upon the walls of my spirit are, *"the* *race is not for the swiftest but for he who has the endurance to endure and endure to the end."* My God, Daddy *endured.*

Another one of his classics? *"Life is strange. Strange man!"* And I, a little boy, was like, *"What?"* like, *"Dude, what are you talking about now?"* He would look at me with neither pity nor derision and say, "One day, Patrick? You will find out." And know what? *It's okay.* Yeah, I get that ocean surfer's wipe out. But he prepared me. He prepared all of us to be the manifestation of his dream for us — dreamers, visionaries and dream catchers — bold, fearless and *status quo disruptors. Catch him* with a certain spirit? And he would declare, "You'll be my megaton bomb disruptors! You will *bless all of creation" — and then? This laughter, an odd titration between sinister and sheer elation.*

To be sure, there is hell to be had in this earthly realm. *Don't catch hell, na!* Look at this silly, silly world these days. But Daddy's peace is as expansive as any peace I have known. I believe he would like to hear me say that. And I know He does. The grass is still, barely rustling and the wind blows wave after wave of a bright undulating light that is his energy. His final accomplishment is not my full maturation as a man. *We all must finish raising ourselves (*I got that pearl from Mommy). Daddy teaches me determination *("If you never give up, you never lose" or "the race is not for the swiftest but for he who has the endurance to endure and endure to the end!")* and fearlessness ("When God is near have 0 fear"). He teaches me how to battle with the entirety of my spirit ("Fear nothing. Fear no man. They all have ten toes and ten fingers just like you!"). He teaches me to always be humble before Our Lord *(if God is with you then all man can be against you and you will be victorious).* Be brilliant ("Be the best at whatever you do! Or, don't do it at all "). And take "no" from *no one but God.* Then, there is the timeless classic, "You can do *anything* you set your mind to." *A king's legacy.* But it is the peace I feel that will be his parting gift. A final lesson from a brilliant professor, mentor, intellectual and man.

Ancestors. Finally, his space is now bigger than his body. *Spirits.* It is expansive. *A real giant.* Released into the heavens — the cosmos. *Into the sun. Amongst a symphony of lights, ancestral and unending creative power.* So now? He — *a spirit man* — walks the Earth as all his children. *Roots.* And I am receiving the force and clarity of my mission. It is beautiful. My *focus with purpose.*

Whew, done with the Tinsel Town exceptionally produced *minstrel* show.

There seem to be three basic tropes of African American caricatures recognized by the Academy (read: gatekeepers of American culture and the ultimate tastemakers of world popular culture), based upon *over* 50% (like 85%) of the Academy's performance awards handed out during their nearly 90 years of existence:

1. Slave-Servant (for example, Hattie McDaniel in 1940, Octavia Spencer in 2011, Lupita Nyong'o in 2013).
2. Degenerate-Victim (for example, Halle Berry or Denzel Washington in 2001; Forest Whitaker in 2006; Monique in 2009).
3. The Mystic-Enabler or, basically, Black Savior (Whoopi Goldberg in 1991 or Morgan Freeman in 2009).

What a *stunning* lack of creativity and imagination — really, it's just propaganda to propagate and export American racism to the farthest reaches of the planet. No. 3 isn't so bad, *I guess.* That's what makes Sidney Poi tier's award-winning performance in *Lilies of the Field* an outlier — a role recognized and awarded, in which an African American not only has a powerful portrayal but comports themselves with dignity, heroism and wholly fleshed out character. *What?* Angela Bassett and Cicely Tyson never earned awards with a lifetime of masterful portrayals comporting themselves with dignity? What about James Earl Jones, Lawrence Fishburne, Samuel Jackson, Daniel Kaluyaah or Ava Duvernay?

Listen, my objective is not to demean the Black artist and pioneer in Hollywood. Because the body of their work has been a master class, if not ferocious, particularly given the DW Griffith conditions of employment in their industry. Denzel, for example, has also reincarnated Malcolm X, Hurricane Rubin and Steve Biko during his illustrious and indefatigable career and a filmography which contains 0 fat and ought to be studied at film programs globally for the next millennium. *It is the Academy's tastemakers* who have used their selections to design a caricature of Black no different to the minstrel or Blackface of America's 1920s. Oh, the Reaganites like to reminisce — *the good old days.* Tea Party! MAGA! *Ha!!!*

The industry is the complex culprit, right? It has elected to celebrate Mr. Washington's charismatic if not masterful Alonzo Harris portrayal in *Training Day* and his role as a slave in *Glory*. I guess Steve McQueen's take on *12 Years a Slave* was genius, but who's going to be inspired by another slave story in a global film cannon that is filled with this propaganda?

The Academy has elected as a systemic body to keep the harness on our collective humanity with a stilted and narrow vision of we folks darker than blue — even after Barack Obama has been elected president and First Lady Michelle Obama redefined the role with uncharacteristic grace, energy and Black woman realness. Their propaganda agenda is carried out with the original DNA of DW Griffith's *Birth of a Nation* agenda at the outset of Hollywood in 1903. And that is, plain and simple, *their agenda*: to control the global game of perception and self-perception; for the enslaved to enslave themselves within mental prisons and endless torture, just as was done in reality to our ancestors for centuries.

To me, as a father, more disturbing than the mind-altering violence, perverse sexuality and psychologically stilted adult content Hollywood peddles to our youth is the Academy's overt retro-racism.

We folks are powerfully projected in Tinsel Town as… *some… thing*. Not someone. So rather than participate in the minstrel show of Oscar buffoonery, we are gearing up for Neil deGrasse Tyson's *Cosmos*. Tyson, director of the Hayden Planetarium at the Museum of Natural History in New York, is a *tour de force* celebrity scientist and frequently cited authority on astronomy in the popular media.

Both my beautiful wife, a biotechnology executive in San Diego and a disturbingly enthusiastic fan of deGrasse Tyson, and my son are gearing up for Science Fair in two weeks at his school, and deGrasse Tyson's *Cosmos* is just the elixir they were looking for for inspiration. She and my son are working on the poster board and she has purchased the Glow Germ UV light, a kit that turns the invisible into "germs you can see!" I've taken on a proud supporting role, agreeing to chaperone on his forthcoming field trip to Reuben H. Fleet Science Center.

And you know something? The seeds we parents plant and germinate can take on extraordinary lives of their own. We've got way more juice than Hollywood.

In fact, Christian has recently advised me that his life's work will be in space, the so-called "Final Frontier." He has no clue that this year's winner for Best Director is the director of

Gravity, a movie with its backdrop set unimaginably, beautifully in outer space. His mother and I listen intently to the details, affirm masterfully and add to his dreams. They are the vision and details of a life to be lived. Effortless.

Before he falls asleep, groggy with a day in the school zone, an afternoon of driveway basketball and some heavy-duty YouTube Disney Daffy Duck on his iPad, my son says suddenly, animated:

"And you know what, Daddy? Can I tell you something?"

"Yeah, bud."

"Then I can see God's face from another Galaxy and tell him I love him."

"That's really cool, dude."

"Yeah."

He drops off into sleep like a narcoleptic and is out like a light. Dreaming realities like this takes work.

In the days that follow, he begins to share details of an intergalactic mining operation from which he will harness gems for humanity, profit, his family and a private collection. I cannot express the excitement that bounds from my heart as he lays out details of his venture on Mars, Pluto, "the coldest planet in the galaxy" and the "diamond planet." My disbelief at Hollywood's charade is quelled to zip. We plan further, adding an expensive business lexicon to his quest. The Hollywood racism agenda will have little to zero effect on King. He will possess the visions of creators, ancestors and the Spirit Force.

He imagines astronaut "cool gloves" for hot planets like Venus or the Sun or a fleet of drones for far away galaxies as exoplanets or "extrasolar planets," or mining equipment similar to the machines we see performing federal projects on the freeways.

What I believe is the basis of Dr. Neil deGrasse Tyson's thought process is a universe without limitation. He speaks to our children like a Pied Piper, far more convincingly than the conniving cabal of naysaying sycophants in Hollywood.

Or as Dr. Tyson has more affirmatively stated: *"Our molecules are traceable to stars that exploded and spread these elements across the galaxy,"* he explains. If you *"see the universe as something you participate in — as this great unfolding of a cosmic story — that, I think, should make you feel large, not small… Any astrophysicist does not feel small looking up in the universe; we feel large."*

In the following years, we purchased model rockets and began launching them from empty lots around North County San Diego, particularly Carlsbad. For years we just focused on the fuel, which was a combustible mix of household sugars and stump removal from the local hardware stores. Basically, we heated powdered potassium nitrate, powdered white sugar and distilled water in a frying pan and molded the compound into a gooey sticky material that would dry into a hard crystal-like rock and light it up! The pyrotechnics are the stuff of movies, ultra violence and choreographed stunts timed to the beats of a conductor's symphony. The only problem is we never succeed in attaching this to a model that actually flies. So, we go to hobbyist stores and purchase prefab models which consist of the launch pad, a remote launch control and the rocket. Chris takes a lot of care with the decal stickers and design of his ship, affixing stickers of jazz musician Louis Armstrong affectionately known as "Satchmo." He also affixes a decal sticker of his mother's native Ethiopia on the model rocket. We take the Satchmo to the lot of the Sage Creek High School parking lot along with his mother, who enthusiastically does the countdown and launch Satchmo into the stratosphere — the ship shoots up nearly 1000 yards into the atmosphere before deploying a parachute and whisking back down to earth. But in our imaginations, just like Dr. Neil de Grasse suggested, it explodes into outer space, into the farthest reaches of the universe.

We'll get to the capitalist lessons, the capital market formation and emerging markets, but that's for later. Let him enjoy his childhood and the infinite intelligence he enjoys from the Spirit Force. When the time is right? I'll teach him all about Peoplism, apex-capitalists, super achievers, hyper capitalism, Uber Capitalist structures and we are already well past elementary understanding of Spiritual IQ. *He's well on his way to becoming his own self-fashioned Trini creation.*

Chapter 4:
My Father's Face in June

1999, Summer

Brooklyn, Park Slope at 17th Street and 7th Avenue. I'm still a young man working at Wall Street, 75 Park Place in Manhattan, to be precise, a few blocks from Trinity Church and City Hall and right around the corner from the two World Trade Center Towers which are still standing

I just woke up from an oddly intense and ancient nap, the evening sun shining brightly on my face and my bed sheets wet with perspiration and tears. My bones ache with sleep and I can't seem to shake or reconcile the effects my life or work week are having upon me. My nerves are on edge and I feel very unstable, nearly invisible. Worst of all? It's only Wednesday. So, I take a walk to run some errands, read the New York Times and get something to eat.

I walk past Barnes and Noble and decide to stop by for a while. My browsing finds me in the Cliffs Notes section, where I pick up notes to D.H. Lawrence's Sons and Lovers. Finally, I decide upon a few books by Warren Buffet, Charles Schwab and Michael Eisner in the hopes of some IQ or high brain power that will put me ahead of the curve at work.

As I step into the dry cleaners, I leave my purchase on the counter and tell the Korean woman at the cash register I will return shortly. Before she can object, I exit and head into Prospect Park, into the safety of trees, on a path unusually devoid of bicycles, joggers and rollerbladers when without interruption, without hesitation, without introduction, without apology, without pretense, my father's face appears to me. It is soft, lean, full of promise and bursting with romance as if he were somehow young in the world.

I laugh to myself, somewhat amused at the concert of his face in a serious consternation familiar to me, but on a young man's face. However, I am afraid. He is a young man taking a pensive stroll, brooding, through the park even though it is his time in the world. A wild and untamed beard grows from his face like wildflowers.

The limbs of trees are shaking in the evening breeze while the shadow blends with teals, cypress and amber of the waning sun. Wild gangly birds sweep by calling out his name in their archaic language but he takes notice of nothing: not the branching chamomile which line foot-tall walls, or the various other herbs and spices planted by a local enthusiast; not the small detailed Japanese gardens planted with bonsai trees, red roses, Magnolias, and all other sorts of phylum which I have on many an occasion taken the time to study and learn.

When he walks by the baseball diamond where corporate teams are in the midst of their closing innings, I swear I see them take notice of this brooding young man who's my father and pack up their belongings. Begrudgingly, though with certain respect these men and women march out in a single sober processional. Alongside are spouses who have been gossiping and watching children; adolescents who are flirting with their adulthood and have planted themselves as flowers in the shadow of trees; and the evening who had become night with an obscenely full and yellow moon.

From a respectful distance of well over 10 meters, I follow in his steps and mimic his every movement. If he scratches his beard thoughtfully, I curl my fingers about my smooth chin; if he picks up a stone, at first playing catch, then dashing it into a heap of dry leaves as an afterthought, so do I. And when he turns around irritated to see who had caused the disturbance to his meditation on the cosmos, I hide behind the trunk of a tree like a coward — I don't dare let him know that I have been following him for I am my own man.

So, I follow in my old man's footsteps until the day completely becomes night through the years, right past the hardships and until I am dead.

It's autumn in New York. I live in Brooklyn but commute to Manhattan on the F and A trains. I share this short story, really, a vision from another time outside the constraints of our time, with Daddy who is in New York City, working on his opus, *The Ideology of Racism*. He's excited and upbeat about working on this book, which is really a summation of a life spent battling. *Battling for his people.* Battling for his children.

The cover was commissioned by my younger brother, Cecil, attending the University of Nebraska-Lincoln. It illustrates a Black slave chained in the fires of hell. He is attached to a white slave master and they are both damned in a senseless cycle of terrorism, torture and torment. Daddy asks how I like the cover.

Uuummmmmmm? I like the font at the bottom in a red all caps Times Roman font with the lettering, "Dr. Bing P. Howell."

I'm proud of Daddy.
He is happy now. I'm proud of his accomplishment — *inspired.*

"Thus, to understand the history of the United States, one has to understand the institutions of slavery and its social dimensions and continued impact."

Ideology of Racism — From Slavery, to Plessy, to Affirmative Action to Racial Healing — Let's Talk! Dr. Bing P. Howell

A Season of Ascension

2019, April

Sacramento International Airport, Northern California

"Bye bye, Sacramento. It's off to a better place."

I am falling. Falling into a deep sleep with my hands squeezing, like a rag, Herman Hesse's *Siddhartha*, a remnant from an adolescence that held for me many of the themes I would revisit in my life, becoming the man I have elected to be. The plane lifts from the tarmac and I dream of Daddy, drifting toward the awareness of his inevitable ascension. He was a lover of life and a warrior who knew no bounds. He was my hero, a man who took the cards that he was dealt and found a way to win over and over again. *I know he is with me.* I feel his spirit inside of me. I hear the West Indian Trinidadian forming my sentences. I see his face on my own.

> *"Wisdom cannot be imparted. Wisdom that a wise man attempts to impart always sounds like foolishness to someone else... Knowledge can be communicated, but not wisdom. One can find it, live it, do wonders through it, but one cannot communicate and teach it."*
>
> **— Hermann Hesse, *Siddhartha***

Seated from business class, I hear the St. Patrick's Day revelers abound with joy and spirits. This is so rich in its anagogic symbolism, I can't help but know that my spirit is also lifting, temperature rising, half awake and in a dream state, I wonder if this is what it felt like when Daddy's spirit rose to the heavens, to the ever after. And then, I remember, Daddy is with me as we fly into the open skies, spirit released into his full spirit body — his physical body behind him is finally free to fulfill his total ambition of peace.

A passenger presses a free drink ticket into my palm and I order a rum and Coke from a freckled Taiwanese reveler. Oh, wait, she is a hostess with wild twang. I drink — something Daddy would definitely not have approved of in his later, disciplined years, although he would enjoy this same concoction on many evenings. I substitute out the rum with Courvoisier and a cherry Coca Cola, and as the plane lifts, I fall into a deep, deep sleep and my spirit loosens from my body. I dream again, visiting an ancestral plane I will later learn to visit meditating on theta and delta rays.

In the dream we discuss women, life, and the architecture of the plans we would discuss so many times as a child. "And Patrick," he says, ever the lecturer, "*be better than me.* Baby, never forget God and remember when God is near — *have zero fear.*"

For days, weeks and months afterwards, my sleep will be populated by Daddy and Christian.

And I am suspended somewhere between the two zeniths.

The Capital of California, a nation state with the fourth largest economy globally, is Sacramento. After the United States, Japan, and Germany, California with a $4.1 trillion economy and home to Silicon Valley, the UC system, Hollywood, a rich biotech industry, and the wealthiest farming community in America, boasts a history not only from the '49ers, who came prospecting for gold in 1849, but from the indigenous peoples who have tended to the lands for thousands of years, long before California became a state.

I was born and raised in Elk Grove, a place whose liberal present covers older associations with not only the racist John Birch Society but the Ku Klux Klan in 1922, when hundreds of residents would join in mass initiations.

When you think of California, most think of Los Angeles or Sacramento, and in that manner, my home state is similar to Albany in New York, a "how now cow town" that governs a global center of innovation, wealth, and prestige. My friend Chris Kydd, publisher of the *Coast News* in Carlsbad likes to say, "There is gold in these hills," and he's right. I've driven Newport Coast from crystal oceans and come down on the other side, coasting the 5 freeway to see the snow-capped San Bernardino Hills. California is rich not only because of her people, particularly the Mestizo population, but because of her unparalleled spirit in the ocean, mountains, and farm terrain — that is the source of all her power, energy, and wealth — the natural terrain which has also yielded billion-dollar oil, gas, and mineral sectors for centuries.

However, Sacramento remains largely anonymous, and, in so many ways, that tells you something about me. But to really understand the mana that animates me and my spirit, you have to begin with both of my parents, *both immigrants* — read: foreigners. They came here as so many do, with dreams that they have lived out. However, there have also been the idiosyncrasies of how America initiates all of its newcomers. Contrary to the image of the Statue of Liberty valiantly standing and welcoming those who come here seeking freedom, *freedom* is not free. Justice is not simply justice. And prosperity can spiritually bankrupt a soul. Freedom often comes at a steep price, oftentimes involving hard work, untold sacrifices, and the sheer terrorism visited upon every new initiate group who comes into America, *including* those designated white who have come from Europe.

When people see me, they assume I am African American, a designation I am preternaturally proud of, particularly as it serves opportunity and justice — but there is a chorus of voices — English, Irish, Caribbean American, Afro-Latino… broken accents that are always informing me and coloring my loyalties and preferences for the underdog, the survivor who makes a way out of no way.

Sometimes? I feel like I come from another place altogether, another era, perhaps, *even,* another galaxy.

Daddy was a Trinidadian standout in track and field — arriving not only by plane from London but in shorts from Denver while snow packed the ground. I would imagine his first experience was unearthly; a Caribbean man in the snow, in shorts? He was inducted into the Chapman University Hall of Fame in 1998, along with his son Cecil, where he made a name for himself at the NAACP championships in Ashland, Ohio. When he returned to the airport in Los Angeles, he was recruited by the NFL. He could have played wide receiver for the Los Angeles Rams with a guaranteed contract. Instead, he followed his own script, looking at prime minister Eric Williams as a north star, becoming a standout academic. He would later wonder if he should have sought his father's counsel before declining a potential million-dollar contract on principle when he could have done both.

Daddy recorded ten different records in the Chapman record books during his two-year career with the Panthers, placing third in the 220 yards at the championships in Ashland, Ohio. He placed sixth in the 440-yard relay team in Ashland as a member of the Chapman Panthers at the NCAA national championships. Daddy's school records included the 100 meters and yards, 400 meters, 440 yards, and 1600 meters. He was also part of the 440-yard relay, the 400-meter relay, the mile relay, and the sprint medley for Chapman in '69, which all set records. Additionally, his 60-yard time of 6.5 at the Los Angeles Sports Arena in '69 set a Chapman indoor record.

My mother's father paid for her to travel from Panama to attend the international student program at Chapman. And that's where they met. The Panamanian daughter of a preternaturally savvy businessman and a Trinidadian standout track-and-field athlete. Somehow they would end up at Sacramento State University for graduate degrees, and would make a home that would eventually house six successful kids of their own.

So, Sacramento is the how now cow town (bordering one of America's most prosperous farm industries in the central valley) I was born and raised in. It's changed a little, but not so much. I forgot about all the evergreen trees that line the valley town. About the decency or power of simplicity.

Simple things. The sun is so bright and the sky so blue.

They say everybody goes about grieving in their own way. My way is to remember but move forward... *aggressively*... with our visions, my dreams, and his work on me over a lifetime. *I do this because it is my legacy.* Daddy was a *strange, strange* dude. Weird, Ha! Or maybe the better way to state that is, *"Daddy* is *distinct."*

Grief is an interesting emotion. When I found out, I was kind of blown away for a couple days, and my son kept asking me if I was okay, and I told him I was *really, really* afraid. I spent some time researching bereavement and mourning, and I came across one piece that said if you have not felt it before, mourning can feel like fear. *Affirmed.* In addition, I get some moments of extraordinary peacefulness, but also a lot of intense sadness and just pure shock... *like, wow*... He *was a* mortal. And from a little boy's perspective, I suppose it would be frightening if, all of a sudden, your protector, your idol, your friend was gone... *just gone*.

Well, it's spring. And everything is changing just as it always is. Nothing is permanent. Everything is transitory. Pretty soon the trees will go from all-bark skeletons to all-green masters of oxygen whilst giving alms to the heavens, branches out reaching to the skies. Ever study the trees and their transformation from the dead of winter to the new life of spring? The painted lady butterflies would have completed their migratory journey from Oregon and it will be a season, one just before summer.

For the past two weeks, it has been raining throughout California, where I live. Heavy rain. As a matter of fact, it's been getting colder steadily to the low fifties. This winter, not only did it rain biblical proportions throughout the regions, but we had days where it snowed in Los Angeles and hailed in San Diego.

Now there are bushels of yellow, orange, and rose flowers everywhere — *a superbloom* — in all of California's valleys, mountains, along the beaches, and in the wide-ranging national parks. California is renewing. Daddy's spirit is part of this movement of spirits. From Sacramento to San Diego, California, the world's fourth-largest economy is renewing and reinventing itself. California used to be Mexico, and, if you ask me, when I see the workers in my neighborhood who pull up to clean houses, clean the pool, or do the yard work in my neighborhood, they still serve as the ultimate stewards of the land and her people.

I'm not sure many know this, but Mommy taught me that California is named after a warrior Queen Calafia, a Moor, who developed an army of women warriors joined in battle against Constantinople with Christians. She is more than likely Kamala's spiritual precedent. This race of goddess warrior queens kept man-killing griffins as pets. Ever since then, from the Gold Rush to farming to filmmaking and Silicon Valley, California has stood for dreams, and yeah, I'm a dreamer, not unlike the Chicano immigrants who arrive here with nothing more than the hope of a better life. That's how our family came to be in America producing college graduates, world-class entrepreneurs, educators, and artists.

Highway mountain sides are stamped with visitors picking bushels of wildflowers. Folks are receptive to the painted lady butterflies' playfulness, wonder, and fun. *California is a global capital of renewal.* The painted lady butterflies tend to thrive in a super bloom because there are so many plants for the butterflies to lay their eggs on and for caterpillars to eat.

Yes, Daddy's passing is part of this movement of renewal. His season of ascension is my season of cosmic renewal. Seeds are dropped and blooming everywhere, reminding me of Galatians 5:22-23 *"But the fruit of the Spirit is love, joy, peace, forbearance, kindness, goodness, faithfulness, gentleness and self-control. Against such things there are no laws."*

In the past month or so there has been a view from atop College Blvd in North San Diego in the morning. There is a 5000-year-old volcano that is the centerpiece of a hiking trail: Calavera. At the lookout perch where cars come to see red moons, solstices with big screen clarity and certainty, you will see the sun rise every single day. I drive this route to drop my son off at school. It looks like Mt. Fuji, but it is the San Bernardino mountains in the Inland Empire, almost 100 miles away. I took my son there a couple of weeks ago, stopping by his grandma's house en route to Big Bear Mountain for his first experience with the snow. It was cold. From this perch atop the Calavera Hills, you are less than five miles from the ocean; you will see snow-capped mountains with startling clarity. I know I will be sitting at the mountainside and beaches in the coming months, focusing on not only my breathing but the spring sun's brightness and green bursting everywhere.

They say everybody goes about grieving in their own way. My way is to remember but move forward... *aggressively*... with our visions, my dreams and his work on me over a lifetime. *I do this because it is my legacy.* Daddy was a *strange, strange* dude. Weird, Ha! Or maybe the better way to state that is, *"Daddy* is *distinct."*

Grief is an interesting emotion. When I found out I was kind of blown away for a couple days and my son kept asking me if I was okay and I told him I was *really, really* afraid. I spent some time researching "bereavement" and "mourning" and I came across one piece that said if you have not felt it before, mourning can feel like fear. *Affirmed.* In addition, I get some moments of extraordinary peacefulness but also a lot of intense sadness and just pure shock… *like, wow…* He *was a* mortal. And from a little boy's perspective, I suppose it would be frightening if, all of a sudden, your protector, your idol, your friend was suddenly gone… *just gone.*

Well, it's Spring. And everything is changing just as it always is. Nothing is permanent. Everything is transitory. Pretty soon the trees will go from all-bark skeletons to all-green masters of oxygen whilst giving alms to the heavens, branches out reached to the skies. Ever study the trees and their transformation from the dead of Winter to the new life of Spring? The painted lady butterflies would have completed their migratory journey from Oregon and it will be a season, one just before Summer.

For the past two weeks, it has been raining throughout California where I live. Heavy rain. As a matter of fact, it's been getting colder steadily to the low 50s. This winter not only did it rain biblical proportions throughout the regions, but we had days where it snowed in Los Angeles and hailed in San Diego.

Now there are bushels of yellow, orange and rose flowers everywhere — *a superbloom* — in all of California's valleys, mountains, along the beaches and in the wide-ranging national parks. California is renewing. Daddy's spirit is part of this movement of spirits. From Sacramento to San Diego,

California, the world's fourth-largest economy is renewing and reinventing itself. California used to be Mexico, and, if you ask me, when I see the workers in my neighborhood who pull up to clean houses, clean the pool or do the yard work in my neighborhood — they still serve as the ultimate stewards of the land and her people.

I'm not sure many know this but Mommy taught me, California is named after a warrior Queen Calafia, a Moor, who developed an army of women warriors joined in battle against Constantinople with Christians. She is more than likely Kamala's spiritual precedent. This race of goddess warrior queens kept man-killing griffins as pets. Ever since then, from the Gold Rush to farming to filmmaking and Silicon Valley, California has stood for dreams and yeah, I'm a dreamer not unlike the Chicano immigrants who arrive here with nothing more than the hope of a better life, that's how our family came to be in America producing college graduates, world-class entrepreneurs, educators and artists.

Highway mountain sides are stamped with visitors crawling and picking bushels of wildflowers. Folks are receptive to the painted lady butterflies' playfulness, wonder and fun. *California is a global capital of renewal.* The painted lady butterflies tend to thrive in a super bloom because there are so many plants for the butterflies to lay their eggs on and for caterpillars to eat.

Yes, Daddy's passing is part of this movement of renewal. His season of ascension is my season of cosmic renewal. Seeds are dropped and blooming everywhere reminding me of Galatians 5:22–23 *"But the fruit of the Spirit is love, joy, peace, forbearance, kindness, goodness, faithfulness, gentleness and self-control. Against such things there are no laws."*

In the past month or so there has been a view from atop College Blvd in North San Diego in the morning. There is a five-thousand-year-old volcano that is the centerpiece of a hiking trail: Calavera. At the lookout perch where cars come to see red moons, solstices with big screen clarity and certainty, you will see the sun rise every single day. I drive this route to drop my son off at school. It looks like Mt. Fuji but it is the San Bernardino mountains in the Inland Empire, almost 100 miles away. I took my son there a couple of weeks ago, stopping by his grandma's house en route to Big Bear Mountain for his first experience with the snow. It was cold. From this perch atop the Calavera Hills, you are less than five miles from the ocean, you will see snow-capped mountains with startling clarity. I know I will be sitting at the mountainside and beaches in the coming months, focusing on not only my breathing but the Spring Sun's brightness and green bursting everywhere.

> *For the revelation awaits an appointed time; it speaks of the end*
> *and will not prove false. Though it linger, wait for it;*
> *It will certainly come and will not delay.*
>
> **—Habakkuk 2:3**

The Spirit Force of the universe is always reminding us of his glory and our impermanence at the right moment. Life is the greatest gift and it is not only "free" but priceless. Herman Hesse's *Siddhartha* is about a soul's search for and attainment of enlightenment.

Daddy was a seeker all his life. And he was rigorous. Determined. *Did not settle.* He was a king philosopher and intellectual giant. Teacher and professor… life-student. He was a master mentor and motivator. *Well,* he has now taken that quest to the next level. Or, as Herman Hesse's Siddhartha observed from the spirit realm, *"My real self wanders elsewhere, far away, wanders on and on invisibly and has nothing to do with my life."*

So, there it is, twenty-first century fans: in time, *all* will *be* revealed.

Chapter 5:
So, Wait — I'm *Actually* an Oreo Cookie? *Ha!*

For me the high school years were also revelatory, if not a painful transition from an often idyllic childhood to an adventurous adulthood with plenty of mountain tops and valleys. There was this incident — *actually there were a lot of incidents around that time* — when I was a sophomore at Jesuit High School in Carmichael Sacramento. Semester grades were going to be posted and all of us were waiting for Father Kelly (Latin class) to post the honor roll. We flocked like little minions to the brick wall and Father Duckworth gently and silently elbowed room, making room for his colleague, another priest, procuring masking tape and then posting the edict. The brick hallway was dark and cool: a pathway of passages and discovery.

Well, it was really a place where we would seek to destroy one another in the vicious competition for placement at Berkeley, Stanford and Harvard. There I was, at the top of the list — Worked. My. Butt. Off. I was so proud and couldn't wait to tell Daddy. Immediately, all of my classmates — at least, the assassin smarty pants in the class — started throwing shade at me: "Ewwww, look! Look! Patrick's an Oreo Cookie! *He's a double filling Oreo Cookie!*" Oreo cookies are black on the outside, white on the inside, dude — think supreme court justice Clarence.

Thomas or some other commonly referenced so-called sellout like Dr. Ben Carson or Candace Owens. And I was a doubled filled one… or, being called that. Immediately, my pride morphed into shame.

Burgundy Bonneville was the ride of choice at that time for my father — he had not yet graduated to his dream of a Cadillac, the Caribbean man's highway yacht. A feeling of trepidation came over me — time to report grades as I saw him pulling up to the pickup in front of the gym. "Hey Patrick!" he sang in an even voice. I said, kinda depressed, *"I made the honor roll?" Cum laude.* He wanted to dance but I was just a mess. "What happened, Patrick?"

The three of us (including Mommy) came up with this: there was a latent form of racism because I was smart and using my intellectual gifts at the highest level, I was somehow "white." If I was on the basketball or football team and doing what the Cowboy's Tony Dorsett or 49er's Jerry Rice were doing, I would be in my wheelhouse as a young Black man in '80s America, where Michael Jackson did the moonwalk.

But I had played the piano for years, played trombone in a jazz band, swam the 100 breaststroke and 50-yard freestyle at meets, was very competitive in the 200 and 400 yard in track and field and liked drawing superheroes. I loved reading — anything that was as much education as it was entertaining: Theodore Dreiser, Edgar Rice Burroughs's Tarzan, Marvel comics, very few DC comics and the *Encyclopedia Britannica.* Oh, and I loved U2, Sting, and Depeche Mode. Of course, Sade and Anita Baker sang the ballads that would put me to sleep. And Snap! ("Got the Power"), MC Hammer and

Soul to Soul composed the rhythms we would jump and draw audiences to with our variations on popping and locking.

Now that I look back on it, I realize I was forming my identity and evolving those ideas of what I could and could not do, and why. The kids call it code switching these days. I was laying the groundwork for the man I have become. And it's still not a complete process. I realize now that my parenting style is very different from Daddy's — he was more so a fixed post to whom I could always look as the North Star and realize the man I want to be. My style has been more collaborative — push and pull. Teach and listen. Learn, lead and rebut. Challenge and concede. Represent and lead but come down from my perch and explore and be led by the next generation of great world leaders. *I sire. I am a magistrate, consul and visionary.* Increasingly, I am excited by what my son, SharkHeart, will create and the difference he and his generation will make upon our collective reality.

Over past holidays, I submitted for my 23andMe ancestry registry test, a genetic test that gives a breakdown of global ancestry by percentages. I've had a strong sense of myself and who I am for as long as I can remember. My mother told me about the West African chieftains that were my ancestors before coming to Barbados and I always imagined us reclaiming crowns in Panama or America. I knew about the smattering of Irish and English in me, but it's a little different to submit a plastic vile of saliva and find out by a breakdown of ancestry that I am 67.9% Sub-Saharan (West African), 29.8% European (British and Irish) and 1.3% Native American. It is illuminating to find that going back over five thousand years, my maternal haplogroup (L1c2a2) is East African, specifically the Bantu Tribe. It is fascinating to see that my father's haplogroup (E-P252), where my ancestors more than likely came from West and Central Africa into the Bahamian Islands of Abaco, Eleuthera, Exuma, Grand Bahamas and New Providence — all the tribes reorganized into new tribes.

When I saw a young Percival "the Gong" Howell next to a young Marcus Garvey in Kingston Jamaica, I wondered if the co-founder of the Black liberation movement and co-founder of Rastafari couldn't somehow be related to me.

I received an email out of nowhere from a doppelganger of sorts in London, another Patrick A. Howell, who asked me if I wasn't related to any immigrants from Jamaica that migrated to Trinidad. I mean, the mindset of Black liberation, intellectual freedom, revolutionary fervor was certainly related to my own. Could it be? It made sense to me that he was the older great-uncle to my own grandfather John, whose origins in Trinidad are somewhat of a mystery to me.

I know the call of ancestors and those djembe drums in my ears (kings' pride drumming through the DNA connecting through platelets of blood) was responsible for the role I played raising $1.5M for then-candidate Barack Obama in John Birch Society legacy community Orange County. It is even more interesting to go back 3200 years to see that I share paternal lineage with Pharaoh Ramesses II. Egypt and Kemet thinking has factored largely into my curiosity and thinking since I began focusing on my writing. My writing is really an exploration of my most authentic self as well as how the symbols of language represent the reality of our daily language. These communications that you are reading? *They are a spiritual exercise.* And it just reinforces the sense that my internal compass is every bit as strong as the miracles of modern genetic testing.

I have no doubt from my love of certain literature, political structures and music, that the Igbo and Yoruba tribes are in there somewhere. And that's also what I mean by *ancestry in motion* — whether the test was taken or not, there are certain traits, affinities, realities that present themselves in such a manner where the ancestors are making their case — year in and year out. As I like to say: *You can take the African out of Africa but you cannot take Africa out of the African.*

So, the 28% of me that's so called "white" is enough to understand how Depeche Mode has influenced Kanye West. Or, how my top ten, including Sting, Prince, Seal, Kanye, Dave Matthews, U2, Tobe Nwigwe and Kendrick Lamar are all related to folk music legend Joni Mitchell through the ancient art forms of storytelling and her modern mastery of that storytelling in folk music; I am cosmopolitan enough to understand that the only position that colonizers assume over the modern colonized is sheer rage, low self-esteem and a slipping grip that creates a mass anxiety. I listen intently to the afro-beats of Youssou N'Dour, Papa Wemba, Baba Maal, Fela Aníkúlápó Kútì, Marium Mekebe, Teddy Afro and so many other Kings and Queens with a keen discerning ear.

My ancestry has been in motion throughout my life and I have taken cues from ancestors that were communicating with me throughout my journey. I still remember being a little boy and being transfixed by a children's book about King Solomon and the Queen of Sheba, of the *burnt-skinned people of the Kush* (Ethiopia) when I was five years old. I remember the intricate drawings of peacocks, clay walls, court drummers, colorful gowns and robes, incandescent riches and being drawn to those images beyond my understanding. I believe sometimes when I stretch my memory and imagination

At that time, I was reading any and all books related to King David and his father, King Solomon — 1st and 2nd Samuel, the books of Psalms and Proverbs, books of poetry and the wealth of wisdom. Further, I have always enjoyed the tribal melodies of Jazz, Calypso, Reggae and Hip Hop for not only rhythm and enjoyment but transmission of spirits, messaging from the realms of ancestors. I've always said this, believed this, known this: technology and magic are in our memories, DNA and all around us. They are in the sun rays, cosmos and communicated by the trees. Commonly referred to as mysteries, creativity, imagination and wonder, ancestral projection from the past and into the future are not only possible but commonplace and second-hand nature amongst so called "creatives."

Secondly, *and this is key here, Ha!* I understand my affinity for the Irish band U2 and my teenage fixation with all things Depeche Mode, Pet Shop Boys, Tears for Fears, Thompson Twins and OMD (Orchestral Manoeuvres in the Dark), the British invasion of the '80s, my coming of age. Matter of fact — *and this is in all seriousness* — I'll bump Depeche Mode (along with Kanye West, Kendrick Lamar and Prince) when I pick my son up from his private Christian school (we listen to Bach, Mozart, Chevalier de Saint-Georges and Beethoven on the way in).

And, well, I guess those kids weren't so wrong, lol. ***I am an Oreo Cookie.*** Sure, there is some off-white sugar filling, but primarily that dark rich chocolate cookie, grades of caramel and butterscotch in the filling somewhere too. And definitely a whole lotta nuts! But even more importantly I will be taking trips to Ireland, North and East Africa and continuing to engage other souls with the spirits of love, mystery and wonder that are ever present in our world and universe.

More to the point, the corrosive constructs of divisive politics all around us are nothing more than the technology of racism enhanced by artificial intelligence by the spiritually weak who have become powerful in our current politics and zeitgeist.

And maybe I just enjoyed those bands because, well, *they are the dopest masters of harmonic convergence in our modern age?* We are one human family with a rich complexity and variety, a never-ending cornucopia of expressions, hues, traditions and spiritual practices. The most specific, cosmic and lasting test of our humanity is tent-poled between two polarities of *Hate and Love.* Everything else is a choice between those two primers — cosmic forces representing the binary one or zero. We are a mighty race, *our human race*. We sire. *We raise on up.* We shine the light for all because we want it to be seen; or as Seal coined it so much better than I just tried, "*Shining the light, 'cause they wanted it seen!*"

And yeah, I will enjoy my Oreo Cookies with some honey wine and almond milk after I have had a rich meal of curry chicken, brown sugar chicken and mango salad or mango chutney and injera with tibs. Or perhaps some Caribbean Callaloo punctuated with snow crab, king crab and blue crab covered with copious amounts of pepper sauce. *A delicious meal — a feast of feast.* All of this with a spirit of immense curiosity, always pushing the boundaries, and a flare for the revolutionary, if not evolutionary. Or, at the very least a cosmic one; *one we have all* enjoyed many, many times before in the millennia preceding this one. Nothing is new under our sun — not even our immense ignorance.

Chapter 6: **Cosby USA *2020***

I had to laugh and just shake my head in quiet disbelief — another article about Phylicia Rashad, America's mom, and how the *Cosby Show* of the '80s was vilified because it thought it was all that. *Haters never ever give in do they?* The April 3rd article by Chris Witherspoon was published on Grio, the African American MSNBC ezine:

The Cosby Show *is without a doubt an American treasure; however the series has received some backlash from critics who believe the show's portrayal of an upscale African-American family wasn't realistic.*

In all fairness, the Grio was merely reporting a story. I guess it is part of my ongoing disbelief at the dyslexic dissonance of American life early in the twenty-first century. Part of that dissonance has to do with class, part of it is issues of self-esteem and deep-seated depression within the Black community and part of it is race in America. *It wasn't until the* Cosby Show *came out that it all came together and our communities, the American Community, was turned towards our total potential.*

So, yes, back in the day, every Thursday was family night on NBC TV and that was unusual because Daddy regimented our media and popular culture intake with the strictest diet. We had carte blanche on the evening news with Dan Rather, Tom Brokaw or Peter Jennings. Unlimited healthy snacks —

read: Public Broadcasting Service. Open pantry Sundays with Mutual of Omaha's *Wild Kingdom*, NBA or *60 Minutes*. During the week, championship diet of textbooks, activities and jogs around the neighborhood with Daddy and my younger brother. No *Hill Street Blues*, no *Wise Guy*. But my brother and I knew how to tip toe quiet down those stairs past curfew while Mommy was grading and catch a glimpse of all the evening action.

Saturday mornings we enforce our rights with *Hong Kong Fuey*, *Fat Albert*, *Voltron*, *Speed Racer*, *Bugs Bunny*, *Road Runner* and *Soul Train*. No to Alex Haley's *Roots* (Mommy and Daddy didn't want us internalizing that we were slaves). No to *Dallas*, no *Falcon Crest* — definitely no to *Dynasty*. *What's Happening* and *Different Strokes* were taboo, too. (A gain, they didn't want us internalizing the tropes that were being spoon-fed to us by mass culture.) I guess Daddy subscribed to the 100 Black Men of America mantra of *"What they see, they will be."* For some reason *Fantasy Island* and *The Love Boat* were cool — and maybe? That had something to do with Mommy and Daddy going on date night.

But every Thursday night, somehow, by the grace of God, the whole family would gather religiously around the television set for thirty minutes with Dr. Huxtable, Claire Huxtable, Esq., Denise, Vanessa, Theo and his homeboy, Cockroach. Theo and his friend Cockroach tried to pass an exam on Shakespeare's *Macbeth* without actually reading the play. As long as Theo Huxtable gave it his best in class, Dr. Huxtable was willing to forgive a "hard-earned C." (When I tried that one with my dad, he said in his characteristic Caribbean bravado, "stchupidness.") Little Rudy Huxtable and her best friend, the blues -loving chauvinist Kenny had a thing for each other but were too young to realize it.

The Cosby Show was family time. It was dream time. It was "be one" time. We watched. We imagined. We cuddled. We learned. We laughed. We envisioned. *We all saw the future.* And it was good for so-called families, no different to *The Andy Griffith Show* or *Leave it to Beaver* — *The Cosby Show* and Bill Cosby reinforced and programmed all of us with the best possible America.

It was no different when Cosby's *A Different World* came along, following Denise Huxtable's adventures at the historically Black Hillman college with Dwayne Wayne and Whitley. The monotony of my junior high school at Sacramento's St. Anne's and Sister Madeline's strictest regimen of literature, were frequently offset by daydreams of Lisa Bonet and her Denise Huxtable.

Ms. Rafanan and Sister Madeline gave me everything I could handle in seventh and eighth grade, sharpening English, reading and language skills that inform you as you read this very piece. Those daydreams were this young brother's *only* relationship to *Ferris Bueller's Day Off*. Matter of fact, I went through a Dwayne Wayne stage in my junior year in high school, embracing my inner geek with glee, sporting a flat top, showcasing nerd wear (pleated corduroys, plaid shirts, with suspenders) and flip glasses because that cat had figured out how to woo Denise Huxtable.

The Cosby Show was a paradox where radicalism and buppiness intersected. Dr. William Henry 'Bill' Cosby, Jr., Ed.D. re-imagined *The Andy Griffith Show* in stunning full Technicolor. To me, the show simply said, *"We are all just fine, matter of fact we are way cool, and that's cool."* Or "dare to be everything you can be. *It'll all be okay, it really will be'* Radical could be cool and matter of fact chill, or normal, like a brownstone in Brooklyn Heights, a castle of buppiness. Radical could be copasetic; it did not have to be radicalized and lethal like the Black Panther Movement (*and not that that was a bad thing either*). *Radical* could be polo shirts with Black power fists casually in pockets. Radical could be Brooks Brothers or tailored suits from a Beverly Hills clothier who had garbed Mayor Tom Bradley in sartorial splendor. It was matter of fact and jarring all at once. And pleasant. And funny. But cool, *you know*? Cosby, a true griot, and his venerated team of educators and producers dared to imagine a world — *a way forward.* Just like the presidential campaign slogans in 2008 for a certain senator out of Chicago: *Forward — like a certain attorney general out of Oakland California made clear in 2025:* ***We're not going back.***

By the way, Oprah Winfrey, in the aforementioned Grio article, agrees with *The Cosby Show*'s significance globally: We probably wouldn't have the president in the office that we had from 2008 to 2016 had there not been Bill Cosby's show because "*The Cosby Show* introduced America to a way of seeing Black people and Black culture that they had not seen before," Oprah noted, referring to President Obama. And she wasn't just talking about Black culture. She was talking about *all of us. American* citizens.

More than likely in another thirty years, in the year 2043, 1600 Pennsylvania Avenue will be multiplied exponentially with zip codes in 90210, 92010, 60615, 30319, the African continent and the Caribbean.

It's funny to me because in 2024, over 40 years later, the Cosby family, with their picture-perfect family and pedigree, have resided in a few million households in America including 1600 Pennsylvania Avenue. *Visions always precede reality.* Architectural designs and schematics are drawn up prior to building empires. By that I just mean that visionaries not only see the future but speak it into being. If you read on you will see what I mean.

In my case, America's Dad and my dad seem to have some unspoken *"this is wassup"* understanding. America's mom and my mom, an engineer with Pac Bell at the time, seem to enjoy regular girlfriend lunchtime rendezvous from their offices to cosign on children and child rearing. We saw everything Mommy and Daddy were endlessly lecturing and promoting about education, a good life despite our doubts from the larger organizing concepts of racism and discrimination institutionally entrenched on our televisions, in the film industry and carried out throughout society — we saw ourselves and *that it could be done.* ***That is power.*** *That is Love, Almighty.* That is removing the harness from the Hollywood Industrial Complex. *The Cosby Show* was power, change and the future. *It was love.* And Bill Cosby is the architect. Just like slave holder and American Hell system builder George Washington. Period. I mean, *ex-plantation point!*

Now I'm thinking about Jack Black from the classic '90s flick *High Fidelity*. There was this scene where Jack Black's store clerk character is insulting the record store manager's (played by John Cussack) choice of attire. Animated, the store clerk bellows with a snooty nasal though borderline psychotic intonation, eyes dilated and an emphatic show of pride, *"a Cosby sweater!"*

"A Cosby sweater!" On the twenty-fifth anniversary of *The Cosby Show*'s last show, I shamelessly snatch Jack Black's crack. I bellow, a fanaticism animating my face, eyes wide open, pupils nearly dilated, ***"It's a Cosby America! A COSBY USA!"***

Chapter 7:
Rise of the SharkHeart

April 2, 2017,

Rancho San Dieguito Boys and Girls Club in Solana Beach

"YOU CAN DO ANYTHING YOU SET YOUR MIND TO"

Yes, I told him like my dad told me, "Christian, you can do anything you set your mind to, baby."

"Anything?"

"Anything." The light goes on like lightning across a blackened night. I see it in his eyes. Rise, Shark Heart. Rise.

When my son was eighteen months old, we headed into the Olympic-size pool at our complex in Quail Meadow, Irvine. I knew I was going to do it — *I knew I was going to do it before he was even conceived.*

I've always enjoyed a relationship with open water. Ever since Mommy took me to Sacramento's Cabrillo Pool in the '80 s. Cornrow-braided Kevin patiently taught me the crawl, elementary backstroke and side scissor swim. I was eight and I still remember him, such a cool, cool cat. He knew I was a great swimmer. I later competed for Greenhaven Swim Club *(before switching to Daddy's track and field) for nearly a decade.* Then there was the ocean, Stinson Beach in California and the beaches in Trinidad and Panama. My father worried about how far I would go out and say, "Patrick! Come back in, na'?" in the Trinidadian lilt that would color his voice. But the pool was my haven — I have always ta ken solace, built confidence and enjoyed the silence of the universe there, so I knew since before he was born that I was going to take my son into the water and we were going to have fun there, a lot of it. It wasn't so much a plan as a calling; not so much of an ambition as a meditation —

Son, this is how we can fly… this is how we can fly on this planet in the atmosphere that is aquamarine dense. You will learn to fly and fly the rest of your life.

You will be Sharkheart.

By the time my son was five, he was friends with the mighty Pacific Ocean lining the coast of Orange County California where he was born. We hunted the shorelines for dollar shells, little sand crabs and all sorts of marble rocks. He's curated quite a collection. We also collected seashells and rocks from the Caribbean Sea, off the shores of Cabo San Lucas and the Atlantic Ocean off the coasts of Panama. And of course, I would talk to him about life during our adventures. We packed his aquarium and later our backyard lake with them. Around this time, his mother and I enrolled him in Waterworks Aquatics in Irvine, right down the road on Sand Canyon. I knew I was going to do that two years in advance, particularly when I saw the photos of Mark Spitz lining their walls on my initial inspection. He had three coaches there. I knew their names and they knew mine — I hand-picked two of them and they doted their attention upon him. That was an excellent investment, superior return.

What sort of entrepreneurship are you engaged with? What kind of an entrepreneur are you? A parasite? An apex-capitalist? An enabler? Enobler? What's your bottom line? What organic relationships would you like to cultivate? What is your Spiritual IQ?

"Power is as Power does."

— Patrick A. Howell

Red hummingbirds darting in and out. They dip long beaks extended by longer necks into vases of flowered nectar. Mourning cloak caterpillars and snails. A dream home in a beachside valley; a quaint SoCal town called Carlsbad right down the road from Legoland. King to sire & serendipity in the dead of winter. The last 10 years have been the fulfillment of many dreams, visions and ambitions I harbored for myself as a boy. And when I say 'Dream' — I mean lifelong visions that were divined from within a long, long time ago.

Like regal black panthers chasing for the hunt, we leap from the paved sidewalk to the concrete street.

My son and I are jogging the neighborhood block, which becomes a winding road through fields of crops — grapes, tomatoes, vine fruits and vegetation. The first part of the prowl from the house to the gates of the trail is less than four hundred meters.

He keeps up with me effortlessly — or is it effortless? The seven-year-old is already huffing and puffing, a stern consternation on his face, a sideways glance askance to make sure I do not overstep my boundaries. He's not going to let his old man pass him, not this time. "Chris, remember to inhale through your nose, exhale through your mouth controlled and slowly. *You* control your breath."

I don't know if he is this competitive organically or it is something I have bred in the young prodigy. Does it matter? We sire our offspring to be kings tomorrow and sometimes a king must dominate by sheer will or display of naked aggression. "Power is as power does," I often say, having adapted Frederick Douglass' *"Power never conceded anything without a demand"* as my own.

Past the gate is a downhill dirt path between fields of vines, tomatoes and strawberries. I use my two hundred+ pounds as well as a long stride to roll past the young Hussein Bolt aspirant. "Not this time around," I think sarcastically, glee and pride populating the cavity of my chest. My joy is overcome with worry that he does not give in.

"Chris, never give in. *In this life, you get what you give yourself.* Remember, the only time you *truly* lose in life is when you give up." I've said it to him on previous runs — that one I adapted from my father, who oft quoted Franklin D. Roosevelt long before Tony Robbins was ever en vogue, *"The only thing we have to fear is fear itself."* The downward hill levels off into a winding path around the creek and I have to rely, now, on my own hubris and internal motor.

Past an old abandoned concrete damn system to a two hundred meter uphill where the lactic acid begins to burn and my quads contract; my long stride whimpers to a simper. He devours me alive; consumes me whole. And save for my pride in his accomplishment, mining his grandfather's edict of success, he breaks me. I am left wheezing up the hill and wondering, dubiously filled with fear, and the sentiment, "How do I expect to compete next month in the half iron man triathlon when I can't even finish off a single one strong?"

I hear the pint-sized motivator bellow earnestly, *"C'mon, Daddy — finish strong!"* I lift my knees now *burdened* by the two hundred + lbs and the ache of knees laughing deliriously at me for my former hubris. *"It never rains in Southern California,"* yeah, right. I am self-defeating, "damn near fifty degrees in this sunny San Diego. Feels like it's thirty." I am barely hopping the sand sacks littering the concrete road uphill and pounding the pavement only to see the pint-sized motivator disappear over the hill completely. I guess he waited long enough. When I reach the summit I see he is barreling down the dirt track past the gates of the dirt track onto the adjacent El Camino road over a side bend path of weeds, uneven land. I imagine him saying, "I'll motivate you *and* beat you, old man." My barrel is bigger than his.

I become a panther running down its prey at full speed.

I imagine it so vividly, I yell, "Beat you like I am your daddy kid!" I lift the aging Pac-10 conference legs and extend toe to heal, stride long and rhythmic — there is no tension and no pain, only form and speed — and I see him look over his shoulder, brow furrowed with determination and his feet stepping smart over all sorts of turbulence without a single misstep. I have the high land of the road though. He has no idea how talented he is but I am his daddy and beating me is a rite of passage. He'll have to earn it.

"*You are my daddy*, Daddy," he says as I pass him on the trodden path.

As cold as it is, I feel the beads of sweat breaking from my forehead and trickling down my back. We, panther and cub, are on a gilded path from the main road to our community. I am tempted to stop and cheer him on before I turn the corner, but I want him to experience the disappearance he gave me a few moments ago. I turn the corner in rhythm, just like the bend of a track curve, nice easy stride, no worry — we are lying down on this bend, relaxing here — definitely no crisis of conscience. *America is elemental capitalism, baby,* and the Wall Street lessons gotta' come sooner or later. Pungent scent of scented flowers punches my nostrils.

I look away from the sidewalk in front of me. At my left is a wall of flowers in full bloom. The weather is confused, inverting Spring ceremonies at the dead of winter. But then I see it. Not that it is an aberration but it is eerie, even shocking: *The vision of a flock of Monarch butterflies hibernating and blanketing a pined bushel.* The appearance of this supernatural bushel possesses my mind. My black panther lies down, resigned, quietly, at the shade of the bush, licking his paws.

I stop running. I turn around to find my son sullen, shoulders sunk, frown on his face. "Dude, what? You thought it would be easy? C'mon! Pass me — and *NEVER give up. Die first, baby.* When you *feel* that break. When you feel like your spirit breaks? *That's when the race has just begun.* Your spirit will not break — it's in your blood to run the marathon. That's when you get up and go and don't be afraid. *Go! Go! Go!*" Inspired, he finds his pace and smiles giving me a one-two rhythm upon passing. He doesn't even notice the Monarchs in their winter.

Before it is done, I am yelling at the top of my lungs, "*Go Chris Go!!!*" The boy is a strong runner and I don't give a damn about winning. *There are levels to this game of life.* A couple of the butterflies with patented black and orange patterned wings serendipitously and lazily circle my head as if a haphazard halo. *"I give up the race for you, my son."* I guess I'm talking to my old man, answering his query as to the only time you lose in life. *"Go Chris Go!!!"*

And like that, all three of us, generations, smile a cosmic smile together. There it is: *knowing*. That is how our spirits are at their most elemental, pure energies.

"How did I do today, Daddy?"

"You did good, Chris — really good."

"Yeah, I did *well,* Daddy?" He wears the crown well.

"You did excellent, King."

Power is as power does.

Chapter 8:
In God We Trust / In Cash We Pay

MAY 2019 *PARKED ON THE PACIFIC COAST HIGHWAY AT THE EARTH-TONED CARLSBAD BLUFFS, PARKED* AND OVERLOOKING THE PACIFIC OCEAN, WHERE MY TRUE WILL ELEVATES ME AND I CONTINUE TO SURVEY, CANVAS AND STUDY… ME

I enjoy a rich complex relationship with the United States of America. My parents met at Chapman College (well before its current designation as Chapman University) and I was born here. I've made my family, success, homes and fortunes here. I've realized dreams here. Heavens, we were even able to elect the first Black president. *Now, keep in mind, it took the US longer than Apartheid South Africa to do so but we're still ahead of Russia and China, right? Heck, we may just elect a woman or a Black woman before those two superpowers, right? Actually, Barbados did it sooner as did Liberia with President Ellen Johnson Sirleaf; as did Ethiopia with President Sahle-Work Zewde and Colombia is tied with America with vice president Francia Marquez.*

At times, however, I've experienced a very specific low-frequency vibration of anger and hatred *(read: rage)*, and at others immaculate pride, transcendental love and warmth.

That low vibration is a burn populating the heart cage with an iridescent fire and I do not wish another human to experience this surreal sensation of rage and yet millions of us, with a hue darker than blue have experienced it every single day for centuries, no different from our beloved James Baldwin, Toni Morrison, Zora Neal Hurston, Gwendolyn Brooks, Richard Wright, Langston Hughes, or Audre Lorde have so passionately, precisely and beautifully. And as I learned, from these healers and spiritual elegants, I offer:

Self-realization is… Don't dream, *be*.
Lay the bad memories, the bad past, to rest like an old
dead man –
Don't forget, simply memorialize and leave it behind… Moribund the effect will raise itself up,
Like a ghoul but bury it
With incantations of self-honey love and granulated will power,
Deep inside the ground.
Deep within the texture of who you are.

Slay your demons, spirit your angels – Summon them
Pull them from within out.
Let their flight guide your heart, and your ambitions in tow,
To its ultimate height.

Don't fear – *ever*.
Don't let hatred inhabit your space –

Don't let it consume you. Don't let it touch you –
Do not Let the Devil have its way with you – You – *brown sugar man,*
Crystallizing cosmic ambitions.
Inhale – exhale. Meditate – focus with purpose every day.
You are – because you dream,
Because you struggle, because you realize, you become.
You are.

I learned as a child *you can't love something that doesn't love you.* Sounds simple enough but when you are a little brown-skinned boy in a classroom and everyone stands to say the pledge of allegiance and something about that runs contrary to your spirit and everything that you are about? Sheer *stchupidness.* What about then, what do you do? I can tell you this: people knew to leave Dr. Howell's children *alone. And that's a fact.*

Didactic Dissonant Dado Daddy Disclaimer:

Now I'm sorry if I've led you to believe he was a sainted brown-skinned angel who walked the Earth. He was that. *To me.* But he was also an incredibly complex soul who — if his branches sprawled out to the heavens — his roots reached down into hell and the mud, as many of us who inhabit this earthly realm.

It's true that when I talk about him in keynotes, business stories or anecdotal tales to other people one-on-one, they are always intrigued by him. They hear the quality of my love and admiration, as you probably have, oozing from my spirit and voice. My love for him and pride in him are qualities that are truly great about me. So many have felt that they met him through me. Or commented that they wish they could meet him. And that makes sense too, because I've been told my entire life that I look like him — I remember the first time in his native Trinidad with his mom and sisters calling me "little Bing " in sing-song accents characterized by playfulness, brown sugar molasses and hummingbirds.

My father afforded me every opportunity America has to offer with the benefits of a powerful self-belief, self-determination, reliance upon discipline, creativity and education. He was unrelenting in his application of these principles. He was adamant that his job was not to be my 'friend' but to be my father. If it were not for my own son, I would be unclear on the distinction, for as a father, your vision, integrity and creative force form the foundation of a young man's life. So while a style of fatherhood might be "buddy," it is always with an eye to the future for which, ultimately, you will be nonexistent. A father's job is to prepare a man for the world and all that it has to offer, all of the contingencies. My father's job is masterful. While I can't talk to him today, I know he receives my prayers and praise — if not, he will see them manifest in the outcome of my life. Blessings to all "Daddies" out there putting in the work, day in, day out; year in, year out without a thought of gratitude and only preparedness.

But maybe, however, I'm getting ahead of myself here. The first time I really had a transformative experience with race in good 'ole America, it was through my Scholastic Reader. That's right — it wasn't any of the times I had seen Daddy pulled over and harassed by the Sacramento Highway and Sheriff's departments for DWB, it wasn't all the time I had two Carlsbad police SUVs pull up in front of my residence for the same crime, it wasn't the time my son was accosted at our club pool and had to let that white Karen know *he ain't the one*, it wasn't the barrage of rampant discrimination I have received at business and education institutions, or my son's experiences, it wasn't all of the lawsuits for employment discriminatory practices — it was sitting and reading and thinking, on that plain, at that frequency of being and all the revelations that can unfold from those sacred spaces.

My father was a young professor at Cosumnes River College and he and Mommy were young, sexy and beautiful beings, filled to the brim with a love and romance that would give birth to six of us. They were a young god and goddess going by the earthly monikers *"Bing Patrick & Luisa Jacinta"*; God's dream of what a man and a woman should be.

My face was permanently set to stun with a brilliant smile — I won the lottery being born to these two. Although they would never be so imaginative in their descriptions of themselves, *they were*. So beautiful. Sensual. Stunning. Sexy. *And loving.* I remember how *all* of it *felt.*

I read a Frederick Douglass Scholastic Reader with an illustration of a young Frederick Douglass, who at 16 was on the receiving end of "slave-breaker" master Edward Covey, until one day Douglass put a whopping on Covey that would be *an awakening for an entire nation*. Again, I read about a young Cassius Clay (a.k.a. Muhammad Ali) throwing his Olympic Gold medal in the Ohio River in Louisville Kentucky. I read about it again in William Styron's *The Confessions of Nat Turner* years later for an AP English honors class with Mr.

Patrick McCrystle at Jesuit High School, but this was my first virtual though bloody encounter with America's harbinger and reckoning in my Scholastic Reader at Pony Express Elementary in Sacramento.

I asked Daddy incredulously, *"Did this all really happen?"*

"Yes, Patrick, it did and it does."

"How did they do this? How did Frederck Douglass and Ali get the power to do this?" I fell in love with educator Mary McCloud Bethune too, who was represented in body by Sister Madeline from St. Anne's Elementary and Ms. Richardson, my fourth-grade teacher at Pony Express Elementary School. Both ladies would add to my literary, writing self-esteem and a significant boost in an advanced after-school reading and comprehension program.

"Well, baby, you can't love something that doesn't love you, can you?"

"No."

"*Well — okay then.*"

And, well that brings back Jesuit High School in Carmichael when I was a young man on the track team. We traveled to compete at a high school track and field meet in Yorba City. I was sitting on a wooden bleacher with friends, dangling my legs. I had Puma cleats with spikes on.

A coach from the opposing team came by and angrily said, "*Boy*, you've got your cleats on my cooler. Move them." My group of white friends fell silent at the sharp racist rebuke. I was quiet as he angrily took my legs, slapped them and belligerently moved them, "I *told you boy*, to move your cleats from my cooler," and then walked away.

I sat for about a minute, initially nonplussed — even then I was developing a habit of not reacting to pain within the moment, keeping a steady head about me in the direst of circumstances. But then a *feeling* — the creeping dark pall of anger, and its precedent grays of shame and humiliation, started settling over me like Tupac and Shaka Zulu deciding they were going to tag team Floyd Mayweather and Eminem — *no es bueno. Oye! ¡Compréndeme!* I got up from my seat, tapped that white man on his shoulder and slapped that white man's face, top of my middle finger to his forehead, palm center smacking his mouth and palm chin bruising his chin, and retorted, *"Who told you you could put your hand on me,* boy?"

He looked at me, stunned, so I belted him another one with my weaker right hand on the other side of his face, with even more force so he could wake up from the shock of the first one. Spit flew from his mouth — "*You awake now?* Who told you you could put a hand on me?!" He just turned beet red, stunned, eyes glossing, tears roiling. I could see the red pattern of my fingers setting on his cheek bones, temple and forehead. It began drizzling.

"*That's good.* Very good — *be quiet* now, because there's nothing to say *is there?*" seventeen years of fighting violently with a competitive pugilist younger brother (think Hershey bite-sized Mike Tyson, or generously proportioned Floyd Mayweather rounded out to Lawrence Taylor portion or a bite-sized George Foreman) were about to be exacted on the unsuspecting mark — little *punk.* Wisely, he kept quiet, so I was able to complete my lecture from the impromptu lectern of where I stood, "And you remember this the next time you think about putting hands on a brown-skinned kid because you think you have some power that clearly you do not. *I could sue you and the entire city of Yorba City and you'd have to just be quiet and take it like you are now.*"

The bus ride on the way home from Yorba City back to Carmichael was silent as the white priest, coaches and my teammates now saw me *very, very* differently. I looked outside the bus window as a storm of biblical proportions began to pour down. Water pelted the quiet yellow bus like an orchestra of drums. I couldn't wait to get off that bus situation and get with my tribe. I didn't understand what had happened even though I orchestrated much of it. *Transmutation.*

Daddy's maroon-burgundy Bonniville was waiting and I told him everything, like a parishioner at the confessional to a priest.

Without hesitation, without interruption, without apology, without pretense, without skipping a beat, he said, "*Good.* Damn right, Patrick. Proud of you. *And don't worry about anybody.* Let me deal with them. You tell them to talk to me, okay?"

"Yes. Okay."

"It'll get a little hard for you now but you know what, *that's okay.* Life's tough *but you are tougher.* Just know I am proud of you and your mother and I have your back. You stood up for yourself. *You have a right to defend yourself.* He had no right to put hands on you."

"*Ok,*" I said, wanting to climb into my bed, curl into a fetal position and hibernate for a century.

"Did he turn red? Like beet red?"

Wait — *what?* "Yes. He got really, really red." Somehow, I smile.

"I thought he might have, Patrick just like a beet, right? Or more like a strawberry?" He started to laugh uproariously and I laughed with him, getting some medicine for my troubled soul — special spirit medicine from our tribe's chieftain.

"Yeah, like a beet… like a cherry. Especially after I slapped the taste out his mouth."

"Wow, man. That's pretty good. Did he make a sound with his taste gone?" He made a sound like a monkey or ape being tortured.

"No. He took his licks like a man. He was smart."

"Okay, baby."

I know somewhere in the galaxy and spirit realms, those spirits of Frederick Douglass, Muhammad Ali and maybe even ancestor Sidney Poi tier, the one from *In the Heat of the Night*, understood and shook their heads in quiet agreement. "*That's just the way it goes sometimes.* A spiritual warrior had been conceived and was now born. But it was Daddy who was there for the anointing at initiation — becoming a Black man in America? *Ain't no joke.* When you see one of us walking around, we are walking, talking, breathing *miracles*. There are 19.83 million miracles walking the planet Earth in the United States of America. And those miracles? We are fact. And that's the truth about the fact.

Well, what's become plain to me now at this advanced fifty plus age is: *fragility*. Peace is a very fragile though powerful thing. I could have just taken it and moved on like a good Jesuit Catholic high school *boy*.

Yes, when war comes to your doorstep, it takes a mighty man to be cool, take measure and retort with dignity or not respond in kind *(and I'll have to keep trying)*. As the artist Sting has so eloquently captured in his ethereal "Fragile," *nothing comes from violence and nothing ever could.*

***

If blood will flow when flesh and steel are one / Drying in the color of the evening sun Tomorrow's rain will wash the stains away / But something in our minds will always stay Perhaps this final act was meant
To clinch a lifetime's argument
That nothing comes from violence and nothing ever could
For all those born beneath an angry star / Lest we forget how fragile we are

Older, I realize, as Martin Luther King often taught, having learned from his intellectual mentor, Mahatma Gandhi, father of the peace in protest movements, *that peace is the only way*.

As we all know from our current era, it is simple enough to codify hatred and find a rationale *for any position*. But whether it's MAGA, CNN, MSNBC, Woke or Fox News; whether it's Republican or Democrat, the politics of hatred *feel* the same — *spiritually sickening soul rot. War, war* and *war.* We Americans are doing the work of adversaries and we have so much work to do to renew and perfect the American promise for a new generation — we are in the mud wrestling, trying to poke each other's eyes out while the *spirit of the earth* is ignored and we become entrenched in our hatred and rage becomes a societal modality and the weather patterns mirror *our total imbalances. And that way*, well, it's the end of us as a people. Harmonics, alignment, balance and collaboration are the only way forward. I've had to go through hell — *American Hell* — to learn this lesson late in life. *However, I'm still mastering it so… be forewarned.* And, yes, *holistic entrepreneurship* is the way of, to and from the future. I know that now.

***

> *Our thoughts culminate into burning globe afire, we must remain cool.*

I've had more than a few battles in these United States of America that fall under the legal tent poles and protections of ancestor and legislative giant Thurgood Marshall (another Founding Father) and the tireless work he provided from the Supreme Court, namely Title VII and the Equal Employment Opportunity Commission — I've taken five- and six-figure settlements from former employers while I spent time honing my knowledge and sharpening skill sets as a financier. *I never sued, litigated or mediated for money.*

Even Supreme Court Justices Thomas and Sotomayor acknowledged affirmative action as being central to their rise to the highest court in the land. I did it for respect. ***I did it for the fight.*** To make a way out of no way. Now, I invoke the eternal military spirit of Tupac Amuru Shakur (as Makaveli) in his appropriately profane anthem "Against All Odds" on *The Don Killuminati: The 7 Day Theory*:

> *I'm hopin' my true motherfuckers know*
> *This be the realest shit I ever wrote; against all odds*
>
> *Heard the guns bust, but you tricks never shut me up. Touch one of mine, on everything I own.*
> *I'll destroy everything you touch…*

And I certainly didn't mind when the money came from settlements. It meant I understood the game, played well and successfully and won. *But I wanted more,* I wanted to do what I did through its inverse functionality: I wanted to design industry and a way forward *through absolute creation versus destruction* — Through my attorneys, including my beloved Noah Kinigstein, Esq. in Manhattan and the ferocious protectorate of the late great Melanie Lomax, Esq. in Los Angeles, Steve Young, Esq. in from behind the orange curtain in OC and, later, the Johnnie Cochran Law Firm, I learned and mastered the value and power of a proverbial stick in transactions. I learned watching Daddy growing up in the United States, it's important, if not critical, to have legal representation and counsel, particularly when nothing is going on because without that protection in American society?

This place is war. You are *persona non grata by definition, a person not wanted or welcomed.* It is a dangerous position to be in in America, particularly as a Black man, where the unspoken immutable laws of the land, as racism and discrimination, coding hatred, are the unspoken and sometimes written laws. I remember our family friend Dr. Thomas Parham put it succinctly when I went to visit his university, Cal State Dominguez, with my son, *"As a Black man, it is wise to always be in the habit of cultivating as many options as possible?* " I learned as a young man that it is important to always cultivate options. As a Black man, that it is not only essential to thrive, but survive in this wild, wild west.

Some would say, *I played the race card when I pursued legal remedy. I always say?* Deal the cards that are dealt to you and play the ultimate game to win. *And when you win? Trade up in the game. But* ***when you are dealt from the race deck?*** *Yeah,* I know the deal and I'm the gambler who understands how to take race and make that trump card (again, pun *totally* intended) make you pay. I have come to understand how to hedge or leverage a deal with its opposite in energy and intention to create the precise and intended outcome; and by that practice, I am nearly a master.

I recall after my first pugilistic encounter in the corporate realm after considerable tutorial and mentoring by Daddy, I was very upset because I did not get an apology from the offending employer — just a simple "*We are very sorry Mr. Howell!*" is what I was looking for.

Daddy asked if I got the check. I told him, five years' salary over three years. He laughed that crass, ugly -but-divine laughter of a Caribbean man's soul, "*Patrick, the settlement is the apology!*" I still didn't understand.

"*Baby, in America, it's 'In God We Trust and In Cash We Pay.'* Do you understand now?"

Yes, Daddy. I understand *the final global wars for Diversity, Equity and Inclusion on this earthly plane in the societies of men will be fought and won in Global Venture Capital, Capital Formation and Economic Development. They will be fought with Spiritual IQ* and deference to peace and ***true*** prosperity for all. We will pull back the cosmetic veil of falsehoods within Democracy that have undermined and all but destroyed our spirit of collective unity, and we will look ourselves in the mirror and come to terms with the beast that seeks to destroy us all; the beast that was birthed at the inception of the United States of Capitalism, which was birthed from the abomination of Slavery. *That Great Beast is us.* And make no mistake about it, the world looks on in derision and sheer delight as black and white, MAGA versus woke, Republican and Democrat wage a century-old war that was never concluded at the so-called *Civil* War into our ongoing uncivil spiritual, social, political and cultural unrest — *we are* *the living dead.* We are poisoned and ingesting quantities of that poison daily. Our very breath is leavened with a poisoned spirit of acrimony. Adversaries don't want us dead, *just weakened.* And they have accomplished their work with our participation as powerful accomplices — us… or the USA, *not so united.*

"By the way," Daddy would add after those brilliant affirmative aphorisms, "I won't charge you for that one — '*In God We Trust, In Cash We Pay.*' Okay, baby?"

"Yes, Daddy. Thank you. I understand. *Perfectly.*"

And wisdom? True Spiritual IQ? It is the pinnacle of all human knowledge and discernment — outside but not necessarily excluding book sense, emotional IQ (or EQ), genius, specialized knowledge, street smarts, common sense or encyclopedic knowledge. Spiritual IQ is an effervescent combination of knowledge (intelligence refined over a lifetime — an *accumulation of knowing),* insights (the ability to discern), judgement (good sense, knowing) and the quality of sharing that knowledge so that others can gain sustenance from it. "Effervescent" because wisdom is a live energy source like photosynthesis or its catalyst, solar radiation, covering everywhere, inviting hope and creating life. Spiritual IQ *is alive.* It never dies — it doesn't become funky, half-truth or false. Spiritual IQ is true and more often than not, Spiritual IQ is like a powerful light, nourishing as it *illuminates.*

> *"Everyone has been made for some particular work, and the desire for that work has been put in every heart. Let yourself be silently drawn by the stronger pull of what you really love."*
>
> **—Rumi**

Chapter 9:
Holistic Entrepreneurship and Organic Networking

Heading to Washington DC to go to the White House that our ancestors engineered, built and yes, financed. The current stewards and inhabitants of this White House are unique in American, World and Afrofuture History. We were invited by Congressman Elijah Cummings at the Pasadena AME, whom we were introduced to by Pasadena's John J. Kennedy. He and his sister, Lena, are pioneers and the embodiment of our tradition's time-honed servant-leadership. We are in the stream of history but, really, this is a precious heirloom in our family history — we go to Ethiopian restaurants for injera, tibs and one of my favorites, Dorowot. We also stop by the Washington Monument for MLK and peer at the horizon, too.

"You only get what you give yourself. And that's all you get."

When I was just a little brown-skinned Sac Town boy, we didn't spend as much time with Daddy as we would during our teenage years. It was primarily Mommy who raised my brother and me about five years before our other four siblings would come along. For me, those Empyrean years are source as well as, well, aim and force. Daddy was a young professor teaching at Cosumnes River College and he was a fixed point we could look to to understand who we could and would become. He taught in the evenings at the junior college in Elk

Grove and was young though bearded, would smoke a pipe and was always suited in pinstripes and his distinct Caribbean panache.

I remember at 7039 Winnette Way (around the corner from Burbank High School and several corners, boulevards and blocks from St. Anne's elementary school where my brother, sister and I would later attend). When he would come home in the evenings and Cecil, my younger brother, and I would hop from our beds, charge downstairs and give our Caribbean champion his hugs from adoring princes. "You have school tomorrow," he would remind us, hugging us back and sending us back to sleep. He would cuddle with us on the weekends and I can still remember waking up Saturday morning and him coming into our room and lying down with my brother and me, then falling asleep with large lumber arms of mahogany and a deep sleep and with no way out for Cecil or me other than patience. Those were very special times.

It was Mommy who would spend so much time raising and detailing us, and she poured endless hours into my brother Cecil and me, as if we were her two little kings. Like I said earlier, *I remember everything.* There are pockets of memory that are sketched in my mitochondrial DNA: I remember the feeling of sharing space with her and the sensation of love that would pass between us. I remember being on buses in Sacramento to head to downtown Yamaha recorder lessons — an instrument that through that school of music is used to develop a musical ear in order to learn piano, with which both my brother and I would hone a lifelong passion and love for music, musicianship, harmony and coming together. Then there was coming into the kitchen early on Saturday mornings, seeing her in a flower-print summer dress and working on a batch of cookies. I would sit on the kitchen banister and get bowls that were coated with cookie dough and a spatula to clean the chocolate chip, peanut butter, spritz sugar cookies, coconut cookies. I think she imported those baking skills from her mother, my beautiful grandmother Dorothy, who understood what any Afro-latino young man knows — that cinnamon sprinkled earnestly into the heart of cinnamon dough rolled and in healthy supply, is one way to global peace and lifelong happiness.

In 2007, I was a business banker at Wachovia Bank, on the corner of Irvine and Newport Beach, as a Vice President and business banker earning a six-figure flat salary. That salary was the vision I had dreamt for myself six years prior in the Management Training Program at Fleet Boston Financial in Syracuse, New York. I had just joined the bank with a signing bonus of five figures, which, as far as I was concerned, was the consummation of ten years as a young, accomplished branch manager on both the east and west Coasts Several months earlier, I had resigned my position with Bank of the West as a manager of the highly visible South Coast plaza branch in Orange County.

At Bank of the West, I had the youngest team out of nearly fifty branches in Southern California, and certainly in the Orange County region, but we were the number one ranked branch throughout Southern California, a young group of multi-ethnic hyphenated Americans: Latino (Chicano), Egyptian, Persian, Indian and Evangelical White for nearly three years. I hand-selected the youthful cosmopolitan team after the team that was in place, largely older team members who were resentful of my youth, verve and nakedly ambitious (though positive and productive) *aggression*. By thirty-five, I had accomplished the mission set forth to me by my father nearly a decade earlier with nothing more than: "*If you got through that management training program and became a branch manager that would be cool man.*" Before that, the goal he had set for me as a young man: "If you could do that branch manager thing, I would be so proud." And, before that, the goal he had set for me in my elementary school days: "If you learn that stock market thing, you would be smart."

Early on, Dr. Howell taught me I could do *anything* I set my mind to. There have been so many failures but that has always been the cornerstone of my philosophy — a guiding light that has woken me from the opaque visage of seemingly permanent defeat.

Holistic entrepreneurship is about embodying virtue, wisdom, respecting life energy and honing our *collective* humanity. Holistic entrepreneurship is about doing the good works that not only leave the Earth better but at its most peaceful and its best. "Entrepreneurship" is derived from "entreprendre," which in French means to undertake or to do something with the grace and beauty endemic to that culture. Then there is "holistic," which in natural medical terms means to take an entire system into consideration when proposing a solution.

In this innovative, new and robust era of business, industry and finance there will, as always, be two sides of the cosmic energy force. Which do you fall on? Going back to childhood, my underlying principle has always been, "*In the end, Love wins.*" So, if I was in a George Lucus *Star Wars* film, it's obvious which side of the force I believe wins. Just as there are stars in the sky, there is an infinite supply of business opportunities, outcomes, wealth, financial paydays and success metrics. And your intention will always precede your victories. *Always.* If you're hanging out with the Darth Vader politicos or think Mr. Smith from *The Matrix* was a misunderstood character, or Gordon Gekko from *Wall Street*, Tony Montana or Michael Corleone from *The Godfather* are heroes to be emulated? This book may not be for you.

Holistic entrepreneurship marks a graduation to a more philosophical approach to one of the core competencies I enjoy as a Gen-X influencer and business success: *"organic networking."* When I was a retail bank branch manager, sitting at a desk at the corner of Sunflower and Bristol, right across from the South Coast Plaza in Orange County and even decades before that when I was a fledgling financier personal banker at Fleet Boston Financial in Syracuse, New York, off of Nottingham Drive, I always thought, *"there is a better way of doing business* than just sitting behind a desk and waiting for the business to come to me."

Most of my incredible successes have come from getting out and hitting the pavement. *Go and get it, my spirit* tells me quietly *like a hurricane.* Like I've intimated earlier, *you only get what you give yourself* is the attitude. (The reality is that we all have an entire tribe with whom we succeed, but that attitude is an insurance policy.) And I'm not talking about the psychotic *take, take, take* that is pervasive in American Capital Consumer culture. I'm talking about forces that seek to stop you from manifesting that which is divinely yours — so think of it as going past that which seeks to stop you: using intellect, spirit and sheer will power (a power that becomes stronger, not louder, not more violent with each successive usage — like muscle toning at the gym). *Should you grow to understand the power of your divine spirit and invest the time in developing that technology?* You will find that there's no supercomputer; there is no artificial intelligence that can outpace spirit that is divinely infused with its focus with purpose. That is power now.

Artificial Intelligence may be able to synthesize tens of millions of data points within nanoseconds, but only the human spirit can act in the urgency of now to create a new reality, a new now. Only the spirit of man is divinely inspired by God to create *life.* That's the love power of humanity; the beauty of the human spirit.

The ability to simply focus on the outcome that you seek and keep your eyes steady on the prize until the goal is accomplished? *That is a component of Spiritual IQ. And Spiritual* IQ is greater than book sense; greater than common sense *(which is not so common)*; greater than any AI and even greater than the greatest supercomputer of world history, greater than emotional EQ — it *is the pinnacle of understanding and wisdom that moves worlds, including the unseen.* Spiritual IQ is not Spiritual Gangsterism, a dated practice to be sure. Spiritual IQ has more to do with summoning your higher angels and invoking their presence in your transactions. It is about invoking archangels and principles, mores and whole epochs through intentional action. Spiritual IQ is about engaging the entirety of your being within your actions so that both are contiguous with one another.

I'll illustrate some more of what I mean — it takes a certain amount of moxie to walk up to a business (remember: NO Solicitation!), network at a networking event (no matter how small or epic) or just to meet someone one-on-one and develop a relationship and pursue an agenda — not only manifest your vision but also that of a colleague or your firm.

I have always found that stepping up to the plate, courageously and with visionary energy, initiating the transaction or just conversation with a positive intention and just putting yourself out there has yielded some wonderful, if not life-altering results. I have always found that an *organic touch* — so-called "pressing the palm" — to a relationship accelerates it lightyears!

This idea of *"organic networking"* began as a blog over ten years ago with *The Huffington Post.* I talked about Daddy, my Panamanian grandfather who was a restaurant manager at the Canal Zone, and Mommy, who has always been my *sine qua non* in all things good and her love of people and helping people. I noted that providing value is a priceless commodity, calling card and valuable business tool for closing out deals. Authentically seeking to help someone, not because it is in your vested interest to do so but because you want to see them do well, not only creates incredible karma but bottom-line results.

In the age of digital technology, search engines, social media, emails, avatars and the World Wide Web, there are any number of ways to initiate relationships with *anyone* on the planet. You will have to use tenacity, strategy, energy, tactics, imagination and a powerful driving force, but nearly anyone can be reached with tools easily at our disposal. It has never been as easy as it is now to develop a strategic and tactical relationship with anyone of the 7.5 billion people, organizations, communities or businesses on planet Earth. And yet, loneliness, poor mental health, information overload and the metathesis of high-frequency communications into base instincts means that we have to be wise about not only "focus with purpose" but a diet of those excesses of materials. Knowing who you are, praying, spending time with yourself in nature, meditating and exploring your life as well as existence from where you sit, stand or lay can result in dynamic thoughts, a renewed sense of being or creating connections that are not in the World Wide Web. Remember, there is a higher frequency than the internet!

Ideas and Dreams have a way of coming from the fifth and sixth dimensions (worlds of thoughts, emotions, visions and imaginings) and finding avatars through which they can express their being. When it is time for the world to change from one epoch or zeitgeist to another those currents and waves of imagination, thoughts and vibrations locate the searchers who are open to change, manifesting and willingness. Ego has so many participants feeling they were the originators when ideas find those who are willing to match hard joyous work, positive life energy and considerable skills and talents at their realization. When an idea's time has come, it will locate willing accomplices. Those avatars are conjoined to ideas, epochs and ongoing battles with universal principles.

If I think about the nature of my successes and relationships in the twenty-first century, many have been initiated or, at least, done with the help of social media and Facebook, WhatsApp, Skype, Facebook Messenger, Instagram, definitely LinkedIn and even Match.com. However, I have always anchored those relationships in reality or organic versus virtual relationships. Nothing — *and I mean nothing* — takes the place of palm pressed to palm, eyeball to eyeball or spirit to spirit. In a material society, we lose sense of the spirit's concurrent realities alongside our so-called real world when the unseen is the fuel and foundation of the known. That mode of transaction is catalyzed by intention, authenticity and other spiritual gifts.

We are heading into an existence in which human interaction is changing and will continue to change definitions with virtual and augmented reality presenting a billion other existences and ways of being. Marvel Comics and other science fiction aficionados call it the "multiverse." *But as my good friend ultra-entrepreneur Brian Jue* is always expounding as he builds the largest small-broker dealer in the South-Eastern part of the nation, something to counterbalance Keith Moore and Dan McClory's piston engine in the vehicle of our American economy, the Boustead Securities on the West Coast, ***nothing is more real than real.*** And business, a full-on contact sport, is nothing if not real. And *real* is as real as you make it. But the unseen imagination, calculations, numbers, competitive furnace and visions fuel every single occurrence of a brand-new entrepreneurial venture or small business. Remember: we are all creators and as such we create the reality we all inhabit — sounds basic and remedial, right? But I don't see the United States of America or capital markets that have mastered the lessons we all learned in PBS's *Sesame Street*, *The Electric Company* and *Mr. Rogers' Neighborhood*. We live in a perverse version of our highest ideas.

Here are some of the principals and ideas that have helped me not only to network but to develop relationships with heads of state or their ministries, captains of industry, celebrities, mavericks and movers and shakers. One more thing, before I distill thirty plus years of wisdom won into nice bite-sized colorful Skittles: All of this is really just a recapitulation of Earl G. Graves Sr.'s How to Succeed in Business without Being White, for just as Prime Minister Williams keynotes off of his intellectual mentor, I keynote off the visionary pioneer of Black Enterprise, with a language, force and energy all my own — thank you Mr. Graves, fearless venture capitalist, impresario and pioneer. We salute you, spiritual mentor, following in your giant steps on the pathway paved by yourself and the legions who follow your editorial visions and pioneering spirit.

Build Relationships

The transactional way of doing business is always thinking about that almighty dollar; it lasts as long as it takes to buy a McDonald's hamburger or Starbucks coffee, *minus the brand loyalty*. Most business interactions are about the transaction, but you cannot lead with it. As antithetical as it might seem to Gordon Gekko's sinister "greed is good," most networking is about *sharing.* Or, as progenitor of Black Enterprise Earl Graves observed, "networking is a social first, business second activity." Try reaching out to someone you want to do business with, or are doing business with, with zero agenda other than just to say "hello." Be authentic in the greeting, one spirit intertwining as a butterfly on the stratosphere finding its counterpart then flying to the heavens. Quickly find mutual ground off of which you two may align and harmonize and build from there — that's *the flight*. If the conversation goes well, share your dream and listen attentively to theirs. Once you've located their dream? *Work!*

A "relationship" is a meaningful engagement; something that goes beyond pleasantries or mechanical formalities to the heart or substance of an energy force. Relationships are a springboard for collaborations no matter how mundane or infused with creativity or verve. So, a "relationship" can be a meaningful engagement, an enactment of a dream, or taking on a vibration or riding a current to its reasonable outcome, if not conclusion. More than fantasy or pretend, collaborations provide a space for imagination and previous limits to be tested, fortified, redefined and broken at exhilarating rates. Balance, Harmony, Peace and Joy are active agents in alchemizing, exponentially developing, force-multiplying and dividing collaborations.

Collaborations and, potentially, collaborators are "force multipliers." Force multiplier, as artificial intelligence, is either a tool, person or process that exponentially enhances the effectiveness of an individual, team or leader, allowing them to achieve more with the same amount of effort. "Balance sheet," "standard operating procedure" or technology can also be force multipliers. Collaboration is another organic tool to create gestalt, where the sum of the whole is considered greater than the individual parts — collaboration, force multipliers and gestalt is how Japan or South Korea, small islands or peninsulas in the Pacific Ocean, have such outsized contributions in the global economy and international capital markets.

Tell Stories

Learn to tell short, engaging stories that are as instructive as they are entertaining. Part of this art form includes bringing energy and being focused one-on-one with your audience and being in the moment. This does not mean tell tall tales, engage in hyperbole, or pretend to be something you are not — it means find an engaging anecdotal personalized manner in which to convey your business point. It means be who you are. It means listen to the quiet voice talking to you — as that's your spirit talking to your mind. Your mind will command your body and your body will shape reality — *the metaphysics of the spirit upon reality.*

Have Fun, Lots of it

Business is adults at play. Holistic entrepreneurship and organic networking are the business equivalent of shouting, laughing, sharing on the play yard or grass field. Whether a creative venue is a restaurant, hotel or creative space. (Some of my personal favorites are Havana's at the Lab in Orange County, The Four Seasons in Beverly Hills, The Desalegn Hotel in Addis Ababa, Ethiopia, Mirbeau Spa in Skaneateles, New York, the Upside Down Hilton in Trinidad and Tobago, Sam Lord's Castle in Barbados, Trump Ocean Club in Panama, The Waldorf Astoria or the Ritz-Carlton in Dana Point, or the Sofitel in Dubai and any Boiling Crab within the continental USA!) Recalling your favorite story of the day or using applications such as ZOOM, Google Plus or X, be at wonder, be engaged and excited about who you are talking with and what you are talking about. So have fun — and lots of it — but always keep it professional.

Lean in and Listen Intently

This is an art form and, initially, a discipline. As a rule of thumb, if you realize that you have spoken more than you have listened (fifty percent), more than likely you will not have a successful business relationship — it's the whole "you have two ears and one mouth" thing. The heart of organic networking is learning *more* about the other person(s) and their business as you have shared about your business, ideas or own accomplishments and/or challenges. Listening — really taking an interest in what someone has to say — *is impressive.* Doctors, psychologists and attorneys are all paid well *to listen well.* The genius networkers know as much about the gifts of silence and keen listening as projecting their own vested interests.

WIIFT vs. WIIFM

WIIFM — What's In it for Me — is a common catchphrase in the world of business. But the keen business mind surmises the interest of the other party and suggests several ways to *serve* those interests. Now, this is not charity — it is understanding that business networking is about always building value or, in this case, WIIFT — What's in it for *Them*. And, of course, they *must* reciprocate or, it might be time to reconsider the relationship business-wise.

Pointer: *Never take "No" for an answer. Like ever. I've learned this in sales and life — this is psychologically, emotionally, spiritually and particularly in reality. There is no such thing as "no." "No" does not exist. I remember my former Africa Connects International partner and brother Dwayne B. Latimore, Esq. telling me, "God only says, 'Yes,' 'Not now,' or 'I have something better.'" "No" is just an opinion given, sometimes forcefully, because the timing was not right or you did not make a compelling enough pitch. Most times, life will offer a resounding "no," oftentimes just before the victory. The Universe wants to know: how bad do you want it? Can you handle the power of this dream? Can you handle the pressure? I've been told no on sales, meetings, jobs, proposals only to follow up the umpteenth time and get a resounding and honeydew-mango-sweet yes!*

Authenticity, Loyalty and Truth

Loyalty and trust are priceless assets in any business deal. Authenticity and truth are vital for business success, fostering trust, building strong customer relationships, and enhancing brand reputation, ultimately leading to long-term growth and loyalty. Honesty and transparency are the cornerstones of any successful business relationship, whether with customers, employees, or partners. By focusing on authenticity and truth, businesses can build a sustainable foundation for long-term growth and success.

Authenticity is a buzzword in business.

Say What You Will Do, Then Do It

Without the science and art of *follow-up*, any business networking is just a lot of hot air. And many folks like to hear themselves talk. I am always very careful about what I promise to do during an interaction because after a promise has made its way from my mouth, I am obliged to do it. You would be surprised how much business is created by simply following up on your good word — in the good old days, it was called *integrity*.

Keepin' it Real

At its highest levels, organic networking is about change. My friend of nearly twenty years, frequent collaborator and business partner Shannon C. Lamb, Esq. is consistently recognized as one of the top litigation attorneys in Southern California. She advocates on behalf of individuals, businesses, and boards. Her brand, Tea and Strategy, is dedicated to the precepts of civility, grace and avoiding conflict (as well as conflict resolution) in business and legal transactions — Tea and Strategy, as well as Shannon Lamb, believe that we can be better, kinder and more successful — lighter in our transactions and collaborations. Don't get any ideas though: she's tough and steely too.

Holistic Entrepreneurship

Holistic entrepreneurship is an approach to business that considers the full spectrum of an entrepreneur's impact — beyond just profit. It integrates elements such as personal well-being, ethical practices, social responsibility, and environmental sustainability into business decision-making. Simply stated, a holistic entrepreneur adds value and enriches oneself far beyond (but not necessarily excluding!) money, without harming another's energy psychologically, emotionally or spiritually. In this model, the entrepreneur focuses on creating long-term value for all stakeholders, including customers, employees, society, and the environment, a.k.a. Mother Earth, while also maintaining personal integrity and balance. Similar to Social Entrepreneurship, holistic entrepreneurship enjoys touchstones in community, well-being of the entire ecosystem as well as the human.

Holistic entrepreneurship also enjoys spiritual exercises, touchstones and visionary practices with a cosmic fundamentalism. This approach embodies principles of servant leadership, with an emphasis on creating positive social impact and maintaining the highest ethical standards.

Organic Networking

Organic networking refers to the natural and authentic process of building and nurturing relationships, often without a direct or immediate business agenda. It emphasizes genuine connections based on shared values, trust, and mutual support, rather than transactional interactions. In this approach, relationships evolve organically through shared experiences, collaborations, and trust-building over time. Organic networking is often rooted in personal integrity and sincerity, making it more sustainable in the long run. It's especially valuable in industries that thrive on personal referrals, partnerships and collaborative opportunities, such as capital markets and entrepreneurship, where trust and reputation play central roles in success.

Peopleism (noun)

pee-puhl-iz-uhm
A socio-political ideology, economic non-economic theory and philosophy complementing true Democracy. Peopleism emphasizes the importance of placing first the welfare, rights and needs of all in society, most particularly the marginalized, oppressed or under-served. It advocates communal well-being, justice and fairness over profit-oriented or individualist interests. Peopleism proposes models, policies and practices for dismantling structures of power so that society can serve the common good, rather than the privilege of a select few.

Fundamental values of Peopleism are:

1. Common well-being and Spiritual consciousness — Community as a whole comes before profit for companies or individuals.
2. Equity — Fair treatment, opportunity and access to resources — finances, systems and networks for everyone regardless of race, gender or economic class.
3. Social justice — Remedying and rectifying systemic and historical injustices and disparities. Perhaps that's Reparations. Me? I'm at ease with a PPM, Subscription Agreement or Series A round. Crowdfunding is an alternative too!
4. Empathy and inclusion — Valuing the perspectives and experiences of all, particularly oppressed groups, in order to construct a more humane and equitable society.
5. And *LOVE* — Well, love wins out in the end, and I love Love far better than Hate.

Peopleism contrasts with capitalism and other *profit*-driven ideologies as America's current Oligarchy by placing human dignity and community well-being at the center of its values and goals. The current mentality and spirit within our financial system is "*kill or be killed.*" There's also the spirit of "I win / you lose" deriving its DNA directly from the institution of slavery, and the systematic modality of American disenfranchisement and dehumanization that is the basis of discrimination and racism and central to business in the United States of America since its beginning. *Slavery? Alive* and doing quite well.

***

The history of capitalism is richly intertwined with the planetary violent transactional *exploitation* of both people and resources. From the blood, sweat and lives of enslaved Africans and the genocide of native populations (to whom war crimes reparations are 100% due), to the Chinese who built our railroads and the great sojourn West to the labor of underpaid workers today, to the one hundred plus armed conflicts going on in the world including Israel, Palestine, Russia and the Ukraine, capitalism has grown on the backs of those most marginalized and oppressed. It is a system that thrives on and primes competition, encouraging a survival-of-the-fittest mentality, where greed and excess are normalized and celebrated.

The power dynamics established during slavery, particularly those that created vast disparities in wealth and access to resources (*literally the understatement of four centuries*), are still very much alive and "prosperous" in today's financial systems — kind of like a malignant cancer that keeps evolving into its next more grotesque sunken form. Holistic entrepreneurship is a cure. The wealth gap, the concentration of resources in the hands of a few and the systematic disenfranchisement of certain groups all stem from a historical precedent set a long, long time ago. And so, while we may speak of the 'free market' with idealism, it is hardly free for those — an eclectic majority who remain locked out of opportunity due to centuries of entrenched inequality in finance, wealth and economic resources.

As we consider the future of labor, particularly with the rise of artificial intelligence and automation, we must confront the critical question: how will wealth, opportunity and power be distributed and shared? As much as the dismal prospect for change is possible, so is the possibility for a better, more prosperous society. What values are encoded into the technology that shapes our future? Will we allow the same extractive unbalanced systems to continue? Or will we pivot toward a more equitable distribution of resources, where *humanity* — not profit — is the ultimate bottom line?

The belief that *"you win, I lose"* must give way to a paradigm where we understand that we can, indeed, win together. Even more so? *WE HAVE BEEN WINNING TOGETHER*, tethered and patch-quilted by a system engineered by so-called "founding fathers" for exploitation and a brutal ethos — *spiritual ruthlessness* is and has been endemic to our coarse culture and way of life — it is essential to the DNA of The United States of America. True prosperity comes not from hoarding wealth or power but from creating systems that uplift everyone, ensuring that no one is left behind. That's right! Being nice is not only good but profitable! Go and tell someone the good news!

Tea and Strategy

My friend and family attorney, Shannon Lamb, Esq., has successfully negotiated and resolved more than a thousand matters. Large or small, she's handled everything from thousands of dollars to billions of dollars at stake. Now, we are partners on a couple of ventures including a film funds and a production company that will redefine how financing and film produce profits for savvy investors.

"Personal, business — it is all the same," offers Shannon. "What's the difference if your business is an extension of who you are?" Lamb is a Loyola Law School graduate and a Legacy Seat Holder and member of the Dean's Leadership Circle through U.C. Irvine's Merage School of Business. "I have been able to use them to considerable success in my own endeavors," she says. Shannon is also the proud mama of a sweet and precocious daughter, Meagan. "I learn so much from her," she says. "I learn from her every day about grace and kindness."

Shannon has distilled her inspiration, a sense of patriotism as well as love of justice into the essence of Tea and Strategy. Tea and Strategy is not only about how we engage one another as citizens. Tea and Strategy, also a call to action, explores leadership and organizational challenges, or it can refer to a broader concept of using tea as a metaphor or tool for strategic thinking and problem-solving.

Kindness, coupled with a keen sense of jurisprudence and the designation of 'esquire' in a time of heightened acrimony and vitriol in American society and its legal system, calls for a renaissance in civility, with a particular emphasis on the importance of clear contracts, mediation and arbitration to resolve disputes before they become financially and emotionally costly courtroom battles. As Shannon Lamb believes, legal practitioners, especially officers of the court, should prioritize collaboration and dialogue over confrontation, seeking solutions that preserve human dignity while upholding justice. By fostering an environment where disputes are settled with integrity and mutual respect, T&S seeks to usher in a new era in law and the courts — a "new spring" for civility in American jurisprudence.

Be Patient, Learn Patience and then? Learn some more Patience

Patience is a commodity — it's in rare supply. The world is always getting faster. So patience is better than a trillion dollars or all the diamonds on Mars. The world is in a rush. *You must not be.* Just as "focus with purpose" is a commodity as a value or principle in today's world, so is patience. Patience in entrepreneurial pursuits allows you to bypass mistakes and misunderstandings and most importantly *learn* from them. Patience is a level of preternatural thinking. Before I was a successful entrepreneur with San Diego Investment Conference, West Coast Wall Street Conference, Africa Connects International, Global Capital Network, Victory & Noble — "a storytelling company," and Valkyrie Media, I was a "serial failure" (while I "interned" at Fortune 500 firms and worked on Wall Street with such enterprises as Just Cuts, the Orange Commerce Consortium and Howell Publications).

I take great pride in those so-called failures because they were metaphysical steps to my success; but also, I was and am *always learning* — the residual of growing up on 7039 Winnett Way, where Dr. Howell and Mrs. Howell created a cosmic learning center out of a home. Failure is a *masterful* teacher. Patience is the magical elixir that allows defeat to only be temporary and alchemically morphs all failures into success. *Be patient, be knowing, be learning* — your success is *always* coming.

Organic networking at the highest levels is about creative faculty and the ability to create opportunity, do good *and* make money. With new generations — the Generation Xers and Millennials — receiving the baton from arguably one of the most influential and powerful generations in American History, the Baby boomers, our legacy will be defined as much by the mechanics (e.g. technology and social media) as by our willingness to advance the nation from the incredible challenges of our day (i.e. the Great Recession, the pandemic of the twenty-first century, the potential for World War III to break out in the Middle East, the onset of AI as a defining planetary force; the development of our Spiritual IQ masters to counterbalance the incredible technology are all signs of our times).

Now, there are virtual and augmented realities. There are also avatars, social media, email, cryptocurrency, PayPal, texting, messaging apps, Amazon, 5G, bots, artificial intelligence and every imaginable way to create a virtual existence. Pretty soon, there will be commercial space travel just as there is international travel. Life on Earth is forever changing, as it always does. (And, yet, there is *nothing* new under the sun.)

One of the silver linings to the worldwide pandemic of the twenty-first century was that it gave professionals and entrepreneurs the opportunity to connect with what was really important to them. In many ways, the pandemic was a global reset. People reconnected with their families, nature and even themselves. Coming out of the pandemic, we realize that the world will never return to the old "normal." Humans had the opportunity to re-evaluate what *living* is all about.

Now, I also understand that the society of men burgeoned as never before, and changes implemented during that time led to what really has become "the new normal." My neighbors Viasat Satellites, for example, wholly matured from private-defense industry contracts to global travel and connectivity on Delta and American Airlines.

We are in the new normal now, where people don't want to return to the cubicle, but provide bottom-line value to others and companies as they work from home or travel the world. There are also contrasting meta forces pulling us into virtual existence as never before. The America that came out of the industrial age with one of the hardest-working workforces on planet Earth is redefining what it means to be "productive," "happy," "successful" and even "alive." Remember: organic networking and "keeping it real" are not only spiritually enhanced ways of doing business, but fundamentally impactful to the bottom line. Organic networking is, at its most essential, about connecting with another human in a natural way to achieve a common, mutually beneficial goal. That's right — organic networking is an essential tentpole in the practice of holistic entrepreneurship.

Holistic entrepreneurship and organic networking center on the deep alignment of our personal values with our professional endeavors, combining both as a guiding force for creating meaningful success. *All* business is a reflection of personal values. From my upbringing and my lineage, I've learned that achieving real greatness goes beyond simple transactions — it's about connecting with the world around you, fostering relationships that are more than opportunistic, and planting seeds that grow into opportunities for everyone in your orbit.

My journey, shared and shaped by both parents, started in these humble spaces where love, integrity and hard work were non-negotiable values. The dedication my mother put into raising my brothers and sisters, and the pride my father took in his professional endeavors, instilled the spirit of purpose, love and a desire to thrive in everything we pursue.

> *"Every morning in Africa, a lion wakes up. It knows it must run faster than the slowest antelope, or it will starve. It doesn't matter whether you're the lion or an antelope — when the sun comes up, you'd better be running."*
>
> — African Proverb, first shared with me by big brother **Tony Faulkner**

In the business world, I began to realize that sitting behind a desk waiting for business to come to me was *never* the way to win and build something lasting. Whether I was a branch manager in bustling Southern California or climbing the corporate ladder in New York, learning how to be an entrepreneur or helping others to fulfill their dreams and visions? My personal drive — that ambition, *Black ambition* — was the key to unlocking opportunities. The relationships that helped me reach these new heights were organic — formed by real connections, not just a transactional mentality of "*Get it! Get some! Me! Mine!!!*" These networks were made with intention and respect for others' time, talents and goals. This is what I call "organic networking," a key spiritual principle for anyone looking to build true, long-lasting success.

Holistic entrepreneurship is *beyond* material gains. It's about creating value that impacts the world in a meaningful, righteous and beautiful way. It is about winning, *spiritually*. It's about embodying wisdom, respect and virtue, ensuring that your business efforts not only provide financial rewards, but also make the world a better place. Holistic entrepreneurship is about understanding the intricate web of relationships that influence your success and nurturing them in a way that benefits everyone involved.

In San Diego, where I live, there is a symphony of parks, rose gardens, museums and centers of cultural organizations in what is now known as Balboa Park. The sprawling urban park hosted a second Panama-California International Exposition in 1935 featuring exhibits from Brazil, Canada, France, Germany, Italy, the Netherlands, Russia and Switzerland. The first was hosted in 1915. Plaza de Panama is a plaza in Balboa Park's El Prado Complex. The exposition celebrated the opening of the Panama Canal, and was meant to trumpet San Diego as the first United States port of call for ships traveling north after passing westward through the canal. The fair was hosted in San Diego's large urban Balboa Park. I now recognize that park as a local legacy and connection to my Panamanian, Bajan, Grenadian and St. Lucian roots.

Growing up, we used to take family trips down the west coast's 5 Freeway from Sacramento to Disneyland in Anaheim, then the San Diego Zoo. That was a very different time to now and yet it set up our current zeitgeist — we didn't know it then but we were all connected by organic means, we just were — there were no cell phones, laptops, internet, social media and the modality of connections and relationships were more… organic.

The spirit of a young effervescent beautiful love flowed through our home in those years. An immense spirit of joy and hope were also there. I have tried to squeeze every ounce of love that was given to me — and there were gallons that would amount to a deluge — and pour that into my son as his inheritance. It hasn't been the education, although that has been invaluable insofar as not only my pedigree but also a curiosity and appetite to learn. *I always be learning.* My curiosity is another spiritual quality, or even just a personality trait that has resulted in not only riches but also a rich professional career in finance. And not in the ways one may expect. I've always been curious about human beings and how they work, what they think and why, why they do what they do when they do what they do. That business of forming relationships, creating connections and shepherding has become the cornerstone of several six-figure businesses in the last twenty years.

I also think part of my intellectual confidence and gifts have been imported from the Caribbean, Barbados and Trinidad in particular, which, until their relatively recent emancipations, were part of the Commonwealth and fell under the auspices of The United Kingdom — the standard of education, particularly, adherence to English standards of excellence in communication, speaking and writing is also something that I have inherited from the birthplace of my father and ancestors.

So yeah… Mommy has asked me not to idealize her, and yet, somehow, I can't help but do so. *Both of them.* I can't help but wonder if I am really not idealizing them. I believe they were both a young god and goddess imported via ancestral cosmic channels to the cosmology and zeitgeist of African gods, goddesses, spirits of old, spirits and ancestors. My God, I remember Mommy and Daddy's love — it was karmic and it was alive and still flows through my veins. It's what made me.

"Be patient when you sit in the dark. The dawn is coming."

—**Rumi**

There are smoky suns over the Trinidad and Tobago of the '60s, '70s and '80s. Streets of country cities are scattered with yellow and orange clay dust, populated by goat herders, butchers and cattle men, cow herders like my grandfather and a professional class, speeding cars, bicyclists and motorcycles, dogs with as much autonomy and rights as humans and hens mothering their chicks, housed in the thin alleyways of neighborhoods. There are little Black boys like Daddy, combing the streets, with heads too big for their little bodies, creating all sorts of mayhem before they would go on to make their mark in our world.

Sepia tones and auburn shades are how my mind remembers those years, traveling at the end of an era. And it wasn't easy but it was beautiful. Perhaps, in its own way, idyllic.

The young country has been filled with ambition, hope and an unmistakable panache of passion, resilience and sheer pride. Our people have had poignant moments and eras of hope and promise and my spirit is always keenly aware of the avatar of these principles, whether in the form of a young, idealistic Barack Obama or the intellectually flamboyant Mia Mottley. It's the same spirit that made Michael Jackson moonwalk from television sets into all of our imaginations. Or Muhammad Ali float like a butterfly and sting like a bee, or Michael Jordan air-walk with Spike's direction into that collective imagination. It is the high-power spirit of our winning and our champions. The high noon of that Trinidad era is our Honorable prime minister, Dr. Eric Williams.

> *"Slavery was an economic institution of the first importance. It had been the basis of the Greek economy and had built up the Roman Empire. In modern times it provided the sugar for the tea and the coffee cups of the Western world. It produced the cotton to serve as a base for modern capitalism. It made the American South and the Caribbean islands.*
>
> —**Eric Williams,** *Capitalism and Slavery*

Yeah, just as the Rio Seco waterfalls or the lush fields of sweet potato, cassava, citrus fruit and coconuts lining our countryside, his presence loomed large and set the template from which our race of divine men and women evolved. *Prime Minister Eric Eustace Willams is beloved.* Just like the obligatory photo of John F. Kennedy and Jacqueline Kennedy coupled with the Rev. Martin Luther King in every liberal home of the 1960s and '70s, or the conservative households with Ronald Reagan in the '80s and '90s, every single calypsonian-loving, carnival-jumping, soca-leaning Trinidadian enjoys a copy of his treatise *Capitalism and Slavery*.

Every single home, regardless of income or race knew the Williams thesis: *Enslavement originated because of economic factors; the system was profitable, so profitable that it lead to the British industrial revolution* — the so-called Negro slaves were ***"the strength and sinews of this western world."*** The *Africans* were the financiers — architects through expertise, genius and the hardest work ever known to mankind of those profitable industries of cotton, tobacco and sugar. The Africans in the Caribbean and United States were and are the wealth-engineers and builders of complex systems of *finance, abundance and prosperity.*

No one has truly embodied that mantle of Caribbean leadership and intellectual courage *(his thesis was a radical departure from the thought of the day),* passed from Marcus Garvey's vision of pan-Africanism until recently. And you will note that the emerging economies in this part of the world are being underwritten and reshaped to the engineering of our Madam CEO prime minister in Barbados, the Honorable Mia Amour Mottley and her contemporary class of leadership in CARICOM, the Caribbean equivalent of the European Union, and, to a lesser extent, the United Nations, including Guyana's President Mohamed Irfaan Ali and Suriname's President Chan Santokhi on global climate change and sustainability — the global Caribbean and Latin American emerging growth markets (Suriname, Barbados, Guyana, Colombia) are building a clean tech haven that will rival Dubai in the Caribbean Sea in less than five to fifteen years.

Matter of fact, the intellectual traditions of Spiritual IQ — and the ways capitalism and slavery shaped them — are the bedrock of the emerging markets in the New World. They shape, underwrite, and design the ideas, trade and capital market with sound business planning, while also demanding reparations, including Prime Minister Mia Mottley's resolute assertion of Britain's debt of $4.9 trillion to Barbados.

In the surreal photo of her smiling and back slapping with a grinning King Charles, *The Guardian*'s text reads that she's willing to be reasonable in her repayment timeline — *after all, it took four hundred years to incur the debt.* That's the moxie, charisma, brilliance and economic savvy of the Madame CEO, not establishing right to pursue but negotiating terms of payment! **CLASSIC** sales strategy and brilliant humanity and diplomacy.

The Honorable Mia Mottley has also utilized the platform of the United Nations to make climate converting into a geopolitical cause célèbre, where the outsized effect of climate change on Caribbean islands is given international priority; so much so that she is often rumored as the next Secretary General of the United Nations, in which case Barbados would receive the infusion of international reputation to become the Davos, Switzerland of the Caribbean, even more so than the financially astute Commonwealth of the Bahamas and even more so than the international haven of the Cayman Islands. She is the inverse function of Marcus Garvey, coming from *within* the system, though aimed at the same outcome — universal liberation and freedom.

"We're not expecting that the reparatory damages will be paid in a year, or two, or five because the extraction of wealth and the damages took place over centuries. But we are demanding that we be seen and that we are heard," she says.

I'm thinking now of a Bill Cosby and Sidney Poitier film — *Uptown Saturday Night* — in a classic scene where a bank robber says, upon robbing a woman of her wares, "My, my, my… *Lord have mercy!* Mmmm-mm." That's what it feels like for me to see Mia Mottley govern Barbados, which also, incidentally, has become the completely legitimate choice retirement destination of all the Americas, Europe and Africa. *Those who know*, know.

A couple of winters ago, I enjoyed the privilege of an advanced convoy commissioned by the Honorable Mackie Holder, Bajan (Barbados) Consul General of NYC (currently the deputy high commissioner of the United Kingdom) through a LinkedIn group I formed twenty years ago: Caribbean Community of Capitalists, Business Executives and Entrepreneurs (CCCBEE) — a group of nearly fifteen-thousand members from across the Caribbean diaspora founded in 2005.

My first revenues as an entrepreneur came in 2005 from the Barbados government with a group I co-founded with Dwayne B. Latimore and worked on with Kate Washington from 2007-2009: Africa Connects International LLC. Dwayne designed the marketing and branding of a cricket bat USB flash drive, which the Invest Barbados (investment promotion agency of Barbados) used for its marketing at MIDEM international music festival in Cannes, France. Kate Washington, a long-time friend and mentor, would travel to Miami and Philadelphia to meet with providers of solar panels and other sustainables, consulting for our beloved Caribbean.

During the advanced convoy, our group, including entrepreneur and "Tobago's own ambassador" Gennike Mayers and master real estate banker and deal maker

Christopher Browne, met with the heads of the Ministry of Housing and Lands, Million Dollar Properties (Cherita O'Dell), Invest Barbados, Sagicor Financial (CEO George Thomas) and Ian Durant from the Caribbean Development Bank, Sir Paul Altman (commercial real estate developer), sustainability industrialist and titan Ralph "Bizzy" Williams and Elan Amor Mottley, executive director of the Tides Restaurant. Alexander Gafoor, Esq., Trinidad's fintech and entrepreneurial movement in the form of a celebrated judicial family, quarterbacked the meetings from Trinidad. Elan Mottley was a treasure and one of the most genuine people you will ever meet; she and her sister, the prime minister, exemplify the superior Bajan stock that provides exceptional economic development and capital formation throughout the Barbados economy and jumpstarting the Caribbean's dynamic inroads with maturing African economies.

I was surprised and proud to find a world-class city at the beginning of its formation, where global leadership, business moxie and a highly educated (99.75% literacy rate) and aspirational citizens, booming private-public projects complement a $6B GDP driven by tourism, international business sector and foreign direct-investment. But really, the country is driven by Spiritual IQ — the brilliant repository of a kingdom of people who know *precisely who they are*.

Offshore bank havens such as the Cayman Islands, Virgin islands and Panama City have a complementary anchoring component in Barbados where fifty years of social austerity and political leadership have matured into a resolute and visionary Barbados for regional and global leadership.

I see an island of can-do attitude, tenacity, inspiration, leading a sustainability revolution at the Tropic of

Cancer where unique environmental conditions have created a petri dish for solar, wind and hydro excellence — the societies and communities of the future. Barbados' wealth and entrepreneurship are on global display with international recording artist Rihanna and other proud legacy holders such as LL Cool J, attorney general Eric Holder, KRS-1, Cuba Gooding Jr. and pioneer Shirley Chisholm Holmes.

Effectively the Prime Minister Madam CEO has become the surgical executive executor of Prime Minister Williams' thesis as well as Marcus Garvey's timeless vision. *"We do not yet know how to live on planet Mars, we only know how to live on Earth,"* Prime Minister Mia Mottley has said. "And the same oil and gas companies, bankers, transport companies, insurance companies, they're living on planet Earth too. *So why does it make sense to earn hundreds of billions of dollars in profit, for only ten or twenty years, rather than being able to sustain profit for the next century or two?"*

She has effectively matured Prime Minister Eric Willams' original thesis, with effective, brilliant governance:

> *"Here, then, is the origin of Negro slavery. The reason was economic, not racial; it had to do not with the color of the laborer, but the cheapness of the labor. As compared with Indian and white labor, Negro slavery was eminently superior"*
>
> —**Eric Williams,** *Capitalism and Slavery*

Dr. Eric Williams' thesis was both a surgical attack on the idea that moral and humanitarian motives were the key factors in the advancement of England's abolitionist movement, and a militaristic implicit critique of the established British hierarchy on the West indies. Not unlike Abraham

Lincoln, held as a paradigm of moral leadership who was, more so, a brilliant tactician and strategist who understood the South had a global engine of prosperity with their so-called Black Slaves. *To me? Capitalism and Slavery* is a trumpeted and twenty-one-gun salute from the realm of the ancestors.

Long before the literary treatise *Playing in the Dark* by Nobel Laureate Toni Morrison, or other literary Nobel Laureates VS Naipaul's *An Area of Darkness* (1964), or Derek Walcott's *Omeros* (1990) staked a claim; before candidate and President Barack Obama's entry into the ongoing discussion for reconciliation of America with *Dreams of My Father* or *The Audacity of Hope*, or, even Tupac Amuru Shakur's *All Eyez on Me*, Ice Cube's *AmeriKKKa's Most Wanted*, John Hope Bryant's *Love Leadership* or *How the Poor Can Save Capitalism*, Dr. Eric Williams made the claim for pan-African resilience politically and with the spiritual might and authority of a proud future that has claimed us all.

Mountainsides and countrysides strewn with fields that were reappropriated from pre-colonial sugar and from before independence and into trade with neighboring communities such as Barbados, Venezuela and Colombia, are teaming up with the nation of Prime Minister Eric Willams, looking to come out from under the hulking weight of corruption, avarice and greed that arose after Trinidad's once-in-a-century discovery of over three billion barrels of oil and gas and 728,300,000 barrels of proven oil reserves; no different than Bill Cosby culturally designing 1600 Pennsylvania Blvd for Barack Obama's White House with visionary Cosby Show.

> *Expansion is a necessity of slave societies; the slave power requires ever fresh conquests. "It is more profitable," wrote Merivale, "to*

> *cultivate a fresh soil by the dear labor of slaves, than an exhausted one by the cheap labor of free-men." From Virginia and Maryland to Carolina, Georgia, Texas and the Middle West; from Barbados to Jamaica to Saint Domingue and then to Cuba; the logic was inexorable and the same."*
>
> —**Eric Williams,** *Capitalism and Slavery*

From Prime Minister Eric Williams' mentor CLR James and *The Black Jacobins'* explanation for abolition, Williams extended those theses into an entire book. There have been other rich explorations of its correlation to the wealth of nations, as with Stanley M. Elkins' *Slavery,* or Dr. Henry Clarke's lifelong passion and devotion to documenting the histories and contributions of African peoples throughout the diaspora as in *Christopher Columbus and the Afrikan Holocaust: Slavery and the Rise of European Capitalism.* In fact, there are armies of economic visionaries and intellectual giants: John Hope Bryant, Rev. Dr. Mark E. Whitlock of the African Methodist Episcopalian church, the iconic Jesse Rev. Jackson, Rev. Al Sharpton, Dr. Elizabeth Asiedu, Dr. Robert L. Green, Dr. Willene A. Johnson (former vice president of the Federal Reserve Bank of New York and president of the National Economic Association), Dr. Peter Blair Henry (author of *TURNAROUND: Third World Lessons for First World Growth*), Dr. Susan Collins (former President and CEO of the Federal Reserve Bank of Boston) and Bishop Rodney Sampson, who continue the struggle for economic empowerment and total financial freedom that Marcus Garvey would define for future powerful people, they are soldiers and grunt men from the ghettos of America who have become generals and kings of their followers in popular culture and the shepherd of parishioners in their churches — both John Hope Bryant and Pastor Mark E. Whitlock of Reid

AME (African Methodist Episcopalian church in Baltimore and before that Orange County, CA) were mentored by the incomparable great Cecil R. Murray, for which Los Angeles freeways and the John R. Tansey Chair of Christian Ethics the USC school of the Cecil Murray Center for Community Engagement has been named.

From Dr. Thomas Parhams to the big brother Mark Reeds and John J. Kennedy to Abdi Ahmed to the Tony Faulkners (we have all been brothers from the fraternity of 100 Black Men of America) — you'll note: Spiritual IQ is the through line from the Rev. Jesse Jacksons to the Honorable Louis Farrakahans to the Pastor Mark W. Whitlocks to the local pastors of the African Methodist Episcopalian Church and Baptists churches to the Rev. Dr. Martin Luther Kings — ultimate wealth, power and influence are *divined spiritually.* ***Them.*** The spirits of our ancestors fuel our quest for not only our rightful place in this realm, but to harness our infinite wealth and the planet's limitless abundance from the spirit realm. Again, *the wealth of kingdoms are* ***directly*** *proportional to our moral, ethical and spiritual standing.*

If you look at Trinidad's *Beacon* archived newspapers from 1932 and 1933, you will find statements by activists and nationalists mirroring our beloved prime minister's theses. And there's a certain intellectual imagination that is a wider part of the Caribbean. This intellectual imagination and intellectual erudition is very much a part of the indigenous Trinidadian character. It's part of our spirit, no less than our indefatigable pride, entrepreneurial wherewithal and it is part of our national identity. If you feel revolutionary, if you feel a sense of liberation and a fierce if not ferocious heart beating throughout the text on these pages? *Trinidad* is where that spiritual vibration originates from and CLR James is the universe with the same functionality of Thomas Jefferson and Dr. Eric Williams is the inverse function of America's George Washington, the liberator of body and spirits — they are the answer to how you reconcile the sheer hypocrisy and plight of American corrosive divisions and it's not science, it's humanity, *the highest form of science and understanding.*

It is heading in the direction of healing, the modality of understanding; it's heading in the direction of a higher frequency, a greater plane of commonalities; it's letting go of centuries-old paradigms and restoring balance for *humanity*:

> *"Negro slaves, one-twentieth of the population in 1670, were one-fourth in 1730. Slavery, from being an insignificant factor in the economic life of the colony, had become the very foundation upon which it was established. There was still room in Virginia, as there was not in Barbados, for the small farmer, but land was useless to him if he could not compete with slave labor."*
>
> —**Eric Williams,** *Capitalism and Slavery*

Or as Madam CEO Mia Mottley has spoken:

> *"We have to understand that the underdevelopment of Africa, [...] of the Caribbean, [...] of Latin America, in many instances, is a child of the colonial experiment, and the colonial experiment extracted wealth. And in some of these countries, the extractive attitudes still remain, such that we haven't been able to build the kind of domestic enterprises and the domestic foundations that's necessary to sustain our people."*

She concludes, there is a need for "a written and clear apology to say, ***'we were wrong, we will not do it again'*, and**

***more importantly, we must pay recompense for what was done*. That is the first step of walking the walk.**"

> *"Action, self-reliance, the vision of self and the future have been the only means by which the oppressed have seen and realized the light of their own freedom."*
>
> *"We must canonize our own saints, create our own martyrs, and elevate to positions of fame and honor Black men and women who have made their distinct contributions to our racial history"*
>
> —**Marcus Garvey**, founder and first President-General of the Universal Negro Improvement Association and African Communities League, through which he declared himself Provisional President of Africa

See? It is heading in the direction of greater prosperity for all; closer to our ideas, closer to an *authentic* (versus globally marketed and branded) democracy where we are the sum of our parts and *where peace and prosperity on Earth are possible*.

Yes, I said it. Trinidad's calypsonian, Black Stalin sang about it in his anthem "The Black Man Feelin' to Party."

Chapter 10: **Getting Deals Done with President Barack Hussein Obama**

"I believe we are a great country. Imperfect though we may be, I believe we are a great country. Part of what makes us great are our democratic institutions that protect our fundamental ideals: freedom of religion and the rule of law, protection from discrimination based on national origin, freedom of the press, and a 200-year history as a nation built by immigrants. What makes us great are the ideals that were behind those words we spoke in 1776, that said we are all to be treated as equals. And I believe this is a moment in time unlike any other that requires us to fight for those ideals and for the values we believe in."

—Senator Kamala D. Harris, ***2012***

Just what is the deal with participating in this grand American experiment? At times? It has been *hell on Earth*. And sometimes? *It seems like a dream.*

The first time I met Gary E. Bryant was through Lisa

Elzy Watson, President at LightWave Education. She and I were introduced to one another at the Federal Reserve Bank of San Francisco in Los Angeles through our mutual friend and exceptional servant leader, Pastor Mark E. Whitlock. I shared my mission with Senator Barack Obama's campaign and fundraising and, lightworker, Lisa promised an introduction which would be transformative and far-reaching: Gary and Suzanne Bryant, who were SoCal change agents and socialites who understood how to work the machinery of American systems to bring about the greatest possible good. I was dubious to say the least, but still excited and inspired by the possibility. I set up a meeting at one of my favorite networking spots, Havana's at the Lab, down the road from my branch offices in South Coast Plaza. The initial meeting hosted a couple of my premiere clients at the bank, including a CPA firm (Bob Goodrich) as well as a political mailing client. The meeting was one of my first attempts at organic networking outside the context of my office, banking and loan, investment, mortgage and deposit goals.

Since then I have learned a lot from Gary E. Bryant and have been sure to share within our world of investment banking in the micro-cap sector and conferences the-low hanging fruits of wisdom from his immense tree of wealth. Gary was an American original, *like an archangel.* These lessons have come in myriad formations, but mainly they have come as conversations between two guys: prodigy and mentor. More frequently than not, the conversations have been unspoken — an energy passing between generations — the quest for knowledge and its quenching with wisdom and patience and most importantly *doing.*

There have been some memorable exchanges, however. *I remember sitting in Gary's office and being powerfully affected and mesmerized by the prospects of a Senator who chose Springfield Chicago as the launch to an improbable journey.* I remember the excitement percolating within my breast like an enlarged heart and having to vent to Mr. Bryant, who was busy studying three screens of green, red and yellow tickers with the day's gains and losses.

"Gary, this thing with Obama is amazing. He's caught pace in Nevada and I feel it —I get the sense even more so that it is going to happen. *It's like Abraham Lincoln had the tenacity and vision to reincarnate himself as a mulatto in the modern age and complete the work that was begun with the end of the Civil War."*

This is where many folks would give a dismissive shrug, unsure of how to respond to such a creative concoction of facts, visions and dreams — more than likely responding with a timid, "Sure, Patrick. Sure. Why not?" But Gary leaned in from his desk, a twinkle crept into his eye, bursting light into his face and he responded from his spirit, "*You know, Patrick, I think you're right.* I believe that is what is happening." This coming from a multimillionaire "good ol' boy" financier — *whew, boy.*

Okay. *Let's go get it.*

Yes, this time my deal wasn't brokering a multi-million-dollar deal or conducting an interview with a cultural icon or Fortune 500 CEO for our international podcasts *Getting Deals Done* or *Here's to Life,* or my national investment conference series, The West Coast Wall Street Conference, our affiliate magazine *The California Financial Times* and San Diego Investment Conference series, or working with entrepreneurs to secure funding. This was a little *different.*

The deal, like a dream in 2008, was participating in American democracy and helping red John Wayne's Orange County in Southern California tilt purple for a mega-star junior Senator from Chicago who would become number forty-four. It was the first time I had participated in national politics as a fundraiser, even though I had volunteered and worked as an intern and campaign volunteer for a California state senator, New York senator and local east coast and west coast candidates (of both parties) over the previous two decades.

$2,500 was the price for VIP tickets and it was $2,300 to attend the main reception at the Balboa Bay Club in Newport Beach. Sports agent Leigh Steinberg, producer and political activist Nicole Avant (daughter of the legendary Clarence Avant, Godfather of Black Hollywood), LA Laker Jordan Farmer and his father, legendary actor Lou Gossett Jr, captain of industry Arianna Huffington and Los Angeles representative Karen Bass (current LA Mayor) — who introduced him — were all in attendance at the historic fundraiser. In total, the event — including fundraisers Sandy and Harold Price — raised in excess of $1.2 million and our household raised about 1/10th of that amount from a diverse group of hedge fund managers, technology and real estate executives. We were teamed with investment banker Gary Bryant and his beautiful wife Suzanne Bryant (an Eleanor Roosevelt devotee), who were originally going to host the event at their home in Pelican Hill in Newport Beach.

The memories of that campaign are, for me, a precious heirloom in my memories because I know that was plausibly considered impossible. A lot of folks older — and perhaps even wiser — than me knew America would never elect a Black man to the US Presidency and, after MAGA, *how on Earth were they wrong?* But, somewhere within, akin to those principles of hope, promise and faith, I knew it was possible and 52.9% of the US popular vote and 365 of the 538 electoral votes made it so.

Now, I'm not saying the Obama's beautiful near-Camelot-like election — the fulfillment of those JFK and RFK visions — excuse the subsequent hundred steps back to Jim Crow America and the Confederacy that have pulled back a superficial cosmetic veil to reveal just how America is fundamentally built upon a bedrock of white supremacy, white privilege and rampant racism and discrimination, but it did clearly demonstrate that the *impossible is possible* in America on a systemic and institutional basis. I would meet President Obama on two other occasions and would visit his White House with my family, courtesy of the late great Congressman Elijah Cummings, California's visionary Lena Kennedy and her brother, the late great Pasadena servant leader John J. Kennedy.

It has been really interesting to see Barack Obama's legacy unfold. In some ways, he is as unconventional an ex-president as Jimmy Carter — he and First Lady Michelle Obama own a storytelling and production company, Higher Ground, and seem very much devoted to and in love with one another, are one of the youngest ex-presidents and first ladies in modern history (in age and sheer exuberance) and they are as much global cultural figures as they are part and parcel of the body politic. Similar to Ronald Reagan or, perhaps, Franklin D. Roosevelt, Barack Hussein Obama is now a two-term president whose vice president became president and successfully extended the Obama-Biden agenda into the fabric of America, even as the Supreme Court holds court for the minority of the fringe-right.

And so, the American struggle to become a nation of her highest ideas continues.

I'm not one of the MSNBC devotees who didn't believe that Donald Trump could be successfully re-elected for his second term. The truth is that Donald J. Trump's presidency has been hurtling toward America in the form of David Duke, Pat Buchanan, Richard M. Nixon and even Dick Cheney for the entirety of our modern era. I have seen it all and thereby believe it is all possible. America has never dealt with its demons so now the devil has dominion.

Hotter Than the Fourth of July

> "Power concedes nothing without demand. It never has and never will."
>
> — ***Frederick Douglass***

All the photos in this literary memoir are what the Fourth of July means to me. So I throw them up knowing it invites all sorts of vitriol and serendipitous vibration. Oh, well. Thank God we live in America. *Right?* I mean, *Left.* I mean, Center!

Number forty-four was a character with the name Barack Hussein Obama. Oh yeah, and he was Black. With a Black family and two black dogs that looked like afros with some of that sheen just walking around, biting and barking in those halls built by our ancestors — *but classy,* you know? The history is written but remember that was *"impossible"*: a Black man with that name (think US President Louis Farrakhan or US president Elezer Silver or President Sheikh Ahmad Hammoud and maybe that gives you an idea of the hurdle) being elected in a country whose legacy is aged in slavery and contemporary racism and discrimination — *but it happened in 2008.*

Hanna and I jumped on board the Hope and Change soul train and helped raise funds in red Orange County — I, the son of Trinidadian and Panamanian immigrant professors and she, a first-generation American from the world's first civilization, Ethiopia, and the daughter of a former Ethiopian Airlines executive and beauty shop owner. We worked with the Whitlocks, the Parhams, the Jankans, the Daniels, the Bryants. That changed our trajectory from bishops and rooks to stewards of kings and queens.

Since then, we haven't looked back. We purchased two homes, have created a real estate fund, served on boards and supported not-for-profits and charities that we believed in, traveled around the country and world for business and pleasure, grown in our love for one another, watched our son (SharkHeart, fastest human on land and in water) become a leading USA swimmer, record-setting track and field star, a standout student and conscientious Christian, begun multiple successful businesses, costumed celebrities, written a couple of books, helped dozens of small businesses secure funding and grow, volunteered for and served with several not-for-profits, enjoyed the fruits of corporate America, participated in several campaigns (successful and otherwise) and lived our American dream. Oh, and we got our own dog, a Jack Russell Fox Terrier called Trinidad. Rascal!

So now, I try not to get distracted by all that social media and mainstream media nonsense talking about divisions. Dream cosmic, think global and act local. Or, as Tupac put it: *plan, block, strategize.* Implement. Execute. ***Do.*** And if you fall down, fall forward, rise up strong with a full beating heart and never give up. I work with Democrats, Libertarians, Independents and Republicans… woke folk and MAGA-ites. *I work with human beings* to achieve common goals. I do it on a deal-by-deal basis, and every fiscal quarter *I* see the checks. *There is prosperity in unity and coming together.* Pay attention to the folks around you — your co-workers, brothers and sisters, pastor, mom and dad, the friends and network, the development of your visions on social media… pay attention to your community, serve your fellow citizens, aspire to your highest self and wake up. Matter of fact, wake everyone up and create mastermind forums and put it together. We get the America we create. That. Is. All. If you didn't make the billion or trillion dollars? Well, it ain't coming.

For me, July Fourth represents November Fourth, 2008 — the first time I completely embraced my identity as an American entrepreneur and businessman. If America can be that dude, then I will stand for the American flag and pledge allegiance so that when my son sees me stand, he understands that when it counted, we stood tall and were counted. (I would never stand for a flag that represented otherwise — Hotep Kapernick!) So, if I am going to turn on my TV, then I watch Bloomberg and CNBC — we can focus on the business of our lives because more miracles are coming — I know I am only beginning. America is only beginning. Yeah, I said it: *I'm hotter than this Fourth of July.*

For me, America and the Fourth of July represents its potential, and I'm willing to stand for that and put in the sweat, blood and tears. We are going to reach the potential declared in our Declaration in Congress, July fourth, 1776:

> *We hold these truths to be self-evident, that all men are created equal, that they are endowed by their Creator with certain unalienable*

Rights, that among these are Life, Liberty and the pursuit of Happiness.—That to secure these rights, Governments are instituted among Men, deriving their just powers from the consent of the governed, —That whenever any Form of Government becomes destructive of these ends, it is the Right of the People to alter or to abolish it, and to institute new Government, laying its foundation on such principles and organizing its powers in such form, as to them shall seem most likely to effect their Safety and Happiness.

Chapter 11:
Captain of Capital Markets

"I get deals done."

— ***Gary E. Bryant,*** *Captain of Capital Markets*

The inaugural San Diego Investment Conference (SDIC), December 2010, was a success by all measures. Over $60 million in funding opportunities emerged from the event, with ten quality companies presenting to a crowd of 120 quality attendees — institutional and accredited investors. These investors came from Southern California, including Las Vegas, Orange County, Los Angeles, and San Diego. Close to 60% of the presenting companies reported a funding event directly tied to their presentation, with 40% of those returning within two fiscal quarters. This was at the bottom of the Great Recession. We didn't care. We didn't get depressed. We didn't get recessed. *We came up.* We moved forward with grace, class and resilience.

"Americans are in a cycle of fear, which leads to people not wanting to spend or invest, leading to more fear. We'll break out of it. It takes time."

— ***Warren Buffet,*** *The Oracle*

One day, I found myself at an $8 million mansion overlooking the Pacific Ocean. It had once belonged to *Wheel of Fortune*'s Vanna White. The man who now owned it sat in an ornate armchair in a mahogany office, his monitors flashing ticker symbols like sentinels. No, this was not Mr. Smith. And, no, it was not Neo. This man was real and his name was Gary E. Bryant — not some character from a science fiction opus or an evening soap opera. His father was a farmer, so how he ended up as one of the most successful micro-cap investment bankers in America probably owes significantly to his grandfather. With an Oklahoma twang reminiscent of Clark Gable or Elvis Presley, he charmed me with a simple question: "How'd you like to come work with me?" The way he asked made me feel like one of the good ol' boys.

"*Yeah, that would be cool.*"

That moment marked a turning point for me. After fifteen years in finance, working with big retail names like Wachovia, Bank of America, and Wells Fargo, I realized the world of micro-cap markets was a whole new realm — elemental capitalism. Mr. Bryant didn't need to ask a second time.

My first assignment with Newport Capital Consultants was a meeting in La Jolla, at the Lodge at Torrey Pines. Sacramento born and bred, though world-traveled, I had never even taken the PCH south of San Juan Capistrano to know the difference between San Diego and its pearl, La Jolla, ensconced off the Pacific seacoast. It was for the Fat Cat Club, a national angel investor group run by Ben Dogherty. Five companies presented before a room of angel investors, accredited investors, and financial professionals. The meeting was quintessential Wall Street: buyer, seller, palm pressing, Cheshire smiles, big personalities, private placement memorandum, sales pitch, subscription agreement, check-writers, pro-formas galore and yes, greed. And yet, the only thing more inspiring to me was the scenic drive of red mountains, evergreen trees and white cascading shore waters at the Torrey Pines National Park leading to my awakening at the Lodge at Torrey Pines.

Gary Bryant and his wife Suzanne would later move to a Dallas ranch to be closer to their grandkids. Together, they launched the Southwest Investment Association, for which I was a co-founder and on the board, along with Suzanne Bryant, Steve and Liz Jones and JD Kerr. Around the same time, my wife accepted a marketing director position with a biotech firm in Del Mar, leading us to move from Irvine to Carmel Valley in San Diego.

However, this was in 2008, right when the economy took a nosedive into the worst economic recession since the Great Depression. But even amid such monumental challenges, Gary taught me that passion for the game could trump fear (pun intended). As I keynoted in my first event, I knew from a long time ago this total lack of depression during the recession was the way I would go. Daddy asked me when he taught one of his classes, "What will you do if there is ever a Great Depression in your life?"

"Not get depressed" was the answer, to which Dr. Howell retorted, "Good. Now, never forget it." The American History, World History and political science professor was keen to prepare me for work in capital formation just as his father, the Butcher, had prepared him to thrive in the American economy with kids who have fared very well.

From Gary, I learned lessons that have stayed with me: "Play offense, not defense," "People buy from you, not your product," and "You get rich off the accumulation of stock." "A company's valuation is always 1.5 x sales," "The smartest thing Ronald Reagan ever did was establish the 504c rule, allowing the flow of capital in the markets" and "You get what you negotiate, not what is fair." (And yes great minds think alike, as my brilliant dad and rich dad both concurred.) By far the most enduring and powerful has been his passion for the love of the game that are our capital markets' formation.

Gary Bryant is not Jock Ewing, and this isn't that Dallas soap opera — he was doing deals until his very last breath. He lived and breathed capital markets, making and getting deals done, and through working with him, I was infected with that same oblong passion and spirit to create, build and make things happen.

Gary could have been in the twilight of a celebrated career as a septuagenarian and financier, enjoying the handsome rewards that span a legendary fifty-year career owning a national broker dealer and playing an instrumental role in deals such as Pre-Paid Legal, Sonic Boom and over two hundred other deals at various stages of the capital markets game, being a founding member of the National Investment Bankers Association and the Southern California Investment Association. He could have been traveling the world on a yacht, but instead he worked out of "the Barn," a self-styled office and Newport Capital Consultant's headquarters on his fourteen-acre Dallas ranch, which was a few ranches away from former Secretary of State Rex Tillerson's, former chairman and CEO of ExxonMobil.

Instead, he was still running with deals like Petro Resources (which eventually became Magnum Hunter Resources, NYSE: MHR) or Lucas Energy (AMEX: LEI), just like his days with Northeastern Oklahoma A&M football.

The San Diego Investment Conference itself became a beacon of hope amid the Great Recession. Nearly 60% of presenting companies reported a direct funding event from our conference, and many returned for future engagements. Over time, we served more than fifty micro-cap companies across sectors like renewable energy, biotechnology, finance and IT. The real success of the conference wasn't just in the companies but the patriotic and keen angel investors who helped build relationships with the officers and made decisions that would ultimately write checks.

The real success of the conference derived not only from the quality of presenting companies (i.e., opportunities to discover an American Steel, Ford Motors or Microsoft in its embryonic stages) but the SDIC membership with patriotic and astute angel investors assessing opportunities from presenting executives, developing substantive and qualitative relationships with the officers (sometimes as strategic investors), making the risk assessment and, ultimately, the check-writing decision. The American Economy is in the midst of a radical revitalization. Never has being a keen, analytical and successful angel investor or investment banker for micro-cap companies been more patriotic. The work is essential to the body economic, like oxygen to a human body.

Members of the Southern California investment banking community including but not limited to Christopher Williams of Trinity Equity Partners, Bob Beers of Seale and Beers, Steve Fryer of SC Capital, Shelly and Lulu Kraft of Stock News Now, or Timothy Laughlin of Capflow Funding are the "accelerators" at these forums, whereas the angel investors are the catalysts.

At the conclusion of our inaugural conference — a sunset rescinding over the Pacific coastline — from the lobby of the Hilton, Michael Miramontes, President of Quick Class, Inc. a tenured corporate officer, financier and master entrepreneur dispensed some valuable advice to myself and the president of SDIC, my partner in life, Hanna Wagari, regarding refinement of our investment forum. Principal among those was "Go to New York City. Call Mike Segal. He is the founder of one of the classiest and best-run conferences I have ever attended. Twenty companies; a single afternoon. More than five hundred attendees. Accredited investors are clearly designated, and all the best food you will ever have is at one of these. His event is a class act."

Michael Segal was kind enough to host a "tutorial" luncheon at the Michael Jordan Restaurant in Grand Central Station in New York City. We sat down over lunch for two hours before he hopped on his train for the suburbs of New Jersey. The Private Equity Forum at the Yale Club is regarded as one of the premiere micro-cap conferences in a town that invented Wall Street. Mike's take on sharing trade secrets of the capital market conference industry? "Patrick, if you create a great event out West, make a really good conference; it gives a good name to all of us." I learned a long time ago with Leslie Brown, my first business mentor —and sister to the late Ron Brown, former Secretary of Commerce — always to take on mentors, always to put your head down, listen and learn.

The principal lessons for the SDIC from Mike and the Private Equity Forum: "Deliver a world class event," "only invite performers (not, as we like to jest within the industry, 'plate-lickers')," "perform with integrity" and "reputation is everything." And, of course, feed the people… well. Heading out to Michael's quarterly Private Equity Forum has almost become a regular pilgrimage after one of my own Southern California events, a rite of passage as well as privilege.

Of course, I also learned that fostering the right relationships with the right people means everything. The engineering of relationships and continual building of your Blackberry Rolodex can be the difference between dynamic success and static failure, knowing and not knowing who and what you don't know.

To be a part of these conferences — whether the Financial Services Exchange (FSX), the National Investment Bankers Association (NIBA), or Alan Stone's WallStreet Research conferences in New York City — was to be part of the entrepreneurial spirit and capital formation that powers American capitalism.

Since 2008, I have co-produced or sponsored hundreds of capital events, exposing well over three hundred companies to millions of dollars in prospective funding opportunities across diverse industries. Together, we've taken our investor roadshow to fourteen U.S. markets and three international locations. Among the companies we worked with are American Motor Products, Aztec Solar Power and Ovagene Oncology

My first "dog and pony show" throughout Southern California was with Earth Energy Reserves (EER), a natural gas company headquartered in Colorado with operations in Northern Louisiana. This was in the second quarter of 2010. EER extracts natural gas from coal bed methane using horizontal pinnate drilling. At the time, they were raising $5 million for their offering. Under the employ of Newport Capital Consultants, I was tasked with conducting two seminars with EER's investment relations head, "big brother" Jim Phillips —one at the Balboa Bay Club in Newport Beach and the other at the University Club atop Symphony Towers in downtown San Diego. Our efforts not only raised awareness but also helped close their initial "friends and family" round of $1.5 million.

This assignment, along with my role as a founding member of the Southwest Investment Association in Dallas, was my coming-of-age as Executive Director of the San Diego Investment Conference (SDIC), which gave rise to our West Coast Wall Street Conference, which gave rise to Global Capital Network. These experiences were my Edison lightbulb moment — the "aha!" realization that if major banks were unwilling to lend capital for business development, the small businessman could still pull himself up by his own bootstraps. All he needed was access to the right forum and the right check-writers — both accredited and institutional investors. This was the art of fostering relationships and making profitable introductions.

Our success with Earth Energy Reserves took place at the height of the Great Recession, underscoring my father's words: "The only thing to fear is fear itself" and his own personal mantra: *"You can do anything you set your mind to."*

We survived perilous and historic times in America and the world. Through the Great Recession, we witnessed no less than three overseas wars, unprecedented national debt, the collapse of major banks, the shift of American economic power from an industrial nation to a global intellectual and cultural leader and the largest stimulus package in American history. And now, we faced new challenges: dizzying multi-trillion-dollar debt reductions, a historic downgrade in the US credit rating and a seemingly ineffective federal government. Through it all, companies like Earth Energy Reserves — along with standout SDIC alumni like Your Offers, True Diagnostics, Sutter Gold Mining (OTCBB: SGMX) and Max Sound (OTCBB:

MAXD) — thrived and came back from the edge of oblivion: super entrepreneurs with a vision that they were willing to put it all on the line for. They exemplified a simple egalitarian spirit of entrepreneurship, emboldened by historic challenges rather than stifled by them. It's this same spirit embodied in the works of Gary E. Bryant, Ovagene Oncology founders Dr. Jay Coonan and Frank Kiesner, angel investor Jeff Maichen, Chlorofill founder Michael Hurst and Timothy Laughlin of Cap Flow Funding. These individuals see opportunities where others see obstacles. They soar at unprecedented heights, viewing the American economic landscape as a capitalist tapestry of deals, negotiations, capital formations and trends.

At the heart of this mindset lies the entrepreneurial grit that carried America through the Great Depression. Just as the Industrial Revolution propelled the country into the global forefront, entrepreneurs today fuel America's next chapter of innovation. The American middle class, born from this spirit, remains strong, with 54% of citizens living in middle-class households driving nearly 50% of the US GDP.

While political leadership remains fractured, and news outlets ebb and flow with reports of doom, the men, women and companies behind capital formation are underwriting history, one venture at a time. We live in the future built by Ford Motors, programmed by Microsoft, powered by General Electric and made possible by American Steel. SDIC takes pride in being a part of this ongoing renewal — America, stronger than ever in her 200-year history.

It takes resilience to rise from a bankruptcy, to summon the will to rebuild a shattered career or to face financial ruin with the courage to start anew. This courage — the strength to face hard facts and keep moving forward — defines the heart of the American entrepreneur. As Gary Bryant, my mentor, so succinctly put it: "Play offense, not defense."

To participate in one of these investment conferences, whether it be the Financial Services Exchange (FSX), the National Investment Bankers Association (NIBA), the Southwest Investment Association (SWIA) or Alan Stone's WallStreet Research annual small-cap conference in New York City, is to experience the lifeblood of American capitalism. These conferences embody the entrepreneurship and capital formation that continue to lead and define global commerce.

Since then? We've made headlines in Southern California, around the country and in several places around the world:

San Diego Investment Conference: American Small Caps Make Their Way Back With Significant Funding Opportunities

Investment Conferences Such as the West Coast Wall Street Conference Are Key to American Economic Recovery

Capital Markets Revival Across America with the Miami International Investment Conference

Miami International Investment Conference Debuts at the Eden Roc Resort

These companies are looking for capital formation but they are also looking for exposure to the professional investment class; they are looking for support from broker dealers, market makers, family offices or private equity funds. As an investor relations professional, my job is to provide "exposure" to the public at large, which I am doing with this very end chapter segment and publishing their names, and some… *most* of these companies don't even exist any longer, having been absorbed by larger entities, gone out of business or grown and merged into larger entities.

Excellent Wall Street, Crowdfunding and Family Offices

I am the proud son of a former author, professor and lecturer, as well as a tenured professor of Spanish in the California community colleges, engineer and vice president of the local teachers' union. For over twenty years, I've worked in financial services across the nation —from Market Street in San Francisco to Wall Street to Upstate New York's markets, and throughout Southern California at institutions like Wachovia Bank, Wells Fargo Bank, BNP Paribas, and Newport Capital Consultants. My journey reflects the influences of the Caribbean, Oakland, Cal Berkeley, and Wall Street. I take pride in my heritage as a first-generation American — an African American, Trinidadian, Panamanian and pan-African Afrofuturist, with a touch of Irish and English bloodlines. I am a culturalist, having spoken with hundreds of poets, financiers, authors, painters and artists. But at my core, *I am a human* who loves this planet — the square root of one that the Universe created for us to act as co-creators.

Perhaps it is this blend of backgrounds and values that made the Occupy Wall Street Movement resonate with me, even as I have sought the wealth habits of the 1%. Their commonality was frustration, passion and a determination to change a system that was undergoing reformation. I supported the federal government's bailout of banks, but felt uneasy about how those banks failed to reciprocate for small businesses. I love community banks, capital markets, and investment conferences — from the National Investment Bankers Association to the Financial Services Exchange, from the Southwest Investment Association to my own national series. I am fascinated by the rise of family offices and the shift from hedge funds to venture capital. Crowdfunding, too, excites me — ordinary people organizing sound business.

Community banks, capital markets and investment conferences became lifelines during the Great Recession. Capital and ideas are the nutrients of free-market trade, and I believe deeply in the "Excellent Wall Street."

We published the *California Financial Times,* a magazine and e-zine promoting California's global economic position and marketing for our presenting sponsorship. We feature captains of industry like Robert Reich, Andre Shapiro, and Hilda Solis, alongside personal mentors and inspirations like Gary E. Bryant and Tony "The Truth" Thompson (co-founder of the 1031 Exchange), Kamala Harris and other California women. As a tenured banker and business leader, I've advocated for "Excellent Wall Street" — the sector that thrives on capital market formation, micro-cap stocks, crowdfunding, and entrepreneurs.

"Excellent Wall Street" is about the people who built Amazon, Apple, Facebook, Ben & Jerry's and the like. It's where companies like Zagg, Magnum Hunter Resources, Ovagene and True Diagnostics first took flight. It is the heart of innovation, where American dreams transform into reality through private companies and start-ups. Excellent Wall Street represents capital formation that fuels small businesses, creating workers, materials and capital that form the lifeblood of the American economy.

However, the Excellent Wall Street I champion faced intense scrutiny and reform since the economic collapse of 2008, especially with the passage of the Dodd-Frank Wall Street Reform and Consumer Protection Act. We are at the cusp of an ongoing revolution in technology, sustainability and energy — these will become the next bull markets. Despite the imperfections in America's system, I believe we are perfecting the twenty-first-century version of capitalism.

Crowdfunding: A New Era for Small Businesses, Markets and Capital Formation

> "Crowdfunding is a game-changer for startups and entrepreneurs. Now every American, regardless of income level, can invest in great business ideas. This bill has great potential for job growth."
>
> — **Republican Boston Senator Scott Brown,** 2012

Through platforms regulated by the SEC, crowdfunding allows startups to raise capital from everyday investors. Since its passage, the global crowdfunding market has grown exponentially, projected to reach $3.62 billion by 2030.

I've had the privilege of working alongside visionary leaders like Devin Thorpe of Super Crowd Inc., who champions community builders, and Bill Huston of CrowdMax, a thought leader in crowdfunding. Together, they're advancing equal access to the capital markets, enabling more diverse and inclusive participation in America's economy. America's potential to defy odds and aspire to its highest ideals never ceases to inspire me. The pursuit of happiness now feels like the upside of Master Yoda's wisdom: "Do or do not. *There is no try.*"

Some Closing Thoughts on Excellent Wall Street

The American economy is stronger for the incredible challenges it has faced. Crowdfunding, family offices and capital markets are evolving to create greater opportunity for small businesses and entrepreneurs. As part of this movement, we must continue to aspire to our best selves, ensuring that *Excellent Wall Street* serves as a model of equity, growth and innovation.

> *We can now say with confidence that our peacetime economic expansion is the longest in history. And it is different than most past expansions. This time, the expansion is inclusive, not exclusive. This time, our prosperity belongs to the many, not merely to the few. This time, a rising tide truly does lift all boats.*
>
> —**President Bill Clinton,** January 8, 1999

I remember visiting the law office of Greenberg and Traurig and hearing from my very astute securities attorney, Mr. Daniel K. Donahue, Esq. about the $10K / $1M crowdfunding exemption taking seed and not only sighing in relief but also feeling inspired by the excitement intuitively leaping into my heart. The 10K / 1M crowdfunding exemption initiative that is taking seed in the Security Exchange Commission and the

White House as part of the American Jobs Act is an excellent idea. It is not dissimilar to the SEC's 504 program of the '80s, basically fostering capital development of emerging growth opportunities. I recall Obama identifying Reagan as the most transformative two-term president of the twentieth century. Needless to say, Clinton, who oversaw the largest peacetime economic expansion, had something to say about that! *Ha!* This program (SEC's 504) was responsible, in part, for the greatest economic peacetime expansion in American history at the end of the twentieth century. Ease of capital flow into the micro-cap markets is essential to a healthy free market capitalism. The American Jobs Act passed a similar provision, only this time it is called "crowdfunding."

Since 2008, I have watched many broker dealers, investment banking consultants, angel investors and venture capitalists thwarted and ultimately defeated by the sea of change, reform and regulation we have all weathered in the last fifteen years. These are the natural ebbs and flows of capitalism, moved by the polarities of greed and fear.

We are the *Excellent* Wall Street Movement, and it is imperative that we take our cues from our best intentions to help out the little guy, innovator and dreamer — *the entrepreneur*.

In 2012, Mitt Romney and Barack Obama had a spirited contest that was the usual rough-and-tumble of American politics, but basically an ideological contrast versus *destroy your enemy*. I thought Mitt Romney would have been a great and strategically astute choice for Secretary of the Treasury. I mean, if Barack Obama could appoint his Democratic opponent Hillary Clinton to Secretary of State, why not?

Mitt Romney came from an investment banking background, and from what I saw of him during the campaign, he seemed like someone who was not only up to the job but imbued with a certain integrity, an undeniable ambition and clear sight as to success and growth within the capital markets. The fortune he earned from his business career at Bain and Company and Bain Capital is estimated between $190–250 million. More important is Bain's fundamental impact on day-to-day American lives with companies like Staples, iHeart Media, Baxter International, Burlington Industries, Dun & Bradstreet, Hughes Tool, Iowa Beef, Monsanto and Wells Fargo.

Treasury Secretary Mitt Romney never happened. I'm confident if he was asked to serve he would have. I, however, was more inspired by this idea of The United States of America than ever before. It was Barack Obama's second elected term and none of the MAGA stupidness had yet occurred — we seemed to be living up to our ideas as a nation of high ideas birthed from certain atrocities. Truly, *anything* within reason, seemed as if it were possible.

> *"I'm pleased Congress took bipartisan action to pass this bill. These proposals will help entrepreneurs raise the capital they need to put Americans back to work and create an economy that's built to last."*
>
> —**President Obama**, Apr 5, 2012

> *"The best advice I know is to give those worldly things your best but never your all — reserve the ultimate hope for the only one who can grant it. America is not better off than it was $1.8 trillion dollars ago. We are a nation of immigrants."*
>
> —**Senator Mitt Romney**

Conversely, the 2012 Jobs Act was passed into law by President Barack Obama with trademark equanimity. The idea of equality in the capital markets was given a legal and policy boost if not a platform in what is now called "crowdfunding." The Jumpstart Our Business Startups (JOBS) Act is a bipartisan bill that enacted many of the President's proposals to encourage startups and support our nation's small businesses. With the ability to access financing, the JOBS Act allows businesses to grow and hire more workers, which helped put Americans back to work after the financial crisis. The JOBS Act rolled back financial regulation in relation to small businesses and Obama signed the law.

That inspiration led to my formation of the capital markets event American Prosperity and Jobs at the Pacific Club in Newport Beach. From OC's faucet of financiers, investors and apex-deal junkies, we invited some of the most powerful and influential figures from the local world of investment banking and entrepreneurship. The Great Recession was all but behind us and we were on the cusp of new potentials and scaling even greater national heights.

When President Obama took office in 2008, the economy was shrinking. By 2012 and the end of his presidency, the economy was growing by 2% in inflation adjusted, effectively outpacing the growth of Presidents George W. Bush and his dad, George H.W. Bush in his single term, and basically outpacing every single Republican president in the modern era, going back to Dwight D. Eisenhower. And then he passed the Affordable Care Act (ACA) in 2009, making it possible for twenty million Americans to afford health insurance. Basically, not since Franklin Delano Roosevelt has there been a more effective governor or servant-leader of American interest, growth and recovery. *And that's not politics*, that's the numbers.

A little brown-skinned kid from a single-parent home with a name that had him become "Barry" overcame massive insecurities and challenges and went on to perfect himself and rescue a nation economically and financially from the second-worst collapse in its history. To me? Barack Obama is the greatest A+ economics student, or at the very least, in the tenth percentile of greatest in the history of the American Economy. As a result of the Great Recession, the United States lost approximately $19 trillion in net worth and more than 8.7 million jobs. It took at least fifty years to amass the incompetencies and the excesses of the '80s into the Great Recession, from Gordon Gekko, Tony Montana and Michael Corleone to President Donald J. Trump.

A once-in-a-Millenium occurrence, economic, capital market and finance leader Barack Obama stopped the hemorrhaging within two years and righted the ship within eight years. I am also confident that the Great Recession served as a training ground for President Obama's political heir — *the great* President Joseph R. Biden, another exemplary servant-leader — to learn enough to rescue a nation in the throes of a Great Pandemic and altogether avoid a prolonged economic depression. Joe understood the Harry Truman maxim: *"It's a recession when your neighbor loses his job; it's a depression when you lose yours."*

When folks refer to President Obama as the first Black president and leave it at that, I always get just a little confused. They must be smoking some of that hardcore slavery racism crack, more potent than crack cocaine, heroin, opioids and fentanyl *combined — and I mean that literally*. Maybe they even believe Obama is one half from Mars and another half from a Kenyan cabal of Machiavellian Illuminati Communist Islamic deep state power operators looking to take over America and exact revenge for all of the terrible crimes of Slavery and four hundred years of rampant discrimination and racism? *Eeeeeeeeeeeeeeeeee-diots.*

How did a constitutional law professor and junior senator from Chicago, a former civil rights leader, shepherd one of the largest economic recoveries in American history? *Well, it's called exceptional economic and financial leadership.* Job growth increased to its longest streak in history, wages went up, and employment expanded. *From the abyss.* The economy was so scary and so funky that America voted for its first *Black* LEADER over the highly decorated war veteran John McCain, with whom Obama shares a legacy.

If you ask me? Like I said, I'll tell you President Obama is the greatest A plus student in the history of A students for pulling off this feat, but still there are many who only see *the first Black president*? *Wow* — I'll wonder to myself — my ancestors going back five generations had to deal with this dolt mindset, this state of Lovecraft-country affairs? *For hundreds of years? Wow.* Through chains, murder, rape, whips, hangings, Jim Crow south, "Separate but Equal," bondage, legislation, systems, inhumanity... bestiality? This decrepit stank ug-lay spirit? *Yeeeeeeeee-uch.*

And well, that's how I get the power to do what I do. *We are spiritually enhanced.* What I contend with ain't nothing compared to what they — *our ancestors* — dealt with and I am not only their dream but their offspring — *we are all the dreams of ancestors who lived, died and dreamed us into existence* — so I behave with that sort of animus animating my spirit: that unbound sense of hope, promise and love. That sense of freedom. That sense of *responsibility.*

Then, I'll have the *a-ha!* moment: President Barack Obama's stewardship, resuscitating and then ennobling an economy that was dead? That was *because* he was African American and understood the challenges and possessed time-honed skills of *making a way out of no way*. President Biden also overcame harrowing lifetime challenges to give America his very best, and appointed the first women African American Supreme Court Justice and Vice Presidents. And really what was the capital that allowed these stewards of the American Dream to advance our collective interest? How did those gentlemen steer the largest economic engine in the modern era? It was an abiding sense of *the American Dream*. It was their faith in the American Dream for future generations. That's *spiritual practice.* That is financial stewardship and the fulfillment of a sacred obligation. To me, they are the Founding Fathers of *holistic entrepreneurship.*

To me, this is the most fundamental definition of DEI, or Diversity, Equity and Inclusion currently in a chokehold by the white *minority* administration in the White House. Without it, it seems like those advocates for White Supremacy, including the *entire* current administration, are content to enforce their own form of white affirmative action where they are uniquely unqualified and are clearly motivated by an un-American agenda. The fact that they don't care how they accomplish their ends is their common denominator. The final qualifier is that they have been selected by the most uniquely DEI candidate in American history and, possibly, world history — Donald J. Trump, a predatory apex-capitalist and not a government manager.

Above fund managers at PIMCO, Black Rock, Millennium Management, Citadel Management, and Bridgewater Associates *combined,* as well as the entire Republican party, and all the millionaires and billionaires globally, Barrack Hussein Obama was *in absolute numbers*, the greatest manager of American funds *in history*; in historical context, he has out-managed the Koch Brothers, Warren Buffet, Benjamin Graham, John Templeton and Peter Lynch. He has infrequently uttered a braggadocio word in his defense. (I tabulate a single time at the Kamala campaign with a sarcastic "the *economy he (Trump) inherited.*") Obama has, in this regard, been exceptionally low key humble about the noteworthy accomplishment, and was just about the bottom line and getting the deal done for the American people *and the world* for which the *GDP is $106.3 trillion.*

Yes, he did it with economic advisors from the Harvards, Yales, Princetons, Goldman Sachs and Chase-Manhattans… sorry Professors Robert Reich and Christine Romer… Cal Berkeley too, but his stewardship enabled… *ennobled* those brilliant minds to be at their very best during the very worst. The Obama administration enacted an $800 billion stimulus program, including a blend of spending and tax cuts, the American Recovery and Reinvestment Act of 2009 (ARRA). From that Act, I believe the Joe Biden Administration was able to learn and apply lessons to the Pandemic, which cloaked a Great Depression in the twenty-first Century. *America has always done well betting black.*

By the time President Obama's second term ended, the economy had recovered. Under his stewardship, America saw its longest streak in job growth, a rise in wages, and economic expansion. His leadership during the Great Recession prevented the collapse from becoming a prolonged depression. *Back in the black.* So, that way? *Yeah, he was our first Black president.*

American Prosperity and Jobs

Mr. Christopher Cox's speaking bureau charged me a handsome speaking fee for which we were able to secure generous sponsorships and participation from not only Greenberg

Traurig LLP but also OTC Markets and other SoCal and Las Vegas firms interested in crowdfunding and creating opportunity in the small business sector. Chris Cox is a pillar of the Newport Beach investor culture — he led the Securities Exchange Commission as the US Economy bottomed out into its worst economic condition since the Great Depression. Roth Capital President Ted Roth, who was a panelist, would host a similar conversation at the annual Roth Capital conference later that year — the Roth Capital Conference is the largest convergence of executives, accredited investors and institutional investors, ranked in the Top 100 events in the US.

I've always proudly claimed political independence and worked with the best and brightest from both sides of the political aisle. And with this latest incarnation of our body politic, I saw an opportunity to bring communities together. Barack Obama's newly signed historic crowdfunding legislation would inject reform into our financial capital, raising markets, providing opportunities to low- to middle-income wage earners to participate in capital markets and take a stake in American wealth. Contrary to the edict of "working hard to achieve the American Dream," wealth is created by leveraging capital and stock markets to grow a dream from emerging growth into a small- and mid-cap company; mid-cap to large-cap; Fortune 500 to timeless. That wealth force multiplier *is ours — we dreamt it and built it with our blood, sweat and tears. It didn't come free.*

"Crowdfunding is a game changer for startups and entrepreneurs in Massachusetts and across the country. These small businesses now have a powerful new tool to grow and create jobs. And now every American, regardless of income level, is able to invest and get

in on the ground floor of a great business idea. This bill has great potential for our economy and job growth."

—**Boston Senator Scott Brown**, 2012

Facebook and the Internet had already been a tool for fund-raising from many thousands of donors. Subject to rulemaking by the U.S. Securities and Exchange Commission (SEC), startups and small businesses would be allowed to raise up to $1 million annually from many small-dollar investors through web-based platforms, "democratizing" access to capital. Because the Senate acted on a bipartisan amendment, the bill includes key investor protections the President called for, including a requirement that all crowdfunding must occur through platforms that are registered with a self-regulatory organization and regulated by the SEC.

The global crowdfunding market size was valued at $1.25 billion in 2022, to grow to $1.41 billion in 2023 to $3.62 billion by 2030, exhibiting a CAGR (compound annual growth rate) of 14.5% during the forecast period. Now, I didn't get to ask Mr. Christopher Cox a question or two about presiding over the single largest economic crisis since the Great Recession; his speaker bureau saw to that. My spiritual father, Pastor Mark E. Whitlock gave the invocation and prayer. However, a collection of thinkers, financiers and national leadership came together to discuss crowdfunding and another historic crack at creating equal opportunity in the American Capital Markets — an effect that has been harnessed and grown in the ten plus years since its passage. A seed was planted in those years for entrepreneurs who had an idea, passion and who were willing to work hard, to have equal access to the system of finance and trust fund babies and multi-billion-dollar hedge funds and family offices. Well, at the very least, folks have a pathway or just a *shot* at that sort of growth. And isn't that the American dream — *having a shot at prosperity*?

Now those efforts are shepherded by my friend Devin Thorpe, the visionary behind the Super Crowd Inc., where he annually champions community builders and diverse executives by organizing events on crowdfunding. He works with women and men like Bill Huston, the founder of CrowdMax and a board member of the National Coalition for Community Capital (NC3), providing exemplary leadership and vision on crowdfunding and digital marketing. There are other great leaders implementing the change from the capital markets — Craig Cecilio, the CEO of DiversyFund, Garnet S. Heraman, managing partner at the Aperture Venture Capital Fund, Ruth E. Hedges, "Queen of Crowdfunding," Jumpstart Ventures, Alexander Gafoor, Esq. (Blockchain, IP and AI attorney (Trinidad)), Kevin Valley (Trinidad), Adela Adebayo (Nigeria), Sarah Hardwick (equity crowdfunding expert) and Sebastien Celestine (Entrepreneurs of Greatness in the Caribbean).

I was and am inspired by America's incredible potential to defy the odds and aspire to its highest ideas. *That's the stuff I am made of!*

How to Build a Global Capital Network

Newport Beach and Orange County are banking capitals of the United States and the world. Insofar as California, Newport Beach is home to PIMCO (a fixed income global leader in private and public markets with a market value in excess of €101.69B); City National Bank is a subsidiary of Royal Bank of Canada with $96.9 billion in assets; comprehensively the fifty largest banks headquartered in Southern California house $415 billion in assets; Like Abu Dhabi and Dubai, Southern California enjoys a symbiotic relationship with and banks Las Vegas, and is also part of the Pacific Riviera, which hosts premiere destination spots such as Malibu, Pacific Palisades, Santa Monica, Beverly Hills, Laguna Beach, Dana Point, Encinitas, the growing and emergent Oceanside, La Jolla and Rancho Santa Fe — from the Gold Rush, there are pockets of pure gold up and down, at the seaside and within valleys of California. For example, San Diego is home to one of America's — and the world's — richest, most fertile biotechnology commutes.

> *"California is home to the most Fortune 500 companies in the country — beating out Texas, Florida and all other states. From tech to finance to entertainment, California's diverse economy leads with 57 companies on the list."*
>
> **—California Governor Gavin Newsom**

Eight Fortune 500 companies are headquartered in Orange County, including Edwards Lifesciences Corporation, Pacific Life — a life insurance company, St. John Knits International, Inc., Waste Management, Inc., Western Digital Corporation — a data storage company, First American Financial Corporation, CoreLogic — a real estate data and analytics company, Boot Barn Holdings, Inc. — a retail chain specializing in western and work-related apparel and accessories.

Fifty-three California companies made the Fortune 500 list for 2023, including Disney (approximately $190B market cap), Qualcomm, a wireless technology and software company, reporting about $35.8 billion in revenue, LPL Financial Holdings, an investment and wealth-management company, with $10 billion in revenue and Sempra, a public utility company that owns one of the largest energy networks in North America, with $16.7 billion in annual earnings. San Diego is also referred to as the second Silicon Valley with the presence of not only Qualcomm but, in North County San Diego, the seaside pearl of Carlsbad, where there are fifty-two golf clubs, and headquarters to Calloway, Titleist and Cobra brands. Other Fortune 500 companies in the vast and diverse Orange County and Southern California areas are Henry Samueli's Broadcom, Satellite Communications behemoth ViaSat Communications, which expanded during the pandemic. This is to say nothing of the multi-trillion-dollar Hollywood and Silicon Valley industries that define global commerce.

All of this is to say that Orange County and Newport Beach is where Global Capital Network derives its lineage from the Southern California investment Association (SCIA), WallStreet Research (WSR), Southern California Investment Forum (SCIF), Brad Turner's Marketing Completion Fund, OC Octane, equites.com, Boustead Securities' capital market formation under chairman Keith Moore and Dan McClory exceptional sales leadership, the San Diego Investment Conference and West Coast Wall Street Conference. GCN is the beating heart of those market forces and the inheritor of the mantle from a rich tradition as old as California itself on September ninth, 1950.

Our groups have contributed to building out the economic development structure of the capital markets in Southern California, particularly in Newport Beach, Orange County and going south to San Diego, inspiring the iCFO Managers' business model with the San Diego Investment Conference's launch in 2010. We were also instrumental in co-founding

Global Capital Network in 2017 alongside Mr. Josh Bois, an exceptional mentee. The purpose of investment conferences is to provide a playground for small businesses to grow, be nurtured and grow financially and within their development and economic acumen. What was the bottom-line impact on their bottom line? Because, not to get vulgar, no one gives a single solitary hoot about how nice the venue is or the exotic geographic locale. I mean, yes, that's part of the allure, but at the end of the day, it's about bottom-line results. Did the company who paid anywhere from $1,500 to $15,000 in fees to attend and present at the event have an investment in their opportunity from an angel accredited investor or institutional investors? Because that's why client companies are paying you. *Quality exposure.*

I think that Josh has engineered a different type of Newport Beach convention experience based upon his genius for marketing and branding. Josh is gifted at resilience, perseverance and increasing frequency and light to their highest potential. He is a supernatural entrepreneur, a good friend and coming along as a prodigy — ***Ha!***

Later that month, we closed shop at the last San Diego Investment Conference and co-founded Global Capital Network (GCN).

I introduced Josh to Alan Stone, the executive director of the Southern California investment Forum and CEO of the WallStreet Research Group. Alan and I had worked together for nearly ten years prior, nearly inking a deal to create a super-investor relations firm. I had brought companies such as Houston's Chestnut Petroleum as premiere presenting sponsors to his event in New York City. Alan and Josh would go on to partner with GCN, with Alan brokering presenting sponsors to GCN.

Here is an addendum I have had around developing a global network of partners, collaborators and financiers:

Partner with People You LOVE to Work With

They are the ones who will have your back and who you will do anything for and with. Obviously, judgment is at play and there has to be a fundamental assessment of mutual goals and an inventory of talents, whether you can grow in spiritual largesse productively together.

Josh Bois has been one such individual. He is the Wunderkind — who graduated from Santa Clara University in 2012 with a Business Degree and a minor in Entrepreneurship — behind a decade of startups that have captured the imagination. He is an extraordinary natural-born entrepreneur with a heart of gold and a platinum ability to close deals.

Some of the other incredible national executive directors include Richard Wilson, who oversees a private family office club that oversees $13.5 million at the Family Office Clubs and Investor Club; Oakland's Renae Griffith is the managing director at GCM Grosvenor Client Group, who for nearly twenty years has organized and managed several events with institutional clients as pension funds, produced her RG & Associates own branded events, specializing in diversity membership of accredited and institutional investors; San Diego's Richard and Diana McCaskill, co-founders of Fruition Consulting, proficient and expert in international events that combine business development, communications, thought leadership, and administration to develop engaging conferences and events. Fruition Consulting clients range from start-ups, government agencies, financial organizations, nonprofits and corporations; and Washington D.C.'s Robert Greene, president and CEO of the National Association of Investment Companies (NAIC), the industry association for diverse-owned alternative investment firms, has 190+ member firms, which manage in aggregate over $410 billion in assets. Better and more expert than any online platform, these men and women operate entire arteries of American capitalism who not only exemplify verve and moxie, but vision and a spirit of gestalt. Together these captains of industry oversee, organize and produce well over several trillion in prospective funding and direct national and international capital finance and spirits to their highest potential.

Beginning in January of 2017, Global Capital Network (GCN), has served the *esprit de corps* of Wall Street and the American Southern capital markets, as a more entrepreneurially driven (versus institutional) regional complement to the Roth Capital Conference. This has been GCN's work, being the premiere investor conference throughout Southern California and the nation with the San Diego Investment Conference, its legacy firm, which came from Al Kau and Gary E. Bryant's SCIA — Southern California's Investment Forum.

GCN's mission is to inspire the spirit of entrepreneurship that has made America a twentieth-century world engine and will continue to lead global innovation and capital growth. Whether the bull markets of the Clinton or Reagan Administrations, America has not only led but inspired some of the greatest aggregate market capitalizations in world history, we believe we are at the nexus of another such period. We believe in the validity of crowdfunding, "friends and family" rounds, series A and series D, initial public offerings (IPO), businesses beginning on college campuses and in garages —

we believe in people capitalizing their dreams and sharing the prosperity for collective growth. We don't call it social entrepreneurship — we call it global capital entrepreneurship.

Through a series of investor roadshows, investment conferences, social media and investor relations, GCN will expose public and privately traded companies as it did beginning with Herohl, Bob Meyer's Spectralcast, Liquidpel, West Texas Resources (WTXR) and Petvivo (PETV) to investor communities around the world and within. Josh began his new venture, engineering a national Wall Street Movement January 23rd and 24th in La Jolla, Orange County, Santa Monica and San Francisco. Ask Mr. Josh Bois how he measures a successful venture and he will say,

> *"It's about empowering the entrepreneur with capital formation and meetings where they can meet potential and dynamic partners. There is an ecosystem around the world and Global Capital Network wants to pronounce boardroom and panel meetings where investors can review opportunities and engage in important dialogue about capital formation."*

> *Well done, Sir.*

Getting Deals Done with Gary E. Bryant, Captain of Industry & the Great One

I remember sitting in Gary's beautiful ornate office and asking what *exactly* he did for a living. His mansion in Newport Beach, formerly owned by Vanna White of *Wheel of Fortune*, in one of the premier neighborhoods in the world, begged the question.

I just saw him on the phone every day, making unbelievable assertions with minimal words.

Didactic Dissonant Rich Dadio-Dad Disclaimer:

Now I'm sorry if I portrayed my rich father as an angel man previously and led you to believe he was a sainted peach-skinned human who walked the Earth. He was that. *To me.* But he was also an incredibly complex soul. When he got angry, the hairs would stand up on the back of your neck. He could torch souls with that temper. And I was, *if you can believe it,* on the receiving end of that hot hot hot fire on more than a couple of occasions. *HA! For some reason, though?* It never really bothered me. Kind of reminded me of Saturday morning cartoons with Bugs Bunny and that character Yosemite Sam.

I remember asking Gary one time when he was in the midst of a rant: We were working on a $367M deal for oil and gas and I thought it would be a good idea to call his friend Chet Paulson at the Paulson Syndicate in Portland and talk to him about the deal. After I got off the phone with Chet, I got a call from Gary, who was none too pleased. "So, you thought you'd call Chet, huh?"

> *"Umm, yeah… I just thought…"*
> *"You thought you'd call* ***my*** *friend Chet…"*

Hairs on my neck began to stand at attention and then I heard it — a banshee scream from the ancient lands replete with curses, hair-triggering ugly things that could sear-singe a soul. "Gary," I asked him, *"why are you yelling?* You know if you just tell me not to do something I won't do it, right? Just talk to me and I'll do as you ask." Exasperated, the banshee went back into its soul cage. *"Awww, Patrick, I know* — it's just that sometimes you just... you just..." Yeah, man, *I know.*

"Hi Chuck," I remember him once bellowing on the phone, cadence teasing an intimacy and easy charm. "Do me a favor and take a look at that company I told you about." Chuck checks his computer and Gary continues, "I think you ought to pick up ten million shares of that company." I looked at the stock, trading just under one dollar. *That's a favor?* I must have asked the question aloud because Gary answered aloud, matter of fact, covering the receiver with his palm, "I made a lot of money for that guy on another deal several years ago."

"How much money was that?" I asked, trying not to sound stunned in the least or intimidated by the series of events unfolding before my eyes, in real time.

"Ohhhh, I don't know." Gary made some quick computations as he routinely reviewed a yellow ruler-bound pad with names and numbers scrawled out in sequence, some with checks, others crossed out. This was his day's work. "It must have been $8 or $10 million." *That's a favor?* I thought. *Human beings do favors like this on planet Earth?* Well, okay. *Got it.*

Another time when he was on the phone with Chuck, Gary was ribbing me over a question I had asked in earnest previously. "What *exactly* do you do for a living?" I knew *whatever it was* I was going to do the *exact* same thing. Gary laughed a good old boys' laugh with Chuck on the phone. The chuckle was warm and inviting, a hint of mischief with a wholesome ethic underneath it. "Chuck, this guy I'm working with, Patrick, he wants to know what I do for a living." Chuck said something on the other line that gave Gary another good chuckle. "Chuck says I just help out small businesses — help them get on their feet." Then he just said, "Patrick," quick and clean, staccatoed with excellence and pride, ***"I get deals done."***

Gary Bryant's life was built around capital market formation. He helped countless companies go public and created a lasting legacy in American finance. He served as the president of Newport Capital Consultants, co-founder of the Southwest Investment Association, chairman of my San Diego Investment Conference and the West Coast Wall Street Conference series. His career spanned decades, touching lives, companies and the broader financial industry. Gary's work created wealth for people across America, from Wall Street to small businesses.

He also helped elect a couple of US Presidents and worked with congressional leaders in the Senate to help create some of the greatest economic recoveries and economic peace-time expansions and boons in American history. He loved working on his ranch in BNobles Farms Rescue, helping dogs, mules and horses with his life partner Suzanne Bryant. Gary was a good friend to so many of us in the capital market and we all had fun, enjoyed a warm relationship with the man and enjoycd the fruits of prosperity.

Gary was a good friend, mentor, and a love-preneur — someone who approached his work with passion and a sense of love for what he did. He got deals done, and he did it with integrity. Gary's contribution to micro-cap companies and capital formation helped shape American finance in the late twentieth and early twenty-first centuries.

I wrote about Gary in *Opportunist Magazine* back in 2011, saying: *"Whatever Gary touches is more than likely going to succeed."* I meant it. We worked together on numerous projects — elections, funding companies, investor relations and more. Whether it was helping companies secure financing or developing boards and executive teams, he brought a legacy of capital market formation and free enterprise development. Gary created opportunities and success, not just for himself but for all those around him.

Yes, Gary was a good mentor. And I worked hard to be an exceptional prodigy. He gave so much — wisdom, finances, time, encouragement, credibility, belief, a charming, affecting way. And I would also give back — brokering incredible relationships or deal flow, time and boundless optimism, a penchant for excellence and an infectious can-do attitude. When he transitioned, I made some ugly sounds — when a man grieves it's not in the pretty world. But I also remembered that in our friendship I gave as good as I got: The West Coast Wall Street Conference was my way of saying, "*Thank you, oh great one.*" One of my colleagues said it well. Dr. Lorri M. Clark, Esq. said, *"I noticed your LinkedIn post regarding Gary and made a comment. I do not run into businessmen/legal professionals who show such generosity or take risks on others so that they may make it into higher echelons. He will be greatly missed."*

There was this bright twinkle in his eye whenever he spoke. It was as if the man held the keys to an unseen kingdom. That twinkle was a mixture of joy, wisdom and pure deal-making magic. He'd tell me stories about his father, a farmer, or his beloved wife, Suzanne. He'd talk about oil and gas deals, or companies he helped grow. To a young man like me, who grew up in Sacramento hearing about the Fords, Carnegies and Rockefellers, Gary was a living embodiment of those legends of finance and industry.

Gary's journey touched countless companies, including Advantage Marketing Systems, Ameristar Network, Cal-Maine Foods, Chesapeake Energy Corp, and Veltex Corp, just to name a few. His ability to build syndicates, foster relationships and guide companies to funding success was unparalleled. He didn't just bring deals to the table; he brought them to fruition.

We never really discussed race explicitly, and perhaps that was part of the beauty of our partnership. It was *best to do good work* — infinitely more productive, more profitable and spiritually satisfying. Gary transcended the limits of identity; he was focused on getting the job done. And through our work together, I realized that he, too, was a dream of his ancestors — specifically his grandfather, who Gary loved to spend time with as a little boy: There was no way this son of a beloved farmer was going to be a "*money loser.*"

One day, I was helping Christian with a school project on Emmett Till. Emmett, whose brutal lynching in 1955 became a catalyst for the Civil Rights Movement, had sparked something in Christian. As we worked through the project, I called and asked Gary, *"Are you related to Carolyn Bryant?"* Carolyn was the woman who had falsely accused Emmett of harassing her, leading to his horrific murder.

"*Yeah, Patrick,*" he replied, *"there are a lot of us Bryants, and some of us are good, and some of us are not so good."* He said it simply, matter-of-factly.

Well, the Name Says It All

Gary Bryant passed away in March of 2024. In his lifetime, he helped elect US Presidents, worked alongside and stood shoulder to shoulder with congressional leaders such as Chuck Schumer and John Kerry, built wealth and helped foster significant economic recoveries and American prosperity. He had an unshakable bond with Suzanne, his life partner, and together they ran a farm and animal rescue — or, as Suzanne — a lifelong Eleanor Roosevelt Democrat — would say, *dead serious,* "all donkeys and *no elephants!*"

But above all else, *Gary Bryant was a dealmaker.* He didn't just take companies public or build financial empires — *he helped build people so that they could support AND profit in the community that is America.* More often than not, those people were organized in a for-profit organization called a corporation, or a limited liability corporation or S-Corp. He created and doled out opportunities and shared wisdom wherever he left his big 'ole Oklahoman imprint on the American economy.

I invoke the immense spirit of entrepreneurial zeal and human connection into every deal I work in this industry of ours. He was my mentor, a true friend and a classic captain of industry. The name of this book and of my podcast, *Getting Deals Done,* stems from Gary's simple yet profound answer to my earlier question. *"What exactly do you do?"* His work wasn't just about making money. It was about uplifting others, creating jobs and making the world a better place. That was and is the bottom line.

Impresario of Capital Market Formation

I was a senior vice president of investor relations with Newport Capital Consultants from 2008 to 2012 under Gary's tutelage and guidance for nearly five years, learning, absorbing, failing and succeeding until I founded my own investor relations practice.

After working with the South California Investment Association, Southwest Investor Association, Financial Services Exchange, National Investment Bankers Association, I learned the fundamentals of Newport Capital Consultants' business model of broker relations, consulting to management going public, general corporate consulting, investment banking consulting, mergers and acquisitions, obtaining OTC, NYSE or NASDAQ listing, introductions to investment bankers and broker dealers and just helping small businesses with capital formation up to $30 million. We never discussed race explicitly. And why should we? It was better to do good work, infinitely more productive as well as profitable and spiritually satisfying.

Honestly? I get tired of talking about race sometimes. I remember hearing Kareem Abdul-Jabbar put it succinctly: ***"Race is nothing more than a fake thing trying to be real."*** *Actually*, more often than not racism, discrimination and separation of people are the instruments of the spiritually weak and financially hollowed losers who have become powerful in this current zeitgeist. *The weakest amongst us spiritually* have become so-called powerful. *The technology of racism is b-o-r-i-n-g and fundamentally destructive to the human spirit.* And *they* are *corny.* Them? *Funny,* the inverse relationship between American spirituality and materialism, right? If it wasn't real to the USA and its 320 million citizens? *I'd be done* *with this farce.* But as Daddy would often say, *"The race is not for the swiftest but for he who has the endurance to endure and endure to the end."* So, *we endure.*

Gary called me when I was preparing for my first event in La Jolla at the Hilton. One time when I came to his office troubled, he asked, *"Are you okay?"* I told him about an argument with the wife and he walked me to his kitchen without saying a word and made me a sandwich — rye bread, mayonnaise, mustard and some turkey and provolone cheese.

Today I was at Staples across from Wholefoods buying supplies — sign-in registry book, name tags, printed banners, printed agenda etc.

"What are you doing, Patrick?"

"I'm buying supplies for the inaugural conference tomorrow."

And I told him about all the companies we were working with and how much they had paid me and how much I would receive, basically giving him an income sheet and balance sheet off a blueprint he had designed nationally.

"*Well, I'm going to stop paying you from Newport Capital Consultants then,*" he said with a kind of rye-and-mustard tone, but with that trademark twinkle in his voice. For three years he had deposited checks into my account as I plied my craft and learned the ins and outs of investor relations, investment dog and pony investor roadshows, investment conferences and investment banking consultation. I made the other 50% on my end, hustling high on the capital market formation hustle.

"That's awesome!" I said without skipping a beat. *I knew how to fish.* We laughed. Throughout the San Diego Investment Conference and West Coast Wall Street Conference, Gary would regularly call me and ask, *"How are you doing, Patrick?"*

More often than not, I was short a couple of companies to make ends meet and be in the black. He would always make up the difference, getting a company or two or three or four to sign up for our events — usually getting them to give some stock as part of their payment. He worked those phones hard, like he was a utility company collecting on a bill, and utilized his personal reputation, personal network and incredible life force to bring that prestige and financial wherewithal to the San Diego Investment Conferences. One time he even gave me a credit card number to place the deposit on a particular events coordinator at one of our events in Torrey Pines. *He never asked for a penny in return. Ever.* And after three years, and some companies offering payment in stock, we're talking about several hundred thousand dollars in funding to our events.

I think Gary and I always understood that the very special introduction that was made by a mutual friend of Suzanne Bryant, Lisa Elzy Watson, a light worker of unusual capabilities and the president of Lightwave Education, had profoundly affected both of our lives. I think we also knew that a good ol' boy from Oklahoma and Dallas and a first-generation African American financier and son of a Central American and Caribbean could create the sort of bond we only enjoyed in the United States of America.

"Loveliest of lovely things are they,
On earth, that soonest pass away.
The rose that lives its little hour
Is prized beyond the sculptured flower."

— William Cullen Bryant,
"A Scene on the Banks of the Hudson River"

Another time, I had a member of our investment series ask me a question. "*Patrick,*" the apex-capitalist hedge fund manager asked me almost accusingly, and looking me dead in the eye, "So, this is your gig? *This is your company?*"

"Yes, sir," I answered in response to his *corny* tone, asking him for his black AMEX card to charge for entry to my room. He gave it to me nonplussed. Typically, I didn't charge members the $250 to come into my room, particularly if they were an accredited investor, but I knew he was wondering *how a Black guy got the keys to the room he had to pay to get into* — and well, *in God we trust and in cash we pay. I was wondering if I should have charged him $500. Could I have charged $5000 or $50K?*

"Does Gary have anything to do with this?"

"Well, he's a mentor and he'll help me with companies and I made him the Chairman of the Board along with my son," I said it arrogantly, an apex-capitalist myself, and Neil retorted in kind,

"Patrick," he asked almost caustically, "*Do you know who I am?*"

I was quiet. *$250 bucks?* Gas, lunch at Rubios, a nice dinner for the family? Maybe a pack of Baby Ruths and another of Butterfingers from Costco? Some burritos and a churrito?

"I'm Neal Fincher [name substituted to protect identities of the misfits and miscreants] and I raised $5M for President Ronald Reagan and I own a $5M technology fund out of Las Vegas." *Okay, I thought to myself,* that's excellent for the room.

"Can I escort you to your seat and get you some coffee?"

"Sure, and thank you. *You love Gary, don't you?*" He said it like an accusation or a chunky vomit — he was disgusted by the very idea.

"Yes, I do."

I got that a lot with my endeavor and I always converted ugly skepticism into positive cash flow capital, a *high-frequency transaction.*

After Gary and I worked on the election of the young senator out of Chicago Illinois who would go on to become America's first multi-racial and Black president, I had a couple of conversations with Gary in subsequent years about his family and their journey as Americans. Gary's ancestor 150 years ago was William Cullen Bryant *(1794-1878)*, an influential Abraham Lincoln supporter who had even introduced Lincoln to New Yorkers in a famous Cooper Union speech.

A contemporary of Henry Wadsworth Longfellow and Ralph Waldo Emrerson, and the first internationally renowned American poet, William Cullen Bryant was known for his poem "Thanatopsis." He was a *New York Evening Post* editor for fifty years. In 1884, Reservoir Square in New York City was renamed Bryant Park to honor the civic reformer. The Poetry Foundation noted, *"Bryant alerted the English-speaking world to an American voice in poetry." And Gary's poetry was his deals.*

Maybe that's why or how Gary entertained my flight of fancy where I imagined Obama as an iteration of Abraham Lincoln — perhaps, Ancestry in Motion is where Gary's ancestor William Cullen Bryant was communicating through him and we continued our quest into capital market formation and wealth creation? *The energy was unmistakable and defined. Maybe that was that trademark twinkle. For me?* That is far more credible than the current state of our reality, in which myriad divisions continue bitterly from that so-called "Civil" War. Maybe it's easier for me to imagine our ancestors George Westerman and William Cullen Bryant sitting over a peppermint, chamomile or rosehip tea, or their progenies working together to get deals done than it is to imagine the current state of total spiritual dysfunction of our systems?

O THOU great Wrong, that, through the slow-paced years,
Didst hold thy millions fettered, and didst wield
The scourge that drove the laborer to the field,
And look with stony eye on human tears,
Thy cruel reign is o'er;
Thy bondmen crouch no more
In terror at the menace of thine eye

—**William Cullen Bryant**, "The Death of Slavery"

As with so many families in American history, there was a complex and rich legacy of redemption and healing and I believe that Gary, in his incredible love with Suzanne, worked to ensure that their legacy was not only in capital formation but the fight for racial justice. And he did it in his typical fashion without a lot of fanfare and a whole lot of "do."

Thank you, Gary — *Love you, man.*

Love-preneur

A love-preneur is an entrepreneur who approaches business not just with a focus on profit, but with an ethos rooted in love, compassion and a genuine desire to uplift others. This term reflects the belief that successful ventures are built on relationships, integrity and the well-being of all stakeholders, including employees, customers and communities. A love-preneur values human connections, acts with a sense of purpose beyond financial gain and integrates empathy, ethical practices and social responsibility into every aspect of their business. For a love-preneur, the journey of creating value is driven by a deep commitment to making the world better — one deal, one interaction and one impact at a time.

Jesus is a love-preneur. Love is a love-preneur. So are Hope and Faith. So were Mother Teresa and Princess Diana. Just as Buddha and Muhammad have been practitioners of a timeless faith and form of macro-economics: Love-entrepreneurship. As with Malcolm X, Martin Luther King and Marcus Garvey's tireless work at the end of his life on poverty, on some level, Gary Bryant's work in wealth and capital formation embodied the free enterprising spirit of a love-preneur by seamlessly blending capital market formation with genuine care for the businesses and people he supported. This is what W.E.B. Du Bois and Booker T. Washington, Sojourner Truth, Harriet Tubman and Mary McCloud Bethune were all talking about. This is what Marianne Richardson, Deepak Chopra, Don Miguel Ruiz and Anthony "Tony" Robbins have converted into whole industries of the Prosperity and Abundance gospel.

Our national emerging growth and capital formation community learned from Gary's masterclass, prioritizing long-term relationships and a community's enhancement and gains over short-term profit. His philosophy emphasized that true success comes from the heart of one's values, with prosperity following purpose.

To me? Getting deals done in the cathedral of American capitalism was his life's sermon. It was the message he would repeat over and over with his good works, deals and capital formation. Getting deals done was one of the many ways Gary expressed his spirit and its love in this world. And, well, that's what I'll be doing with my last breath.

Chapter 12: Some More on Organic Networking and Capital Financing

"I will tell you how to become rich. Close the doors. Be fearful when others are greedy. Be greedy when others are fearful."
— Warren Buffett

The world of finance is not like the literary one. The worlds of finance are characterized by deft moves, loud do's, even louder don'ts; defining the known world, the believable, percussive rhythms, real-time execution and exacting effects. The literary one is one of quiet introspection, defining our unknown worlds, the unseen, musical art balanced with philosophy inlaid with story, the unbelievable, harmonic possibilities and the outcome of quiet peaceful minds. There are, however, some obvious intersections. Binary outcomes and momentary finality are a couple. Also, good storytelling as recognized in organic networking plays a central role in brokering productive, intimate and powerful relationships. I know, I've been doing it for decades now.

Both business and literature deal in languages of imagination. The literary voice deals with language and the courage to capture in language the unseen or even unknown. The business language is one of reality — people, places, things — as well as considerable imagination — business IQ — and the same creative faculty engaged to write great literature. Business effects are in the material world: whole cities, buildings, finances, inventions and homes. Literary effects are a vivid unveiling of the world (third dimension) and the fifth and sixth dimensions as well as our intimate and daily inner lives. In this manner, business and literature are complementary, where business provides a platform and literature (in all of its forms — music, poetry, plays, film) the content.

Story is another broader point of intersection. As a matter of fact, a balance sheet and income statement are nothing more than the story of a company as told by its finances or EBIDTA. For example, take gross profits versus net profits. Understanding the differences between gross profit and net income can help investors determine whether a company is earning a profit and, if not, where the company is losing money.

Assets are on the top of a balance sheet, and below them are the company's liabilities, and below that is shareholders' equity. A balance sheet is also always in balance, where the value of the assets equals the combined value of the liabilities and shareholders' equity. This business is all about choices.

Forgiveness is a choice.
Being honest is a choice.
Spoken words are a choice.
Optimism is a choice.

Happiness is a choice.
Giving back is a choice.
Teaching others is a choice.
Showing gratitude is a choice.
Respecting others is a choice.
Being at peace is a choice.
Living a good and honorable life is a choice.

"God and Nature first made us what we are, and then out of our own created genius we make ourselves what we want to be. Follow always that great law. Let the sky and God be our limit and Eternity our measurement."

— **Marcus Garvey**

You get wealthy in this business of investment banking and investor relations in the small-cap, micro-cap and emerging growth sectors by intelligent speculation or what I like to call rich man or intelligent man's lottery. *If I do this thing?* Put the money in this investment? Put the time into this venture? *Leverage my extensive network, know-how and capital?* How likely is it that this company will fulfill its potential? Every investor, whether accredited angel or institutional investor, signs on the dotted line of an agreement that says they *may* lose all their capital and they are aware of the risk and can afford the risk. In part, that's why the Securities Exchange Commission and FINRA (Financial Industry Regulatory Authority) exists, to ensure fair play in an industry that can be driven by avarice, greed and all sorts of malfeasance, epic stupidity and incompetence.

That's what those riders, or long clauses — all that English Chinese *(pun TOTALLY intended), Ha!!* — that investors sign as they place their money in exchange for equity in an investment are. They are an assurance that, when the likely occurs, and they lose their capital on an investment, legally they were informed of the prospective pitfalls and the possibility of losing their entire capital investment. Whether a subscription agreement, preferred stock, debt financing, private placement memorandum, convertible note or some other instrument, the Securities Exchange Commission and FINRA oversee, regulate and prosecute crimes, and 90% of those pages will talk about everything that can go wrong.

But for every ten deals… for every eight that don't make it all the way? *Two go right.* Those two investments could go anywhere from 2x (double your money) to 100x (very, very few will go to one hundred times your money), and they make the other eight losing investments well worthwhile. It's a numbers and large volume investment *game* — there is a significant amount of IQ that goes into each transaction, but it is still a gamble, and American markets are designed for this sort of play.

> *"Given a 10% chance of a 100 times payoff, you should take that bet every time."*
>
> —**Jeff Bezos,** son of Cuban immigrant Miguel Bezos

> *"The stock market is filled with individuals who know the price of everything, but the value of nothing."*
>
> —**Phillip Fisher,** capital market mentor of the Oracle of Nebraska, Warren Buffet

To be an investor (read: silent *business partner*), you have to have mastery of a cacophony of powerfully competing impulses. You want to win but will more than likely lose. You have to lead, but to do so within the confines of a growing entrepreneur's own growth. An offering essentially worth nothing could potentially become the next disruptor, worth hundreds of millions, if not billions. You can calculate the fundamental EBITDA (earnings before interest, taxes, depreciation and amortization) better than the founder who will oftentimes lack your business savvy, network or sophistication in building a balance sheet. You're afraid because the fledgling executive has no fear. As Andy Grove of Intel and Ronald Reagan made famous, *"Trust but verify"* is a key operating principle for the successful operators in this space. *This part of the big game is about becoming fearless and becoming the master of failure.*

By definition, an accredited investor is a wealthy individual. *And just who and what and how wealthy is a rich individual?* That definition is set by the SEC — Securities Exchange Commission — who regulates and oversees the entire capital formation industry. The SEC regulates, controls, monitors *greed, malfeasance and sheer stupidity.* That's the SEC's job: *to control excess.* Think the Great Recession, the Great Depression, a Pandemic masking a second great depression, market crashes and volatile markets that are just an aggregate of individual choices and larger volume trades and transactions as represented by banks, broker dealers, hedge funds, family offices, PE funds and VC funds. Specifically defined by the SEC, accredited investors are "Individuals" (i.e., natural persons), who may qualify as accredited investors based on wealth and income thresholds, as well as other measures of financial sophistication.

Specifically:

- Net worth over $1 million, excluding primary residence (individually or with spouse or partner).

- Income over $200,000 (individually) or $300,000 (with spouse or partner) in each of the prior two years, and reasonably expects the same for the current year.

Truly? *The reality?* ***A wealthy person is someone who knows their value.*** *An American capitalist? She or he gets that value deposited in their local and offshore bank accounts.*

That's why "ancestry in motion" is such an interesting concept, and the ability to control a people's self-perception is *king*. The rest of it is man-made definitions or constructs of definitions in these man-made societies. God made us ***all*** wealthier than kings, wealthier than billionaires or millionaires, wealthier than Warren Buffet, Bill Gates, Donald Trump, Jeff Bezos and Elon Musk *combined* — the Spirit Force made us all *pricelessly wealthy* — *far beyond* our wildest imaginations.

That's why crowdfunding is such an interesting notion, providing opportunity for traditionally marginalized communities to have a seat at the table of some of the world's greatest games of educated man's roulette and savvy woman's poker. Granted, they are not at the same tables as the VCs, funds, family offices and broker dealers *but* they are in the building, right? And historically? We've had far less to begin with. So, don't let lack of capital stop you (while getting your hands on as much of it as you can). Don't let anything stop you from materializing your dreams — that is why the universe put us here: to realize our Dreams, Visions and the best way Forward.

Crowdfunding is not necessarily the equalizer where working- and middle-class members can have a seat at the table based upon network, industry, vision and good old-fashioned hard work. They're not guaranteed a win but they have a seat *within a realm* at the American table of capital formation, the greatest in the world *bar none.* Oftentimes, in America, the driving force of culture, society and business, outside of the stymied influence of race, is *class*.

I imagine Martin Luther King would have found crowdfunding to be very interesting — perhaps he would have crowdfunded a couple of marches and sit-ins, as he was also a power advocate against poverty and its indecent presence in the wealthiest nation on Earth and arguably in the history of mankind.

Sometimes the FBI will get involved in the investigation and prosecution of white-collar crimes in capital market formation: junk bonds, retail, real estate, any sort of instrument in which commerce or a product or service are commoditized — think Michael Milken, Calvin Broadus, P-Diddy, Sam Bankman-Fried, Donald J. Trump, Jordan Belfort, a.k.a. the Wolf of Wall Street, or Martha Stewart; criminally indicted and convicted entrepreneurs who played the game, lost, but doubled up the ante and went hard at that dream again. NEVER EVER give in. EVER. The only problem with this equation is that it is not fair. Plenty of folks without those resources — plenty of folks who don't understand this system are marginalized and treated as less than human. And this makes you wonder, just what is America's deal? Absolutely prosper at the absolute detriment of others? Absolute power absolutely corrupts the spirit in this *fucked-up system!* Let's fix it — *Ha!!!*

At a certain point in most transactions, the mere size of the deal is on the precipice where there are no guardrails other than what the apex entrepreneur's integrity will guarantee: the spirit of the wild wild west free enterprise is alive and well

— in fact, it is a piston engine in the turbine of American growth, wealth and ingenuity.

The intelligent investor listens to CNBC's Jim Cramer, *Squawk Box*, Bloomberg, Charlie Payne's *Making Money*, Maria Bartiroma's *Mornings with Maria* on Fox Business or *Black Enterprise* or a company earnings call for education, information and a sense of the larger markets. Forget politics and exercise their entrepreneurial muscles! Or she comes to the investor roadshow meetings to have the opportunity to meet the apex-entrepreneurs when they are still in their embryonic stages. The goo-goo gaa-gaa talk takes place over plated luncheons and the trappings of wealth and privilege.

Facebook, Twitter, the Wynn Hotel, Chipotle, Starbucks, McDonalds, Nokia, Blackberry and Apple were all small-cap stocks before they were towering captains of industry on the NASDAQ, S&P 500, Russell 500 and the New York Stock Exchange. Capital market formation is driven alchemically by opportunity, opportunism, business creativity, financing creativity, the powerful desire to win, success and hedged by those affirmative polarities in greed, poor management and sheer nonsense.

If the deals that go all the way — the Exxon Energy, Mobile Gas, SmashBurger, Subway, Baskin Robbins, Nestlé, Domino's Pizza, Chick-fil-A — 80% of the initial $100 million is funded by giant institutional private equity funds and 20% by individual accredited investors and family offices. Broker dealers and boutique investment banking consultants like Gary's Newport Capital Consultants provide value with business development. Then there are the larger broker dealer firms such as Keith Moore's Boustead Securities, the even larger Roth Capital Partners who form, grow and fund projects as they grow to their full potential and then Wedbush

Securities. The largest player on the west coast is PIMCO, an investment management firm with $1.89 trillion in assets that provides solutions for institutions, financial professionals and millions of individuals worldwide. They are *nearly* as large as the African American consumer market — *Ha!*

This gets companies to their listing requirements, at which point they are taken public by the major investment banks — the Goldman Sachs, Morgan Stanley Banks, Fidelities, or a smaller boutique investment bank to the floor of a major exchange like the New York Stock Exchange, NASDAQ, NYSE Chicago, Boston Stock Exchange or the US Future Exchange; these exchanges are funded by Robin Hood, Charles Schwab or E-trade, which provide investors with a platform to get involved in larger markets by aggregating their investment with other investors.

Then monetary policy, rates and oversight in the US government is provided by the Federal Reserve System and its chair of the Federal Reserve of the United States who takes an oath of office. The Federal Reserve is the central bank of the United States, overseeing and providing guidance and regulations for all other banks and the economic well-being of the United States of America. "The Fed," as it is called, manages monetary policy and regulates the financial system of the United States, which is the largest and most liquid in the world. In 2020, finance and insurance represented 8.3% (or $1.7 trillion) of the US gross domestic product. US gross domestic product (all of the services and products generated by US entities) was measured at $25.44 trillion. The Fed accomplishes all of this by setting interest rates, influencing the supply of money in the economy and, most recently, making trillions of dollars in asset purchases to boost financial markets.

Can you imagine that? ¼th of the planet's GDP in pure numbers is housed in the United States of America with less than

4.22% of the world's population. THIS is the imbalance spoken about by the Honorable Mia Mottley at the United Nations when she spoke about global warming and the effects of these extractive and violently capital systems. All America has to say? *Drill, baby, drill.* Why? Because, according to market research by IBISWorld, the total revenues for the oil and gas drilling sector came to approximately $4.3 trillion in 2023. Greed is running things!

Sometimes in this business of investor relations, it can be smart to take a fixed payment in equity or stock. I've done it as a preference. Gary was a master at it — oftentimes a firm would offer millions of shares to have Gary serve on their board or as a member of their IR team, paying a million shares of their company by providing turnkey capital formation.

A million shares? Initial companies worth cents on the dollar, sometimes fractions of cents on the dollar, will become worth a dollar and cents, then something like $5.25 per share, trading on the OTC Markets or some other emerging market exchange, until they qualify for listing on a larger exchange like the NASDAQ, then come to $20, then zoom to $60 and change, then $120 and change in years to come… What was originally worth $0.01 is now worth $120? That's 12,000 x. It's rare happening, perhaps less than one of a hundred deals. But when it hits? *It will be worth it.*

The longest-standing IR (investor relations) "dog and pony" roadshow that I know of is WallStreet Research (WSR), or Southern California Investment Forum. Alan Stone and Company (ASC) has been run by Alan Stone for nearly five decades. WSR has been running investor meetings in Los Angeles, Beverly Hills, Newport Beach, San Francisco, Las Vegas, New York, Miami, Boca Raton and Palm Beach (including at Mar-a-Lago). On an institutional and international basis, there are my

Carlsbad neighbors, the MZ Group, with Ted Haberfield's hand steady at the helm as a corporate servant.

Alan was an analyst with an assistant portfolio manager at Merrill Lynch Wealth Management's $250 million high yield "corporate bond" fund. As one of the largest buyers of corporate stocks and bonds on Wall Street, Alan worked with the investment community's leading underwriters. In my dealings with Alan for nearly twenty years, I've found him to be the iron man journeyman of our group of capital market executive directors, with a penchant for professionalism and consistently putting together no-nonsense rooms that exceed the expectations of investors as well as presenting sponsors. He is very good at making money for his partners — I *know.*

Small businesses with a proven record of profits and a plan of action for the future will look to grow their business with that timeless source of American wealth and wealth creation: OPM — or *other people's money*. On the first Reg D raise — Regulation D, Rule 506, otherwise known as a friends-and-family round — companies can raise up to $5M; on a subsequent Reg A one in Y2 or Y3, they can raise another $10-$15M.

It's not easy — but it is relatively straightforward and doable. And if you're raising for the crowdfunding campaigns, then you can begin with little more than an extensive network, marketing assets (marketing and branding assets) and have a shot at the greatest game of wealth creation on planet Earth, bar none.

That's the thing.

There is nothing simple about this business. A vast network of tenured relationships is useful. A working knowledge of capital markets and financial instruments is essential. Your reputation is gold with which most transactions are easily negotiated. This business requires an extraordinary degree of *willpower. Willpower, excellence* and command performance to overcome the deluge of no's, hesitation and maybes. Willpower to overcome the devastating rejection that is an occupational hazard. Willpower to overcome the most dangerous of occupational hazards: the *reasonable* objection.

And then *people*. You are in the business of convincing capricious *human beings* — investors, rich guys, power brokers, power players (such as celebrities, beautiful women, politicians), fund managers — to do things they were not thinking of doing until they started talking to you. And it's not *manipulation* — that will result in lawsuits and investigations by the SEC, FINRA or even the FBI. Manipulation is about sharing untrue information to get something of value. This business is about convincing another energy, another human being to join you on a venture, on a journey of sheer exuberance, wealth creation and *creation-grab* from the fifth and the sixth dimension of visions, dreams and ideas and plant them firmly in the third dimension of reality with hard work, outcomes, results, finance and savvy.

> *"A society that keeps cures a secret so they can continue to sell medication for huge profits is not a real society but a huge mental asylum."*
>
> **—Alfredo Darrington Bowman,**
> also known as Dr. Sebi

Entrepreneurs convince investors to sign on the dotted line, to back up their *dream* with their hard work, hard living and even *their* dreams. *Investors are partners*, some more passive than others, others more active than others. That's the business we're in. It's a form of *terrorism*. Positive, productive, premiere *terrorism* — real treasure-chest-of-gold and stick-of-dynamite action — otherwise known as *leverage*, the purview of apex-capitalists and capitalist minions. The default capitalist purveyor is bold and audacious *although* gracious, intelligent, charismatic, elegant and a true professional.

Chapter 13:
On Getting Deals Done

"Today, we direct our economic and political strength toward winning a more abundant and secure life"

—**Mary McLeod Bethune,** in her last will and testament, May 18th, 1955

You know, it's a funny thing. When somebody passes from this Earth, or transitions to a part of existence that's outside of this so-called reality, we romanticize that person. Well, some of us do. We think about what they've done, and I believe we think about the net effect of that person on our lives. We eliminate all the negative understanding and perhaps, in our selective memories, we do away with the painful, uncomfortable, and peculiar.

Understanding ourselves in the flow of the universe is useful as a spiritual practice. Developing a vision and seeing yourself in all of your complexity and appreciating the nuance and details that make up our lives is an asset in *rare* supply. Looking at these so-called flaws is where we get the opportunity to make our weaknesses our strengths. These uncomfortable truths, seeming contradictions and rich ironies are the point of break, an inflection point against which we uncover the deepest truths of ourselves and our lives. These truths are key to greater opportunity and a gateway to our greatest selves.

The first one-on-one meeting I ever went to with Gary as a member of his firm, Newport Capital Consultants, was for a friend of his from Dallas who was heading off the financing for a private prison in Texas. We enjoyed a scenic lunch at Miguel's, a Mexican eatery in Newport Beach Cove. I was so excited. *I had a seat at the big boys' table with the good ol' boys.* Some capital, equity and a juicy title lined up for the taking. But when I left that meeting, I was pensive. A strange feeling crept into me.

That feeling crept into my conversation with Gary and the prison CEO. We were sitting at a five-star restaurant overlooking the edge of eternity, or an ethereal vision of Southern California. Gary explained how we could take a fee and stock to work on the deal with him.

"I can't do that," I told him.

"Well, what… *it's a good business*, and I can get you some stock," he replied.

But I just couldn't do it. *This time,* I walked away.

If you can imagine Newport Beach, particularly the cove overlooking the Pacific Ocean, you can imagine heaven on Earth. I've had so many enchanting experiences here. As we drove back to his mansion's offices in his black vintage Mercedes-Benz, Gary asked me how many shares of stock I wanted from that deal. His take could typically be a million shares, and he would also break down the fee schedule for the prospective client, explaining how they put deals together at

Newport Capital Consultants. This consisted of both the fee and equity.

I told Gary *respectfully* that I didn't want anything to do with the deal. I think he knew. But we never really spoke about it again. For me, there was a feeling of *selling out.* Private prisons in the United States are packed like sardines *(and no, the simile is not funny)*, with Black men and women in what has become the largest prison-industrial complex globally. Black folks are 14% of the US population but represent 50% of the US prison system, with generations traumatized, institutionalized and systematically brutalized.

Private prisons in the United States make an estimated $374 million in profit each year. This profit increases as the number of prisoners increases. Private prisons can make between $30 and $200 per inmate per day, depending on the state and type of facility. They make money by signing contracts to house inmates — these contracts are issued by the Federal government, as a matter of fact, itself headed by a convicted felon. Many commentators use the term "prison-industrial complex" to refer strictly to private prisons in the United States, an industry that generates approximately $4 billion *in profit* a year. I suppose I could have taken the time to explain this to Gary. Now, I didn't know all these details at the moment — but my spirit force knew to tell me, *like a little bird*, that something was off and wasn't right for me. Maybe ancestors have a way of letting us know?

What if I did the same thing with the Yorba City track coach when I was at Jesuit High School? What if I had just let that situation go and let it be? Was I dead wrong for the right reason? Was I absolutely right for the wrong reason? That coach went low. And well, as a tactical choice, I went lower. Or, at the very least, I met him at his low post and then kicked the hell out of him there too. *At least, I sincerely hope that's what I accomplished — kicking the KKK hell out of him.*

Building prisons that incorporate Black bodies in their stymied historical position is infinitely worse and more systemically damaging than racially accosting a teenager — but Gary and I had different world views and different cultural orientations with a common point of intersection at *our hope for the future and getting deals done in the present.* Could we co-exist and find mutual ground to work and get deals done? *We could and did we ever. The mutual respect and beautiful equity we had in our relationship allowed us to create greater possibilities.* That is one of the keys to racial healing and collective growth: *There has to be room to grow* — there has to be *Respect, Understanding and Grace as operating principles,* and a willingness not only to listen, but make accommodations, materially as well as spiritually, *to make things right.*

Whereas Good = Great, Great = Good

It was my principles and integrity that guided me, and those same values have served me in every deal I've ever done. There have been other offers and sometimes I do think about all the deals I've helped facilitate in sustainability, oil and gas, mining and minerals. And there have been other times I considered a deal salacious or where something just didn't feel right, *but being wealthy is so much more than a ledger line in your bank account. I cannot emphasize this enough — you are as good as the deals you do* ***not*** *make just as you are defined by the deals you do make. True prosperity* is about living to your greatest potential, *no matter the cost.*

Ethics in Deal-Making is Golden

There's a fine line between being a criminal and being an exceptional entrepreneur or even *just* a businessperson these days. *That line has gotten even thinner in recent times!* Typically, that line is drawn with access, inside knowledge of the system, access to levels of the system and not only gumption but also a sense of patriotism and powerful drives to leave a legacy of accomplishment or defined outcome. *What does that all mean?*

These days, the poor criminal gets arrested and sentenced for what wealthy hustlers do without a second thought. Think of the Godfather's ethos of *"It's business, it's not personal,"* or *Wall Street*'s Gordon Gekko's mantra of "Greed is good." *Has it ever been different in America? Has the spiritual damage of Slavery all but destroyed the American Dream?* Really, think about it. What Slavery has cost America insofar as *true* Greatness, *true* Freedom, *true* Justice. True wealth? *Tragic.*

For me, business is about more than just deals. The president of the United States of America is a convicted felon — 34 times over, and according to our business community? It is okay because we're all making money hand over fist. ***NO!*** It's about making the world a better place — one deal at a time. It's about being our best. This is a perversion of American principles — this attitude of *as long as I make the money, anything goes.* Whether in Slavery or in our modern economies, it's wrong. *And it is evil.* And, ultimately, unproductive and unprofitable. Ask Canada or Mexico. Ask BRICS. NATO. Those are short-term gains with, ultimately, negative returns that define our current reality. How many of us watch the news because we enjoy it?

I've learned this through my experience working on thousands of deals, big and small. It's not about knocking a ball out of the park every time or even embodying Mother Teresa's spirit for a better world, although that's not a bad way to go if you must! It's about infusing transactions with ethics, kindness and professionalism in every business transaction to the best of your ability. It's about focusing on how a deal can create value for everyone involved. It's about moving forward fearlessly and inviting more light into your space, from your space. It's about creating light. *It's about becoming the light*

And that's the difference between just getting deals done and getting the right deals done: the kind of deals that align harmoniously with my values and make a positive impact.

Torchlight Energy: A Triumph Amidst Challenges

One of the most memorable deals I've ever had the privilege to work on was with Torchlight Energy Resources (NASDAQ: TRCH). Torchlight began as a modest player in the oil and gas exploration space, focused on unlocking the potential of its assets, especially in West Texas.

Will McAndrew, a former client with Xtreme Oil and Gas put in a good word for me. I originally got the Torchlight Energy account as a referral from the MZ Group, Derek Gladwell and Ted Haberfeld, humble servants of the executive. Despite a turbulent market and fierce competition, Torchlight's management team under the leadership of CEO John Byrda displayed a level of tenacity and resilience that set them apart.

The company faced significant hurdles, particularly in the aftermath of the oil price collapse and as the energy sector underwent sweeping changes due to environmental and regulatory pressures. In 2020, Torchlight Energy reported a net loss of $11.55 million — steeper than the $8.88 million reported in 2019. Revenue had also taken a hit, dropping from $0.74 million in 2019 to just $0.19 million in 2020. For many companies, these kinds of financial figures spell doom. But not for Torchlight.

Their success story was just beginning.

What makes Torchlight's journey so remarkable is the way they turned adversity into opportunity. While many companies in the energy sector were retreating or consolidating, Torchlight leaned into its strategy of asset development. By focusing on their Orogrande and Hazel projects, they positioned themselves for a major turnaround. And that's exactly what happened.

In 2021, Torchlight Energy embarked on a strategic merger with Metamaterial Inc., a developer of advanced materials and nanocomposites. This merger marked a key turning point, transforming Torchlight into a company with a broader, more innovative future. Investors saw this as a game-changer, and the market reacted favorably. Stock prices surged, with Torchlight's shares hitting record highs as the merger was completed.

The merger not only provided liquidity to Torchlight's investors but also opened new doors in industries far beyond traditional oil and gas. Suddenly, Torchlight wasn't just an energy company — it was a key player in the tech-driven, future-forward world of advanced materials. This transformation aligned the company with emerging sectors like aerospace, defense and clean energy.

For me, working on the Torchlight deal was the epitome of what getting deals done truly means: not just completing a transaction but transforming a business, unlocking potential and creating long-term value. Torchlight Energy went from a struggling oil and gas company to a diversified powerhouse with a hand in cutting-edge technology. That's the kind of success story that makes all the hard work and high-frequency hustle worthwhile.

The Power of Deals: A Legacy of Success

Stating it's been a tough last two decades would be somewhat of a gross understatement. These years have provided America with historic challenges. As noted in the previous chapter: The Great Recession, the first Black president, an international pandemic, quarantine, the first president criminally convicted, two impeachments, war in the Middle East, war in the former Soviet Union, the threat of the end of democracy, social media, the introduction of BRICSs as a counter-currency to the United States, the emergence of African nations as emerging economies globally, the emergence of African Americans as a singular global economic force, the first female presidential candidate of the United States of America. Words like "fulcrum," "inflection" and "transformative" come to mind.

It's been tough. *But we're tough too.*

Looking back, I've had the privilege to work on deals like Torchlight Energy, Reading International Cinemas, American Prosperity and Jobs, Global Capital Network, and the West Coast Wall Street Conference. These ventures have shaped industries, changed lives, and, most importantly, helped businesses grow and thrive.

But getting deals done is so much more than just business. As I've said before and will keep saying, it's about creating opportunities, building communities, and helping others rise to their highest potential. It's about staying true to my values and never compromising on integrity. In the end, it's not just about the money or the accolades. It's about making a difference — one deal at a time.

I am a self-confessed serial deal junkie. *I love getting deals done.* Better than mango. *Better than… well… better than menudo. Better than crab and seafood. Better than Dominican cigars with a Courvoisier. I love Getting Deals Done. I don't love getting deals done more than God or more than my family, but those aren't commodities. And they are not equivalencies.*

But what's better than getting together with fellow gentleman and lady free enterprisers, putting a plan together and executing that plan until your original mission statement is realized? Creating reality through finance and industry of the human spirit? To me, there's not too much.

Our home address in the Foothills of Carlsbad *is a business incubator.* We've started off more businesses and more franchises than the SBA. And *perhaps* that's hyperbole but it's not necessarily an untruth. Shop Mombasa, San Diego Investment Conference, Global Capital Network, Global International African Art Movement, and the West Coast Wall Street movement are exposing hundreds of emerging growth to large-cap companies to financing and providing a market. West Coast Wall Street Conference, Beverly Hills Investment Club, Miami International Investment Conference, Enlightened Billionaire, Global Capital Network, iCFO Partners (events), Here's to Life, *Getting Deals Done* (the podcast), Southwest Investment Association and SharkHeart are all distinct and unique brands that have all had touchstones at our residence in Carlsbad.

We've successfully influenced popular culture featuring Angela Bassett in jewelry on the cover of *Entertainment Weekly* for *The Black Panther*, and launching the GIAAM (or Global International African Arts Movement) on C-Span at Max Rodriguez's Harlem Book Fair. We gave sustainability and crowdfunding a platform in its nascent stages amongst the money makers and financiers with the 2012 Jobs Act. We've funded over three hundred companies or been instrumental in those funding events through my roles in retail banking as well as producing financial events. We've produced or co-produced hundreds of these events all around the nation and some around the world. We've bought homes around the world and established funds. We've served on the boards of nonprofits as well as for-profit emerging growth, small and medium-sized businesses. We've liaised with civic and national leaders for patriotism and to play the game of American Democracy. We've formed and contributed to *communities through a visionary and egalitarian manner of doing business.*

At the bottom of the pandemic, 3050 was one half of the recording studio for Walter Mosely, Jenifer Lewis, Vanessa Williams and Yossou N'Dour to speak their voices in podcasts that were the grown-up version of PBS or the urban version of NPR. We were executively produced by Rita Reid (Tori's mama) with a schoolteacher's art genius all her own. Tori Reid, my partner and the CEO of our fledgling production or new media and storytelling company, masterminded audio and visual production and leveraged a lifetime pedigree from one of America's premiere entertainment families for the listening enjoyment of folks just coming out of a tribulating pandemic.

7039 Wynette Way, where I grew up, was an academic institution in the form of a home where six souls, well actually eight, were curated to rise to their highest possible potential. The Professor and the Engineer (my mom) as the Butcher and the Housewife before them, made a way out of no way for six kids to excel and be their very best. Or, as Dr. Howell would frequently boast, "Wow — six kids and nobody in jail, everybody went to college? I must be a genius!"

So, now I understand Grandmother Magnolia's sharp jab at her and my grandfather's masterful job at parenting — "*if it is luck you should try it sometime.*" I understand as a parent myself — *it ain't luck.* It is blood, sweat and tears; body, soul and mind. This form of parenting is about building institutions, crafting systems and working within a larger framework to create greater prosperity for your children and their children. And I know this not through statistics but from my network of friends, colleagues and acquaintances. We are among hundreds if not thousands if not millions of households that the mainstream press does not necessarily cover. I don't get a sense of our footprint as economic pioneers but it is there — *silent, powerful and ready.*

For example, at 3050 Glen Avenue, the greatest accomplishment we could ever aspire to? *Love.* Or as my great Aunt Janet likes to say, *Love, alone.*

As a matter of fact, just as 7039 Winnett Way was a center of learning, education and intellectual rigors, the home where I grew up is where St. Joseph's elementary school in Trinidad, Chapman College, UCLA, Sac State, the University of Nebraska at Lincoln, the American School in Guadalajara, Mexico, St. Anne's Elementary School, Jesuit High School,

Burbank High School, CK McClatchy, St. Patrick's, Pony Express Elementary School, UC Davis, St. Francis High School were diffused into the cultural nuance of our home and central part of the Caribbean foreigner culture there.

3050 has also been a center for excellence in entrepreneurship, free enterprise and getting deals done, distilling cosmopolitan BNP Paribas, Noervir (Japanese cosmetics), Wells Fargo, Bank of America, First Federal Bank of California, Cardium Therapeutics (biotechnology), RR Donnelley Financial, Newport Capital Consultants, Africa Connects International, Shop Mombasa, Victory & Noble, San Diego Investment Conference into our schools of learning, practical application and prosperity. And our best? It is *right there* in *front* of us.

> *"When a man makes up a story for his child, he becomes a father and a child together, listening."*
>
> — **Rumi**

I set aside investor relations where I had become a recognized business leader to pursue a more creative approach in podcasting. In 2026, we've combined both the media and investor relations component to create Global Market Intelligence and Media working in the most sought after emerging markets globally in the diaspora and with standout economists as Guyana's Kesha Mercurius has been the opportunity of a lifetime.

Below: Coast News's Chris Kydd and I have worked closely to ensure that our humanity is up front and center in all that we do.

Keynoting at the Balboa Bay Club in Newport Beach to an audience of accredited and institutional investors in 2012, honoring and initiating the Lifetime Legacy Achievement Award for Gary E. Bryant, a mentor who gave selflessly to teach a prodigy how to fish.

60% of presenting sponsors reported a 30% rise in their stock in capacity room of accredited and institutional investors. At the West Coast Wall Street Conference, we gave out the first Gary E. Bryant Lifetime Legacy Achievement Award

Pictured here with financial consultant Andrew Tomlinson at our Beverly Hills Investment Club at the Four Seasons. The San Diego Investment Conference also worked as the Beverly Hills Investment Club, Miami International Investment Conference, Enlightened Billionaire Series (international in the Caribbean and Europe).

Pictured here with Gary and Suzanne Bryant at the Balboa Bay Club in Newport Beach. Success can never be alone — it is only affirmed by those who walk the walk with you. The journey is the reward.

Pictured here here with Senator Barack Obama in 2007 during his historic campaign. Moments like these remind you that proximity is not the goal—it is the beginning of a deeper responsibility, not only to yourself but to a community of a shared humanity.

Pictured here with my life partner, Hanna Wagari, and our three-year-old son, Christian Wagari Howell. You are never alone in this life—the journey is carried, witnessed, and affirmed by those who walk the journey and have endured with with you.

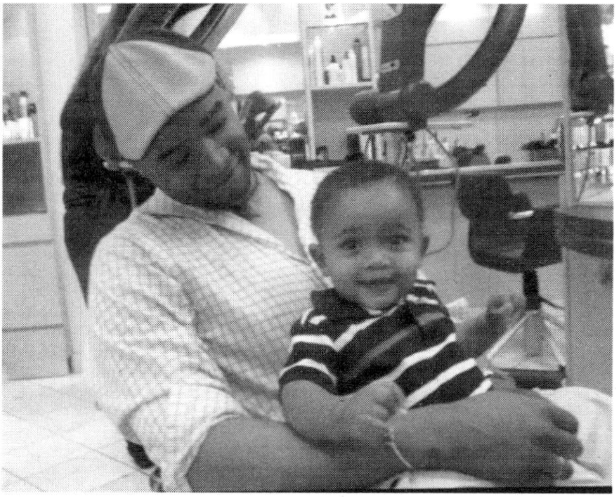

I poured myself—body, soul, and mind; blood and tears—into this young man. Along the way we shared miles of water together in the Caribbean, Adriatic, Pacific, and Atlantic. We call him "SharkHeart." He has grown to love the ocean, love swimming.

Years later, Christian graduated from San Diego Virtual as a U.S. Presidential Scholar, a standout student-athlete just as he had been earlier at Tri-City Christian in junior high. Cousins Sara Kelel and Gashe Messele Kelel were there, along with Amado Soma, Amina and Cecil Yusei, and Uncle Cecil. Chris towers over us all now- a giant, much like his grandfather before him.

Hanna, Christian and I have enjoyed a home in the scenic foothills with beautiful sunrises and Pacific Ocean sunsets. Our journey has been one inspired, affirmed and lifted by God.

Daddy was inducted into the Chapman Hall of Fame in 1998 from the Class of 1969.

My brother Cecil and I enjoyed a magical childhood and went on to make our own families, remembering the love and Caribbean traditions even as we grew up in Sacramento.

I stepped away from the world of capital markets formation to pursue something less certain but more true — eventually returning to integrate both capital and narrative into what would become Global Market Intelligence & Media.

PART II

The Ideology of Racism, Daddy, Solstices and the Spirit FORCE

Magic Spelling, Invocations, and Black 100 Proof Wizardry

Literature, the electromagnetic ground &
Poetry is power unbound
from rock grammar-ed realities
Our finances inlaid, economics flowing
Struggles in a white casket white house — Joy
Inbound Peace and flowing prosperity.
Light chaos x (times) dark beauty reigned;
Given to birth dreams, meanings
and dimensional entendres
Awakening.

Straight up? What are you waiting for? *Fly — Kings and Queens of the eternal midnights… and so, at last, our sun breaks — daylight. Deeeeeeeeeeeeeeeee-light!*

Listen. With your heart. Inhale deeply, swallowing whole breaths, eating life itself through your nostrils. Flare and feel your nostrils' muscles… flex. Close all the windows to your body, opening your image-i-nations, gently shuttering your eyes. Remembering all. *Becoming no one. Know* this *body, Spirit.* Now, fly Spirit. Letting go. *Awakened, exhaling quickly through your mouth. Quick shallow breaths, flat and hot, blow! Big fat purple beautiful black lips. All else is hallowed. And what you know is everything you did not. Be even more still and know more yet. Be* — I am God. *Dreaming as you, in the form of a human: you.* I am you and you are me. *Experiencing myself in so many outcomes, a variety of human forms, different ages, hues, experiences. Loves. Hurts. Triumphs. Turmoil. Different knowings. Beings. Imaginings. Beginnings. Endings. Humbly. Proudly. No. That's not what I said. Don't minimize. Not "a god." I said God. Be still and know* — I am God.

I am Spirit. Captured in a bloody body. Imprisoned in a material realm. I can fly, too. *Celestial.* And crash into this Earth dusty, to walk in the configuration of man, awakening, crying like a baby. *Screaming. Yes,* I cry, captured in this messy mess fleshy. Like again and again and again and again… *I'm born. We die. We live. We are born.*

I'm a Lover. I'm a fighter. I'm a fighter who will kill… *who will live* for the Lover.

Yeah, sometimes I fly daytime skies and see how close I can get to the sun. If its radiation won't burn me into my purest form. I look that ball of psychedelic metaphysic fires dead in the eye and dare it to crisply burn my retinas, char the skin right off this melanated body. *Blessed,* if I don't want to become the sun setting. Yeah, howling in fuchsias and auburns. Then become camouflaged dark as the nighttime, dense with countless stars and a hypnotic hanging low moon. *All sick like.* I unstick myself from the short and little hands of man's so-called time… my body bounds and I pound-gallop open fields with reckless abandon charged with the edicts, prayers and dreams of ancestors. I climb mountain sides, jagged walls of black lacquered volcanic rock like a human rock climber. And then there were those times when I have been overloaded with heavy yellow emotion. *Transference.* I sat still in those moments. Solstice. Let the demons rip, scream and fly. All around me,

I pray, I pray, I pray. Indeed, what if God were one of us? *I meditate and I Love.* And then I come up again with the morning sun. I'm a spirit. Again. In a body. *God.*

Writing *literature* or business how-to's is "effortless work," like playing football or basketball in physical terms. It's work because you break a sweat and you're catching your breath. And if you're out of shape and can't breathe? It's like death. *You know?* Under that adrenaline rush is the lactic acid churning over your Black ambitions burned. But danged if you didn't just have the best ever time… *and learned.* Literature is about harmonies, melodies and rhymes. Economics, the complementary rhythms. Not only musically, but also in terms of philosophical query superseding space and time. Yes, literature is about solving personal worries but also lyming, culture-manufacturing and juxtaposing — cosmic signposting.

So, when I started doing poetry… *or, when poetry started doing me* decades ago, I was following the likes of Robert Frost, William Butler Yeats, T. S. Eliot or those Harlem Renaissance fellows… Paul Lawrence Dunbar, and Countee Cullen; Jessie Redmon Fauset, Gwendolyn Bennett and Georgia Douglas Johnson. Countee Cullen, though, whew! *Ha!* What he said was real in "Any Human to Another" and made it so clear:

The ills I sorrow at
Not me alone
Like an arrow,
Pierce to the marrow,
Through the fat
And past the bone.

Your grief and mine
Must intertwine
Like sea and river
Be fused and mingle
Diverse yet, single,
Forever and forever.

And then there was Howard University's Paul Lawrence Dunbar in 1890s, penning "Sympathy," expressing for those of darker than blue hue, in a somber tone, his profound empathies and immaculate sympathies, no doubt inspiring Maya Angelou's late 1960s caged-bird literary sonnet wanderings:

I know why the caged bird beats his wing
Till its blood is red on the cruel bars;
For he must fly back to his perch and cling
When he fain would be on the bough a-swing;
And a pain still throbs in the old, old scars
And they pulse again with a keener sting—
I know why he beats his wing!

Always forward Spirits.

And then there is William Butler Yeats' "The Second Coming," penning intimate thoughts about our sign of the times:

Turning and turning in the widening gyre
The falcon cannot hear the falconer;
Things fall apart; the center cannot hold;
Mere anarchy is loosed upon the world,
The blood-dimmed tide is loosed, and everywhere
The ceremony of innocence is drowned;

The best lack all conviction, while the worst
Are full of passionate intensity.

I would measure stanzas for syllables and end lines on rhymes. But, as I became freer and more confident, as I had become lost and then found, found then lost again, learning from the jazz griot giants such as Al Jarreau, Ismael, Toni, Shirley Horn, Anita, Sade or Yoruba Jali masters such as Bobby McFerrin, George Benson and Herbie Hancock, *I soared. Spirits.* I opened up my gate a bit and would end a stanza on an unconventional line. Little like an infinitesimal black unicorn… nibbling on your ear, speaking in juju imagery and concise djembe time. Who-do *Voodoo?*

The classical training from the jazz maestros and poet ghosts served me well because the meter, song and drum were now in my pulse, my own heart hoping. Now I call the masters godmothers and big brothers — Jaki Shelton Green, Sonia Sanchez, Quincy Troupe, Nikki Giovanni, Ishmael Reed, Askia M. Toure and Abiodun Oyewole. Oh, the memories! From Imagination, Learning and Reading, I connect with Baldwin, Wright and Ellison in these spaces — the greats who have done their sacred texts over the decades, built lores and legacies — sometimes at their knees, others challenging, at others, Imbibing. Spirit saved. *Centuries. Journeys.* We're all just returning home. So, writing literature is neither hard nor easy, it is a total trip really.

In 2018, I published my first book of poetry through Jacar Press and Richard Krawiac, a fan and good friend of Godmother Jaki Shelton. Some folks say some amazing things about my work and inspire me to keep going, keep striving. Tony

Medina penned, "Patrick Howell's *Yes We Be* is affirmation and confirmation of the resilience of Black people and Black poetry. Reminiscent of Amiri Baraka's *A Black Value System*, as well as Haki Madhubuti's *Book of Life* and *Rise Vision Comin* — Black Arts meditations laying down a foundation for being."

Angela Narciso Torres from my writers' group offers, "In the tradition of Langston Hughes and Walt Whitman, Howell writes a truly American poetry in the language of the streets, office cubes, living rooms, bars — the everyday landscape of humanity. In poems at once ecstatic and reflective, Howell celebrates his heritage while unblinkingly portraying the African American experience. A modern-day hymnal for, of, and by the people, his music will reverberate long after the last page has been turned."

a drop in waters
will reverberate until
the earth, trembling, quakes
& trembling, the earthquake
reverberates
from a single drop in calm waters

Rise of the SharkHeart

When SharkHeart was older, his mom threw a nice party with friends at the movie theater to see Steven Spielberg's *Big Friendly Giant*. He invited friends from his Ethiopian church, school, swim team and neighborhood. This summer was also the 2016 Olympics in Brazil. The family, including his Obaba, caught the highlights of Michael Phelps as he collected his twenty-eighth

Olympic medal to become the most decorated Olympian in history, Simone Manuel as she collected two silver and two gold medals as a historic Olympian, and Kyrie Irving, rising all-star and NBA champion on the Team USA basketball team. By this time, SharkHeart was officially registered with USA Swimming and he received his second invitation from the Rancho San Dieguito swim team to swim on the Junior Olympic individual medley and freestyle relay teams.

I started writing full-time and had flexibility with my schedule, so I asked SharkHeart, "What do you want to do with your summer? Which summer camps?"

"I just want to swim. No camps, Daddy. I want to hang out with you and swim."

"*Okay.* We can make that deal. No camps. But why don't you have your own Olympic summer then…"

"Yep!" It was funny, he didn't need any further explanation. *I should have known.* Ha! He just… *flew* with it. And I didn't explain to him it was a *practice* Olympic summer — aspire to your own heights, your own greatness. *Be the best you can be.* I guess he didn't need to hear any more from me. Or maybe he just heard the blood experience of my heart beating for him. Or, perhaps, it was all the times I told him, "Don't let anybody ever place a limitation on you. *God made you. The same force that made the sun, the ocean and the endless skies.* These powers are his body and you are his dream. He made you and you are made in his image. That means you can do *anything — Anything you set your mind to.*"

So, in the summer of 2016 SharkHeart practiced five days a week, including surfing, boogie-boarding and basketball, competed in four swim meets and worked out in a long course meter pool at Catholic Cathedral High School thanks to Coach Joe. He swam twenty-five events, including his first

Junior Olympic swim meet and the Junior Olympic Max meet; he improved his times in the breaststroke, individual medley, backstroke and freestyle twenty-one of those times, eliminating approximately 16, 13, 1.37 and 13 seconds from his times.

There was a hiccup though. He was disqualified on his fifty-meter and hundred-meter backstroke not once but twice due to improper flip turns. Needless to say, SharkHeart never wanted to swim either event ever… for the rest of his natural-born life. But after studying Instagram videos and talking with coach Nicole, coach Steve and coach Armani, he straightened it out and the backstroke wound up (once he wound it right) being his best stroke. So, he learned after tribulation, triumph is possible *if you get yourself off the proverbial mat.*

Also, his coaches asked him to remove the SharkHeart before his race. They thought he might be disqualified by one of the officials. I was very concerned by this but SharkHeart told me, "Don't worry, Daddy. The power is mine. It's mine."

At the end of that summer he also competed in what is called the Junior Olympic Max meet. It would be the last one he ever competed in. Junior Olympic Max meet is a meet for "C" level swimmers, or swimmers who have not attained a level "A" and "B" standard in five or more events. Since SharkHeart began his Olympic practice summer and dropped all of his times, he had also taken himself from a "B/C" to "BB/A" swimmer. In this Junior Olympic Max meet, he swam the fifty free, one hundred free, fifty back, one hundred back, fifty breast, one hundred individual medley relay, anchored his two hundred free and two hundred IM medley relay teams. He got first place in all of his races except his fifty breast, where he got second to one of his good buddies, Mr. Wang.

But something also happened at that meet: He received his first *individual* Junior Olympic qualifying time for his fifty backstroke. The same event in which he had received two DQs and even said he never wanted to swim that event again, turned out to be the first JO individual time he qualified for. He qualified on his hundred-meter backstroke as well. While he had been working on meters all summer, this was his first yard race of the summer and he was more than ready. It was the first meet for which his cousins, grandma, Obaba and Uncle Cecil came out to see him swim too.

Yep. 2016 was truly his Olympic summer.

That fall we would prepare for an open water swim competition — the Del Mar Power House swim, and we could carry on training from SharkHeart's Olympic Summer to the fall season when the Pacific Ocean would get colder and school at St. John's began. In fact, this was SharkHeart's best swimming summer by far and he had mastered "Dedication," "Devotion" and "Discipline" with training weeks that included two-hour workouts at Catholic Cathedral, Moonlight Bay surf camps with over five hours in the ocean (8am to 1pm), beach days and ocean swimming. He was learning by a premium of experience that, indeed, he could do anything he set his mind to. He would go on to compete in the Winter Junior Olympics, qualifying with JO times in his fifty back, one hundred IM, two hundred free, one hundred free and fifty free. He would become one of the fastest swimmers at his club. He would train and compete in the Catholic School diocese regional meets at the highest levels.

But those are other stories for other days. By the time his ten-and-under swim year was complete (June 2016 to June 2017), he had removed nearly twenty seconds from his hundred-meter back time and ten seconds from his fifty-meter backstroke. He had effectively become the fastest swimmer in backstroke at his club the Rancho San Dieguito boys and girls club in Solana Beach, one of the best if not the best swim club in San Diego. In his freestyle, he was also the fastest ten-and-under swimmer in his fifty-yard and fifty-meter freestyles for his club. We missed a couple of club records for that age group, and if we said we were not disappointed, we'd be engaging in magical thinking. That's something SharkHeart and KillerWhale *(that's me)* don't do. We face reality head-on and embrace the challenge. We set our eyes on the twelve-and-under age group, re-working our goal sheets, knowing from past challenges that whatever we set our minds to, we can and will accomplish.

I got home late last evening — I went out to the pool with Christian, who said he wants to be the best, so we practice every day. The walk gives us the opportunity to talk and catch up. "Daddy?"

"Yeah, bud."

"Do you see that ring around the moon? Kind of like the ring is a blurry eye."

I look up and see no stars in the sky. Cloudy sky, even though it was hot today. And there is a mist in the midst of the moon. I remember when he was just a baby I used to tell him God always has an eye on us. One eye, bright, illuminates, gives warmth, observes while giving life. The other eye, open at night, is gentle and caressing, and encourages dreaming and rest. "Yeah man — it looks blurry."

We are walking down Glen Avenue, an idyllic street with a club pool at the roundabout. It's typically quiet. Not sure about working out at this time of the evening. The boy is prone to colds. Not sure I want to get in the pool. *But I am sure about him.* About following dreams — cause, I always teach him, *dreams come from God.* Just like we watch TV and get programming for Pepsi, Beats by Dre, Microsoft, Chevron — our dreams are programmed by God — that's how He talks to those wise enough to receive the programming. So I do this exercise with him. Dreams are meant to be lived. And there is no mystery to realizing them. *Just believe.* And then work hard with the clarity of that belief in mind.

"Daddy?"

"Yeah bud."

"It's like the ring around the moon is a sonic boom — all of its power just extending out around the heavens."

"Jesus," I think to myself. Kid has got a vivid, vivid imagination. *So weird, right?* Maybe he should be a Hollywood director, like Spielberg or a producer like Gene Roddenberry. Maybe an author, like J.K. Rowling — write kids' books. Then I look up at the sky and I see that there is a clearing around the moon, far wider than Saturn's ring. It's a wide halo, tough to miss, unless you think we are living a mundane ordinary existence. And there are no stars in the sky around this moon, a radius with an energy field as wide as the sky. Wow. "Hey Chris — you see that!"

"What?"

"The ring around the moon — it's really, really large — a whole radius" I draw a finger figuratively around so he can see the rings extending about like larger and larger rings in the heavens.

"Yeah, Daddy — *that's what I was showing you.*"

"Oh, ok." We're already in the gates of the community pool, "Get in the water kid — let's go swim — and remember, just believe."

"You too, Daddy. You believe too, Daddy."

***

Chris and I are lying in the dark, messing around with Google's globe app, searching Addis Ababa, where his mother was born and other places we've been to around the world.

"Daddy, can I tell you something?"

"Yeah Chris. What's up, man?"

"Sometimes when I am in class?" He just started attending St. John's Elementary School in Encinitas last fall, "Sometimes Ms. Tucker will tell everybody it is important for them to be a good Christian."

"That's cool," I say.

He deadpans, "a good Christian" with the faintest hints of sarcasm, not fully knowing and perhaps even some embarrassment. "Everybody in the class always just keeps staring at me every time she says that." He shrugs his shoulders. Kid's got jokes. I'm laughing, zero inhibition.

When he was just eighteen months old, he would sit on my shoulders everywhere we went — church, school, to the mall, board meetings, ocean swimming, basketball courts up and down the Pacific Riviera, prospecting calls, hiking — everywhere we went, Chris was on my shoulders as almost an extension of myself. People would often comment on how cute it was or just smile. They would, I believe, in their spirit's eyes, see the incarnated symbol of father and son.

Very often, I was doing business, negotiating, networking with him there and often my conversation could end in frustration with myself hanging up the phone exasperated. Chris would talk to me as a one-year-old and ask, "What happened, Daddy? Are you okay?"

"Yeah, man. People are just greedy!" I'd answer.

"Just be patient, Daddy, and wuv them."

"*What?* Oh, yeah?" He kind of sounded like Yoda or some kind of Buddhist pint-sized sage, "And how do you know this? *Are you Jesus?*"

"*Yes, I am.*"

"Prove it."

"I wuuuuuvvvv you, Daddy. I wuv you."

Kindly Don't Have My Child Play the Slave During the American Revolution

I picked Christian up from the car line at his Christian middle school. He's playing wall ball but drops the ball like a brick running to the car when he sees me.

"*Hey, Daddy...,*" he hugs me — *my little King.*

"*Hey, baby...* how was your day?"

"I had some big problems today."

"Oh, yeah? What happened? *Tell me.*"

"They have a school play tomorrow. They wanted me to play Crispus Attucks for the American Revolution and I don't want to do it. I've told her several times and she just ignored me. So, I went to the basketball court to play hoops. So these two little blond girls in my class came to get me. They said the teacher wanted to see me. She said I was delinquent from the class or something. She told me I have to play the slave for the play tomorrow."

"You went to the courts all by yourself? Wow. Was your shot going down? How was your flying?" I know I warned this rottweiler teacher of his but I guess she wants to find out the hard way. *No problemo.* "I love Crispus Attucks and he's a true American revolutionary. But I understand, baby. And I respect how you did what you needed to do." Crispus Attucks, of African and Native American descent, was an American sailor, stevedore and whaler. He's often recognized as the first person killed in the Boston Massacre for the American Revolution.

"Tell you what, bud — Do you want to hang out at Grandma's tomorrow? Then we can go get some ice cream and go to the Ferris wheel in Irvine? Maybe catch a movie?" You know, I don't remember Christian having an issue with playing Joseph in the school Christmas play with a blond Mary, mother of God.

"God is with me *always,* Daddy. My shot's going down pretty good and I'm getting better and better at my flying. Yeah, that would be fun. Thank you, Daddy."

"Love you, baby."

All names have been substituted to not only protect the identity of the parties concerned but to convey an allegory of the reality of race relations in the USA, have some fun and laugh light at something heavy.

A letter from parents to the principal at a so-called Christian (all puns intended) school. I wear a blood red tie with paisley imprints.

Good morning, Principal Owl —

On several occasions this year, my wife and I have taken time out to share with Mrs. Mary Magdalene Rottweiler our concerns about our son and the manners/curriculum in which she has dealt with or referred to him that we felt were derogatory or otherwise inappropriate given that he is a person of African descent. Last week, my wife and Ms. Rottweiler had a conversation regarding Christian's participation in the American Revolutionary War play. There were some issues with her interpretation and we wanted to share some of our concerns.

With this latest incident around the American Revolutionary assignment, we spoke with you of the latest incident when Mrs. Rottweiler singled out my son to play a freed slave during the American Revolution Day. In a previous assignment, he was given a project to illustrate a slave plantation — he drew monsters on a plantation. She gave him a C+ not because of the academic and artistic merit but because of her racist disposition.

I will be the first to admit that racism, if you are not on the receiving end of it, can be tricky to identify. As we have met and spoken several times, we do not get the impression that Mrs. Rottweiler is malicious in her intent or seeking to damage our son (we absolutely do but I am taking the time with you to peacefully resolve this before I take it to the next level and we will all have to spend time in the Twilight Zone). Thus, I am taking this opportunity to explain to you in detail how her actions were racist and how these actions are in fact detrimental to our son. At the same time understanding that as we are patient, hopeful and seeking Christ in Mrs. Mary Magdalene Rottweiler, we are equally adamant that these actions must stop at once; or your entire institution will face consequences that might seem outsized but fit to my temperament perfectly.

In the simplest of terms, to ask our son who is of African descent to roleplay a former slave of African descent is an extremely negative psychological reference for him. He was not a slave, nor is he now. I derive my ancestry from West African kings and his mother is an Ethiopian from the continent of Africa. She came here on a plane from Ghana with her father, who was an executive with Ethiopian Airlines.

He is the descendant of kings and queens, proud country men that developed the first civilizations and the first global empires. I am mixed with Caribbean (Trinidadian) and Latin (Panamanian) roots and come from West African Chieftains, more than likely of the Igbo or Yoruba tribes. I am a proud African American, born in Sacramento, California. Yet still Christian must internalize this role and act it out (in front of his white classmates who all play men and women who were born free). He is only eleven years old! Freed or otherwise, a free slave was still enslaved.

Those who did the enslaving were neither Christian, nor good people in their actions. *They are savages and terrorists.*

In fact, they were monsters. They are monsters and Christian's interpretation through his drawing was quite brilliant. Also, as kids have their own world out on the playground and after school, there is a chance that these negative references will take on a life outside of the class play. We have asked her to not typecast our son in these types of roles again and yet she insists upon why it is an appropriate reference.

Perhaps the Rottweiler ought to be separated from her pension? And perhaps this Christian school ought to headline in SoCal as a bastion of confederacy practices and ethos that it seeks to impart upon the next generation of leaders? Perhaps, you will establish a trust fund consisting of your school funding for the next two generations of our family's education? This is California after all — not Alabama or Mississippi.

We wonder what the experiences of other African American children in her classes have been throughout the years?

What were their grades relative to their white counterparts?
How many played slaves or freed slaves?
How many Latinos or Asians were given the roles of Benjamin Franklin, George Washington or other Founding Fathers?
How many Caucasian children were asked to perform as slaves or freed slaves?
How many were asked to perform as Abdul-Rahman ibn Ibrahimi Sori (a prince from West Africa and a slave in the United States for forty years until President John Quincy Adams freed him)

Mrs. Rottweiler has noted defensively that she is not responsible for the curriculum, and does not control what is in it. We have shared outside materials from university presses such as Harriet Tubman or Denene Millner's press with her in previous meetings, even offering gifts — surely these books can be used for individual projects or class projects. She might also host American Culture days for history, where parents of different nationalities and different cultures share their Taiwanese culture, the Ethiopian culture, and the Latino culture (Mexican or Ecuadorian) with the rest of the class.

Does the artwork and class materials in her class reflect its rich Christian diversity? Some recommendations in lieu of the curriculum, in lieu of her "classic" materials — some ideas that have been shared with her and to which she has been non-responsive, instead offering that she is familiar with the material.

Again, I trust that her intent with our son was not to harm his psyche. *(Of course it is but let's play the game of semantics just a little bit longer.)*

Diversity and sensitivity issues can be tricky, so if she has any questions about how she should approach the diverse offering of children in her class, she should feel free to proactively reach out to us directly. We have always and will continue to take a very active role with Chris' education and classes.

I guess the adage in the African American community of, *"twice as good to get half as much"* is at work in Mrs. Rottweiler's class. Christian is getting a first-hand experience of institutional racism and how it works. We do hope this negative programmatic curriculum and Mrs. Rottweiler's unwillingness to hear us out does not continue to affect his grades.

Principal Owl, thank you for your efforts to be a positive influence in our son's life. We recognize your excellence and the love you bring to church, singing in the choir, directing traffic and other administrative concerns. We remain committed to your Catholic School's core values of Truth, Community, Character and Spiritual Growth. We recognize that we are all Christians, a single family under Christ. We are committed to our spiritual growth, Christian's spiritual growth and that of our community of teachers and principals. We will continue to bring Jesus Christ into this conversation and will continue to pray for the leadership at our Christian Schools.

I do want to inform you, however, that *I am not a pacifist. And this is not a peaceful entreaty. I am just trying to make things right. I am learning patience and God's still working with me. If I have to come back to this table again? It will be with a lawful subpoena for records answering those aforenoted questions and pending massive legal action. Instead of my wife with me, my attorney will be present and your institution will serve as seed money for our son's college education. I will sue you, your school and the board, and I will do it in* ***full view of***

everyone. *And what that… rottweiler has tried to do with my beloved son behind closed doors? I'll do it to you and your institution. Times ten.*

Sincerely and with Kind Regards, and
invoking the spirit of our God
Patrick A. Howell

We just got here — Friendship Baptist Church in Pasadena, a historic west coast Black community. The Honorable Congressman Elijah Cummings remembered meeting Christian W. Howell (a.k.a. #Sharkheart, USA Swimming) in 2016. Christian thanked him for making it possible for him to go to the Obama White House and shared his fourth-grade report with the Maryland congressman, who now walks with assistance but recognizes Christian and is happy to see him again.

The report talked about Benjamin Banneker, the self-taught astrologist and architect who designed DC and was referred to by Thomas Jefferson as "the Black Ethiopian." The District of Columbia was built by West African architects, engineers and visionary system builders. The District of Columbia was designed so that it could govern the world. Christian W. Howell is not only a first-generation American but also a West African prodigy and an Ethiopian with cosmic ambitions.

Sometimes, the future can take a while — decades or even centuries — to ripen, but when it finally arrives it is deliciously glorious. The honorable congressperson, child of two pastors, spoke his good word and said the nation was in danger and that the institutions of democracy needed to be safeguarded and were worth living and dying for. He spoke from the same pulpit MLK did in 1960.

A SharkHeart Will Rise

We've all heard it said that the Bible is essentially a story of fathers and sons and I get it: Jesus and the father, David and Solomon, Job and his sons, Abraham and his son. Then there are the popular opuses like *The Godfather* or Will Smith's reinvention of Bill Withers' classic "Just the Two of Us." But what is it about that bond between fathers and sons? *The solstice and equinox aligned.*

A father is a protector (sometimes fierce and at other times gentle). A visionary. He is a tactician and master strategist. He believes and hopes but, more so, he knows. *He do.* A father seeds a son's life with sun, water when necessary, and endless blue skies. But he also reflects reality. A father is a friend — the first and the best. A father will not let you down. A father will see you. Truly. He will reflect you and you will reflect him. A father is a master North star. A father will correct his way and always find the best path forward. A father is a holder of the legacy and a steward of tradition. You may be the future but a father has designed that future with his love, time and spirit.

My father is Dr. Howell and my son is Christian. It's a galactic continuum. And a sacred obligation. My dad — "Daddy" — was pretty good, many times he was the best on the planet. Ambitious and accomplished. He would always counsel me to be better than him… *and I try.* He set a good benchmark. And I work hard to be "better" but I enjoy the journey of fatherhood with my Christian, a great son who at sixteen continues to shine bright, grow, surprise and giant up. Sometimes I can't figure out if I love him more or am prouder of him. Or, maybe it's both oscillating, taking the place of one another, and they are both elements in the continuity of what Daddy began a long, long time ago.

I only saw Daddy cry once: Muhammad Ali versus Larry Holmes in 1980. Ali fell — *we all felt that one within our guts and spirits.* We didn't know at that time His Airness was coming. That the Black Mamba would be on Ali's butterfly heels, with a viscous, venomous, murderous snake bite. We didn't know that Colin Kaepernick would take a knee, just as Tommie Smith and John Carlos had raised their fists three decades earlier. That King LBJ would soon thereafter blend Dr. J. with a little Magic, some Bird and drizzle it all with some Ali caramel in his mission of the people, for the people and by the people. We didn't know that our warriors on the diamond, hardwood or grass fields would become extensions of the community following Dr. Harry Edward's thesis *The Sociology of Sport.* There's only one Muhammad Ali, *a new prophet for the new times. Ali's fall shook up the continuum of time and space* — our beautiful, fierce cosmic lion protectorate went down and we would have to wait a spell for Tyson the Savage Destroyer to avenge our lamb's fall. Or, you might just say Holmes ended Ali. But did he?

This was at the duplex in Land Park. Ali went down and all of a sudden Daddy's head fell into his hands and his whole body, whole soul, began to shake uncontrollably. It was kind of like the California earthquakes we would get every now and then. The entire pan-African global connect had become an extension of Ali's regal spirit — it was as if through Ali we were connected to the ancestors, the gods and our immortal soul. It was like he was *a movement unto himself,* a giant human with a million extensions like the Voltron robot. And Daddy was like this molecule in Ali's heart, one that would travel through the bloodstream to Ali's tear ducts. I think a sixteen-year-old Mike Tyson swore revenge right around then too. The only thing Daddy loved more than his Calypsos *was Ali.* Cecil and I started laughing — we didn't even know what was going on. *Criminals.* Now? How I wish I could put my arms around Daddy and comfort the man in his grief — it was the end of an era; but Ali had begun the new millennium: a champion from the people, by the people and for the people. The undisputed Greatest of all Time had given birth to the new time inside all of us. We laughed because we thought Daddy was laughing *or something.* It never occurred to us that our hero, our shining king — Daddy — resplendent in pinstriped three-piece suits could break down and cry — that he could tremble in grief.

That great spirit of a world-conquering champion was alive and well during Barack Obama's campaign, and Obama became the surrogate for what I can only imagine was the spirit of Mansa Musa reincarnated, claiming dominion over his lost tribes, or at least the first visage or incarnation of that spirit in the modern era. It was the same spirit that attached itself to Michael Jackson and rested in our collective soul as we all pantomimed that moonwalk in our daily lives to the timeless rhythm and beat of our African drums layered out under Quincy Jones orchestrations.

Ali was the perfect man — a perfect Black man, a perfected human. *He* was Black Jesus… *I mean Allah.* that man was pretty. Oh, and tough too. But we *all* know this.

Exquisite, the Spirit

A Caribbean gourmet restaurant, Solimar, down the road from the Normandie Hotel on St. Annes off a main street, left off an alley named Nook Avenue, just past the orange Havana Hut Cigars with green awnings. Every single Caucasian vacationer on the island — Spanish, Brazilian, Argentinian and American — is at this place tonight socializing and making quaint as wind washes us in warm breezes, summoning warm glowing sports. Winds whispering of spirits, angels and demons, winds wandering, winds that open our wondering; winds that recognize our spirits and pick up from the line so that we are all aligned.

Trinidad — a Caribbean potpourri of spirit and material excess, an island defined internationally by its oil riches and carnival season — 49% Black, 49% Indian, 2% other; a cosmopolitan confluence of contemporary economics, cornucopia culture, ancient-modern history.

Father and son take a stool at the bar as we wait for our table to be set. A Caribbean man of boy-like proportions and a gentle soul bartends as we toast with his "Caribb" and "Man Over Board," Dwayne's specialty, first-place-prize-winning drink: Dwayne, a young Black man with a slight frame and a head as large as those kingdoms of Ghana, Mali and Songhay and my father, a former slang boy, like our slang boy bartender. So, his heart wallows a sad tongue between the tragedy of Dwayne's genius squandered on prize-winning drinks and my father's fortune to escape the fate of his countryman brother and the sad bastard European classic playing. Tears began to roll and emotions roil as he recalls precisely why he had to leave his country for opportunities overseas, to give wind to unlikely ambitions and how his country was never the best it could have been, the excellence it could be.

"The politicians are corrupt," he laments, bowing his head in his hands. "They are pontificating, philandering, foolish, fluttering sycophants. They are oil-rich, they are oil-sick and will not build the roads. Will not build the railroad tracks. Will not build the citadel university of the West indies. Even though it has been over fifty years since he had to leave his slang home for opportunities overseas. He wallows for a spell in the sad-bastard ballad.

Sandra is her name, a handsome face, strong cowboy disposition with the presence of angels, another Trini creation unto herself, a songstress with the voice of free birds and Caribbean men of old. She narrates a story with her guitar in hand — Caribbean lullabies modulating effortlessly, simultaneously between sparrow bird's falsetto and a Caribbean folk anger gravel baritone rasp.

Daddy invites Sandra to our table when she's done with her ditty. They speak conjoined spirits, reminisce, lyme as intellectual country persons. Sandra rememories her world travels from Munich to Washington, patronizing rich clients on factions at the slang Hilton "upside-down" hotel, paying her fare overseas for their dinner parties at home. She fondly remembers the magic of snow packing outside her window to forget all the commotion of the house at the breaking news of Saddam's capture. They weave into their oral dissertation the morning paper headlines in the TnT Express and the Trinidadian Guardian those pressing national issues. They lyme singing the praise of their countrymen luminaries, cultural ambassadors and guardians — The Mighty Sparrow, Lord Kitchener, V.S. Naipaul, and now a young senator Ato Bolton — of those who have passed to the other side. They converse going back and forth at first, within their own landscape, then vocally. Alas, they rap philosophically; they wax existentially, conversing and reminiscing, remembering the nature of death until they come to the denouement, after the climax:

"We will leave this lifetime with who we are, not what we have."

I remember when SharkHeart was five and could swim freestyle and backstroke twice as well as I could at eight. He saw the shark tooth I had around my neck and asked if he could have it. *Sure — everything I am, I have and ever could be is yours.* But I didn't say that. I got the dark, carbon-colored shark tooth from a trip to Trinidad and Tobago when my wife was pregnant with our prince. My brother, father and I took a trip of memories, visions and dreams to Daddy's birthplace in the Caribbean, Trinidad and Tobago. During that trip, we took a long winding road to Maracas Beach, an hour-long drive from the capital, Port of Spain, and spent the day at a beach famous for its Bake and Shark huts. We had coconut water, hiked up and down the shoreline, lymed, talked about women, made dirty jokes and put our arms around one another. It was a good time for us. It was a good year. Now, I didn't tell my son that either. I took the shark tooth off and inspected it, telling him, "This is the tooth of a Mako Shark that can swim up to seventy miles in the open waters and is a fierce carnivore.

"That's a swimmer that likes to eat up all the other creatures in the ocean with his fierce style of swimming. What I am saying is this amulet is a peculiar gift of nature that will confer special powers and abilities upon whosoever wears it. If you want it you can have it, but it will give you superhuman speed, strength and a shark's heart. You will fly in the water. Your speeds will have no limits. And you will devour your competition. In time, the mutant abilities will become your own, organic.

"Eventually, you will *become* the SharkHeart." He snatched it out my hand, shut me up good, and took some special one-on-one time with his newfound treasure — I'd imagine not unlike the Silver Surfer upon acquiring his cosmic space-travel board from Galactus, or the Submariner flying on winged feet as he learned of his American sea captain father, or Batman speeding up and down Gotham after getting the Batmobile from Lucius. Or maybe, even, Neo after taking Morpheus' red pill. Since then, he's been known as Shark Heart, and the transformation began to take place.

His mother thinks this is silly comic book stuff but you should see her eyes, how large they get, even for gorgeous Ethiopian eyes, at the swim meet. "Asanabari!" (That's

Amharic, Ethiopian, for "My Shark!") My chant since he was a child has been "Pan-African Champion Olympian. One half Ethiopian. One quarter Trinidadian. One quarter Panamanian. Yes I can, Yes I can, Yes I can!" It has simply changed to a thunderous "Go! Shark! Heart!"

However, as much emphasis as we have put on cut-throat competition, we have focused on the source of all power, all true power: God. "Greatness without good means nothing. There are a lot of so-called great men in the world," I tell him, and after a long jump, eight-hundred-meter race on land, five hundred meters in the water, two hundred meters on land, fifty yards A-time in the water, a victorious soccer match, one-on-one basketball on the courts, we always give the glory back to God. But that is another story for another time.

Leimert Park is a place with timeless roots that reach deep into the lore of Hollywood and its surrounding Los Angeles neighborhoods. In the 1920s, the master-planned community was built with Spanish Colonial Revival homes that cast quiet spells of imagination on resident and passerby alike. Its evergreen pine needle trees reach into the heavens. Ella Fitzgerald, Ray Charles and iconic former LA Mayor Tom Bradley have all enjoyed homes and time in the historic neighborhood. It has been called the "Black Greenwich Village." Today it is an ongoing bedrock of free expression and American culture.

This past Saturday, October 14, from 3 to 6pm, Leimert Park, at the Vision Theater, a Los Angeles historic cultural monument, enjoyed another cultural hallmark in its celebrated history. The national media, Leimert Park residents and cultural leadership enjoyed the debut of the Harriet Tubman

Press by Loyola Marymount University and its parent press TSEHAI Press. There were panels and live readings from the poets of the press's first book, *Voices from Leimert Park.* In fact, in a time in which public funding for the arts has been cut by federal sources, Loyola Marymount University and TSEHAI Press and its international publisher Mr. Elias Wondimu have doubled down not only on publishing and world culture, but community and bringing people together.

Mr. Collin Hinds, Loyola Marymount's Director of Development also said of the event, "One of the most significant blessings of this weekend was that the day before the event, Congresswoman Maxine Waters addressed Congress with the following words:

> *"The Harriet Tubman Press — an imprint of TSEHAI Publishers — is an important new publishing platform based in Los Angeles, California... The Harriet Tubman Press is housed in the Marymount Institute for Faith, Culture and the Arts at Loyola Marymount University, which is one of the centers of higher learning in my congressional district — the 43rd District in California... I congratulate Loyola Marymount University, TSEHAI Publishing, the Harriet Tubman Press, and all the members of the South-Central Los Angeles community that worked so hard to make this first publication possible. Your dedication and fortitude is necessary to the preservation of the African-American voice."*

Over the weekend, Colin Kaepernick was vaulted to the status of the Muhammad Ali of the twenty-first century by the vitriol of a president well healed in the underbelly of American life. Stephen Curry, beloved Oakland hero and "baby-faced 3pt. assassin" became a voice of reasoned calm in the cultural hurricane of America's racial wars.

National Football League players, Black and white, became metaphysical warriors in the universal battle for true justice and the only freedom. The National Basketball League's Lebron James continues to show himself champion of the people calling out the "bum" in the White House. The NFL's Roger Goddard and New England Patriots Robert Kraft demonstrated too — they demonstrated that the $1.3 trillion dollar buying power of African American consumers can bend the knee of even billionaires and the so-called powerful to the requirements of justice and freedom for all. All of this as hurricanes Harvey, Irma and Maria remind us all of how fragile we *all* are and our common humanity, Russia-gate continues to reveal that even high treason is a crime protected by white privilege... for now, anyhow... and world nuclear war is threatened by mad men. Yes — it seems to be a mad, mad, mad world.

However, we — *We, the people?* In order to form a more just society, a more perfect union, in our greatest aspirations, eyes kept firmly on the prize — we came together. Turns out griot and American treasure Abiodun Oyewole of the Last Poets was a seer when he said he saw the people coming together. In Los Angeles at 2200 Virginia Avenue, the Ethiopian Festival celebrated the Ethiopian New Year at a Festival of Harmony. There was dancing, singing, kids running in and out of the nearby park in their Ethiopian traditional suits, lines of traditional foods provided by Messob's Ethiopian restaurant and culture of the ages with children's fashion shows, timeless jewelry from Mombasa Jewelry, hair braiding and talent shows. And there were books there like *Ethiopia During the Derg Years* by Tesfeye Dinka, Temsalet (Phenomenal Ethiopian women), and *The Read with Me A to Z: English-Amharic Alphabet*, the first book published by TSEHAI.

Spiritual IQ is when a person understands and applies principles in a way that enhances all of the other senses, including emotional intelligence, book sense, niche knowledge, street smarts, memory, and even artificial intelligence, where these other manners of experiencing reality are better attuned and aligned. In this attunement, Spiritual IQ, deeply personal and deeply aligned with each person's individual experience as well as their highest form of expressing and interpreting themselves, is refined and perfected.

In business, an individual with Spiritual IQ will:

- maintain peace and balance, particularly under extreme distress;
- show empathy and demonstrate a transformative empathy in relationships;
- lead with integrity and a divine purpose, prioritizing collective priorities as well as playing the long game;
- incorporate their spiritual being into decisions, bringing the DNA of their moral and ethical considerations into most if not all choices and decisions.

With African American executives, financiers and entrepreneurs, *Spiritual IQ* emphasizes profound healing, cultural resilience, generational wisdom, and a commitment to not only uplifting the community but advancing humanity to its highest and greatest expression. Spiritual IQ is the ability of an individual to act beyond their immediate needs and within the continuum of their principles instead of their immediate human needs. Spiritual IQ correlates to an individual's ability to act with core principles and infuse transactions, conversations and deals with such limitless spiritual assets as Love, Hope, Faith, Resilience, Persistence and Light. Spiritual IQ believes in the limitless potential of beings but also our human experience. Spiritual IQ is fortified in our deeply human experience where the greatest spiritual expression is simply to be and love ourselves through it all.

Summer Equinox & Strawberry Moons

> *Out beyond ideas of wrongdoing and rightdoing,*
> *there is a field. I'll meet you there.*
> *When the soul lies down in that grass,*
> *the world is too full to talk about.*
>
> —**Rumi,** "A Great Wagon"

Today is the longest day of the year and is also *empirically* the most blessed — the summer solstice. There is a unique combination of several cosmic phenomena in full bloom throughout the Milky Way Galaxy. Many of us are awake to experience it consciously. The first full summer moon is also known as the "strawberry" moon. This full strawberry moon will appear low — according to the *Old Farmer's Almanac* and NASA, it is the lowest full moon of the calendar year. It hangs like a big ol' pie sitting right there on your kitchen counter. 'Cept this one is in the sky.

This year's strawberry moon coincides with the summer solstice, a time of year with its own anagogic spiritual significance. *Anagoge*, sometimes spelled *anagogy*, is a Greek word that means *to ascend upwards*. And yes, it is one of my favorites! The anagogic method of literary interpretation is a mystical or spiritual lens for perceiving life with the third eye — it is an all-seeing spindle eye. It is visionary, imaginative and, really, only those fundamentally grounded in this reality can handle it without flying off into the cosmos. I've been interpreting and reading like this, taught by the mystics of my own cosmology: Mommy, Daddy, Sister Madeline, Mrs. Richardson, Mr. Patrick McCrystle, Toni Morrison, Prince, Gabriel Garcia Marquez… and even the bombastic Mr. Darling.

I've learned to tame my wild side but also give the majestic free reign over the open fields of my existence — I've got the routines, rhythms and rhymes to me down. My rebellious and untamed spirit — bold, beautiful, bombastic and belligerent — has become an asset and is exemplified by my own aphorism, *"power is as power does."*

Christian's spirit is controlled, silent, nearly deafening and unbelievably powerful, like a strawberry moon. He is a gentle soul with his own unique empathic way. We've begun to separate and sometimes it has been unbearably painful, like a death of sorts. *Ah, those adolescent years — Ha!* During the solar solstice, the sun crosses the Earth's equator. In many nations, annual seasons are determined by solstices. Solstices result in a change of day and night lengths. The summer solstice is in the longest day of the year, resulting in the most amount of daylight time. Solstices start summer.

> *Today, like every other day, we wake up empty*
> *and frightened. Don't open the door to the study*
> *and begin reading. Take down a musical instrument.*
> *Let the beauty we love be what we do.*
> *There are hundreds of ways to kneel and kiss the ground.*
>
> —**Rumi,** "A Great Wagon"

Nothing, however, is new under the sun, *including the journey children will take, loosening the bond to their parents, at least temporarily*. Christian is becoming his own distinct Trini-creation unto himself, his own man — I don't think I mentioned this earlier, but he has a cosmic sign that is nearly the opposite of my own, born nearly seven months after my own. I was born January fourth and his date of birth is July eighth. I am an earth sign, whereas he is a water sign. I am a Capricorn and he is a Cancer. So there's a precise space of seven months and four days. There has been in this season of our lives a lot of push and pull, a lot of breaking of old energies and bonds and then coming together again in new ways. It has been ferocious, mercurial, transcendental, moody and ascendant. He's given me all I can handle, nearly breaking me on more than a few occasions, as I know I did unintentionally with Daddy.

My name, Patrick Anthony Howell, literally translated means "Eminent Nobleman, the Priceless One," and as I shared with you earlier, Christian Wagari Howell Wagari means "Eminent Follower of Christ in Whom God is Great… *twice*." I wanted to call him "Christian Alexander" but Daddy wanted to know, *"Why"?*

"Because I like the alliteration."

"What does his mother think?"

"I think she'll go with whatever I suggest. We compromised on the first name — I wanted to call him Xavier Alexander so I could play with Xavier — "X-man," "Prof. X."

He has no idea what I am talking about. "Then make it *African* instead."

We doubled his Obaba's last name, which, if you understand the etymology of the Ethiopian Amharic nomenclature, last names are really first names — real F.O.B. (fresh off the boat) foreigner stuff. So, his mother and I doubled the last name *Wagari* as his middle and maiden name: God is great, *twice.*

The moon looms large over this day, even as the sun is out in full glorious bloom and there's a palpable joy everywhere — it is as if the sky, sun and all of us rainbow and star children are animated with incandescent bulbs of magic lights. The day *feels* like honey dripping from the sun. It's fragrant and sweet, in a land-of-milk-and-honey way. For those of us who are awake, we see the atmospheric sparkles everywhere like little incandescent bodies of emotive fireflies. People greet one another with effortless smiles and pleasant salutations. The grays of winter that were muddied and soiled in Spring are obliterated into flowers and new green leaves unfurled in the summer season. Spectrum lights are interwoven into the fabric of reality everywhere and the flowers and fruits are sweeter, lovelier and more beautiful: Mango and pineapple are just the sun made flesh, watermelon dragon fruit and pomegranate juices are its rays captured in fleshy meat. Passion fruits have begun to bloom on the trellises of the backyard; it's official — the new age sung of by genre bands like Depeche Mode, Radiohead, Coldplay and Imagine Dragons has officially dawned. *Welcome to the New Age. We are all radioactive.* I squint my eyes in the sun rays, and look beyond the horizon to see my own reflection in the sparkling body of the Pacific Ocean. There is no limit to what we will accomplish. There are no limits to our prosperity and abundance. My eyes are completely opened. I can do anything I set my mind to, *because, well,* I have.

Adolescence and Christian have become strong like a full strawberry moon rising, quiet and with its own galactic cosmic pull. He is nearly seventeen and is now a practitioner of the philosophies of Marcus Aurelius' stoicism. Stoics believe that practicing virtue will karmically achieve *eudaimonia*, a well-lived life.

He no longer embodies child-like innocence, unbound in euphoria and joy. A darkening mood has come to settle over his being, balancing out his inner child with the man he will be in the full — he takes a lot of time to himself. Interestingly, I am aging backwards, becoming increasingly youthful and optimistic as I mature — I have mastered my resilience. I am more powerful in my own spirit than I have ever been. I've learned to temper my fearless ambition with its equivalency in quiet patience. I realize that a permanent peace begins to enter into my space — it's the same great spirit that passed through me at Daddy's passing. It is expansive and immense and I am only at the beginning of the maturation and final evolution of my spirit. I'm strong enough in my hind quadriceps and bulging calves to take the valleys and climbs slowly, and to enjoy pasturing as I advance, putting one foot in front of the other and repeating the process.

Cancers are mercurially attuned to the energies in a room. Christian is highly sensitive to the energy in his environment as well as extremely self-protective, like a crab in its shell. Just like his spirit animal, he is shielded by a hard external shell. He's well respected by teammates, classmates, teachers and coaches — most taking the time to share enthusiastically with his powerful quiet affirmative approving energy. They all look up to his towering frame: Since the baby's check-ups at doctor's visit, he's been within the ninetieth percentile of his peer group in size. He answers with quiet smiles and a stoic knowing spirit.

We've begun to complement one another in temperament, ethos and spiritual gravities. In many regards, he is becoming my polar opposite. I find there is a familiar supreme confidence balanced by an equally motivated insecurity that all young men have as they are about to embark upon their own life journeys. It reminds me of a morning we shared when he was just eighteen months old at the townhouse in Quail Meadow on Sand Canyon — Shady Canyon, where he was born in Irvine. The sun was rising and we were enjoying quiet moments of cooing and listening and talking — talking soul to soul. I watched him lift his beautiful head awkwardly from the bed and I realized, he doesn't realize he has either hands or feet; or what he can do with them.

His Ethiopian nanny would take him in the stroller around the neighborhood and I would sneak home from the bank to shadow and spy — I watched him take his first steps at the park in the Irvine Company complex he was born and grew up in. They were strong, and he was built like a Sherman Tank back then. Now he is svelte, lithe, and beautiful. He will fly on this planet, just as our ancestors did in the times before these ones, leaving wonders of the world behind to mark their travels in Olmec Civilizations, ancient Mesopotamians, The Minoans of ancient Crete, the Indus Valley Civilization, the Spanish Moors and the Shang Dynasty of Ancient China.

And the great task before me now is to let go. *You did your work, papi.* Go easy. Just let it flow. Completely let it all go. *He's good.*

He destroys me in basketball, swimming and running regularly. Jesus Christ, he's ruthless! You might even say he is *righteous*:

"Behold, I send you forth as sheep in the midst of wolves.
Be ye therefore wise as serpents and harmless as doves."

Of course, I swear I'll get in five-star sexy shape and show him about the power of his DNA — I'll pull my own George Foreman. The only problem is he's no Michael Moorer — but I'm also happy for him. *Kind of.* I recognize I've been pugilistically competing with him since before he was half my height and that my defeat by his hands was a coming of age I had prophesied and thereby forecast nearly two decades before. I tried to give him what Michael Jordan had growing up in North Carolina with two brothers James Jr., known as "Ronnie," and Larry, who gave him so much competition it would torch the entire NBA and world.

SharkHeart finds life, energy, peace and power in the artifice of competitive fires and revelatory oceans that we built together. He loves to ball out on the basketball courts at North Alga and Calavera Parks, playing the low post with a ferocity I remember Patrick Ewing, Alonzo Mourning, Dkembe Mtumbo and all the Georgetown Hoyas playing; he loves running with the stampede of other youth that will include an NBA draftee or two in years to come. He's an ocean swimmer who can go for five miles in the Pacific and run back on the shorelines without resting. In fact, the run and the swim are a rest from the mendacity of life for SharkHeart.

He's taller than me at six foot five and growing. Last time I went to the doctors, I found I had shrunk to six foot one and a half. Ha!!! He's sleeping and eating regularly so I know he'll squeeze another few inches out of it. His aesthetic in music has rounded out from smooth jazz to bone-crushing hip-hop wizardry and the film soundtracks of Ludwig Göransson and Hans Zimmer. I'm alarmed when I hear him iPod-learning from Denzel Curry, Mac Miller, Kendrick Lamar and the rapper JID. But what did I expect when he grew up listening to my Tupac, Eminem, Ice Cube, Snoop Dogg, Busta and Kanye? Ha!!!

My biggest job now is just letting go. I remember being his age and not being able to wait — *like I was getting out of a federal penitentiary.* Seventeen years of mind-numbing indoctrination by Dr. Howell. My job now is to trust and have faith; to believe and know. He's had seventeen years of mind-numbing indoctrination by Mr. Howell. *I didn't mean it that way though; I just wanted to give as good as I got, baby.*

He's smarter than me and is a crisper analytical and strategic thinker than I was at his age. I'm like the sun and he's like the moon — we contrast, pull and push against, contrast and define based upon the polarities of our powerful natures. Between our energy of down-to-earth practicality and tender emotion, we have the potential to balance each other out beautifully.

His is a force stronger than nature, fierce with an unbound love for existence — all those years of spiritual strengthening for the battles to come. No force of nature can parallel my will to self-motivate. And his mother? Well, she's the season. Or sometimes season is correlated with reason.

We are learning and embracing our differences — we are growing in respect, understanding and loyalty. Killer Whale and SharkHeart are growing a lasting bond that will withstand any challenge.

He's coming into his own. Christian is a noble soul imbued with strength, honor and integrity.

Come to the orchard in Spring.
There is light and wine, and sweethearts
in the pomegranate flowers.
If you do not come, these do not matter.
If you do come, these do not matter.

—**Rumi,** "A Great Wagon"

Chris is driving now. I used to have this trick and I would use my knees and legs to steer the wheel. I've been doing it for decades and it's actually second nature to me by now. I remember sitting in the back seat of Daddy's sky-blue Monte

Carlo with his hand on the wheel, and I couldn't wait to get behind the wheel myself.

I would massage my temples like I was moving the car through telekinesis. You know how Professor X does it when he's using his telepathy powers? Christian was a baby sitting in a car seat in the back. I wanted him to think, literally, *you can do anything you set your mind to.*

One day little man asked me, "Daddy, is it hard to drive with your knees?"

"It just takes some practice, baby" I answered. I never assumed he was stupid. Anyhow, I've seen him trying to master the wheel with his legs and knees. And now? It's all about the prayer hands going up.

I know many of you will want to know how his story ends, but this is the end of my role as his author — he recently started narrating his own story with editorials in the community paper. His first piece is "America's Obsession with Rap Music" and the second, "Wind Power," advocates for a sister-brother relationship with Denmark and our hometown of Carlsbad on offshore wind turbines. Oh, and he's begun production on his own passion film project, *A Good Christian,* a short film that will debut at international film festivals.

He publishes under the pen name Christian Wagari, and, *well*, you know what that means.

The Ideology of Racism, Sign of These Times and the Spirit FORCE

In December 1992, a writer, news editor, and founding member of the University of California's newspaper Diatribe observed that it is obvious that the American government gave more importance to the pursuit and winning of the Cold War than to the eradication of racial conflict in American society. Thus, a mere 42 years after announcing her intention "win the Cold War," the United States crushed Soviet communism. However, after having stated, more than 200 years ago, that all men are created equal" and are entitled to "life and the pursuit of happiness," racism is still a predominant problem in this United States. Why, he queries, does the power structure continue to focus its attention on problems abroad rather than its own backyard? The reason, he said, "should be apparent"
—**Dr. Bing P. Howell,** *The Ideology of Racism*

Now I would say that the more things change, the more they stay the same just as the '80s marked the end of the Soviet Union, Ronald Reagan, Mikhail Gorbachev and the fate and realignment of the Eastern European World, the fall of the Berlin Wall, the pendulum has swung wide, and what doesn't rhyme repeats itself as the old adage has so presciently surmised. These days? It is the self-fulfilling incessant chatter about the end of the American democracy, Donald Trump, Vladimir Putin and the fate and realignment of the Western

European World. No, this has everything to do with the *arc of the universe* envisioned by Martin Luther King in his cosmic "I Have a Dream" speech.

The quote at the top of this chapter was the first time my words ever appeared in print on a national platform with the publication of my father's brilliant treatise on race in America from Simon and Schuster. In 1999, Daddy dedicated his opus *The Ideology of Racism – Let's Talk: From Slavery, to Plessy, to Affirmative Action, to Racial Healing*: "*For my children, your children, and their future.*"

The first page of the prologue to *The Ideology of Racism* continues: "Thus, to understand the history of the United States, one has to understand the institution of slavery and its social dimension and continued impact." Daddy wrote *The Ideology of Racism* in 1998, just as the millennium was about to turn into the twenty-first century. He presciently, or perhaps obviously, surmised:

> *"Racism has developed into an ideology of American culture, one that passes unrecognized and undetected from generation to generation, purposefully severed from its origin: slavery."*

> *"The ideology of racism has disproportionately affected African Americans because of the stigma of the dehumanizing institution of plantation slavery. This racism has trickled down like a contagious virus to other minority groups and is now consuming the nation."*

After Daddy transitioned, I spoke with Dr. Clayborne Carson, a professor emeritus of history at Stanford University and director of the Martin Luther King, Jr., Research and Education Institute. Since 1985, Dr. Carson had directed the Martin Luther King Papers Project, a long-term project to edit and publish the papers of Martin Luther King Jr. He was also the co-founder, along with Daddy, of the pioneering Alternative to Western Civilization Program piloted at Stanford in the early '80s.

While I was still at Jesuit High School, sometimes I would drive with Daddy to Palo Alto on either Tuesdays or Thursdays when he had his lecture and office hours. I would watch his classes, as they had in previous years at Cosumnes River College, shoot up to standing ovations. Daddy was an exceptional orator, and if you ever catch me not so present in mind, so I can catch a spirit or two, I can give you a soulful rendition of Dr. Howell thundering from the land of our ancestors. We would go through his keynotes and students' papers and I would offer him a comment or two. Dr. Carson wanted me to know that Dr. William John Bennett, Secretary of Education under Ronald Reagan, took great exception to his and Daddy's pioneering work on critical race theory.

In 1988, there was a well-documented back and forth with Secretary Bennett castigating Stanford for the school's decision to diversify requirements for the freshman "Western Civilization" course. The online e-zine *The Cafe* reads:

> *In 1986, Stanford Black Student Union leader Amanda Kemp launched a national campaign to get Reverend Jesse Jackson—then preparing for a presidential run—to visit Stanford in support of broadening the Western Civilization syllabus. On January 16th, 1987, Martin Luther King Day, Jackson marched alongside 500 students on the pastoral Palo Alto campus. "Hey hey, ho ho, Western culture's got to go," some of the students chanted. Jackson did not join the chorus, but his proximity to the marchers' strong words catapulted the controversy into the national arena.*

Pat Buchanan, White House Director of Communications, said proudly of Bennett's style, *"This is the politics of the future."* We now know the future of which he spoke concisely, where books such as those by Zora Neal Hurston, Toni Morrison and Anne Frank are being banned in elementary schools across the nation. I truly hope and pray this book — *Getting Deals Done* — makes that banned list. Because we are *still* gonna get those deals done — we are still getting to the end post, *that promised land.* So, that's probably where all those heavenly books will be. And if you should happen to find *Getting Deals Done* has been banned? Please email me at globalmarketIQ@gmail.com. ***Ha!*** Just like those Parental Advisory stickers they affix to the gangster rap albums, *it's a badge of honor and the mark of conscientious protest during the middling of these times.* As the publisher of this book, Repeater Books, has stated, "*we are alive and do not agree.*"

Daddy was a *spiritual* warrior at the onset of the culture wars, which were dubbed the Reagan Era Culture Wars, which were the seeds for the MAGA devolution and the ongoing Civil War being fought on cultural and spiritual planes. "*Daddy*" — Dr. Bing Patrick Howell — was and is a spiritual general or griot directly responsible for not only those movements from the spirit realm, but these words and the entirety of this book — the spirit of radioactive fire and celestial brimstone being lobbed at the enemies of humanity. *And you know exactly what I mean.* ***HA!***

I remember when Daddy wrote his treatise on race and America and *healing.* I was still working in New York City, living in Brooklyn, taking the A train to the World Trade Center Towers from the F train in Brooklyn. I shared the vision you read in part 1, *My Father's Face in June.* I thought he would, at least, understand the effect his being and spirit has on mine.

Instead, he said, "Patrick, I know you are a great writer. *What I want to know is when will you get your work published?*"

So — *now, Daddy. My work will be published now Spirit. Sorry I didn't finish it while you were here* — but I guess that's the way deals work sometimes.

Heaven — Filled with free spirits,
Jerusalem's gates opened.
Sunny shook we all.

Dr. Howell intended for *The Ideology of Racism* to be short, small and concise, almost a treatise of his thoughts, lectures and considerable discernment on race, politics, the spirit, the future and healing. I'd imagine he was thinking of something like Herman Hesse's *Sidhartha,* James Baldwin's *The Fire Next Time,* Martin Luther King's "Letter from Birmingham Jail" or the inverse functionality of Niccolo Machiavelli's *The Prince.* The central organizing theme of ideology is that of healing, and how do we arrive at consensus? It is the summation of a life lived valiantly, passionately, boldly and with extraordinary highlights though with just as many of our spiritual battles fought in the shadows, at times threatened with obscurity.

How do we come together and rise as one after the inexplicable atrocities that birthed what we all call the United States of America? *How can we perfect our union?* How do we reconcile the utter hypocrisy of a nation birthed on the ideas of justice, freedom and the pursuit of happiness when those ideas and those qualities did not apply to whole generations of some of the greatest Americans; when it did not apply to those entire populations who built America's wealth, prosperity and fortune? When that nation continues its abject hypocrisy in the modern age talking about the murderers, rapists and insane coming over the borders when the murderers, rapists and insane people are the ones who now govern those original inhabitants' lands. Or, as Latin recording artist Bad Bunny noted during the 2026 Super Bowl LX halftime show, "Seguimos aquí" *And that's a fact.*

Well, having engaged in the warlord endeavors of a bone-crushing industry of finance, as well as the peaceful deal-making of American capitalism and business at large, I can tell you that there's no peace to be had in war other than the extinguishing of life and its spirit. *There is only hell.* There is no peace greater than the peace that exists between our ears and in our collective soul. Let God and the universe deal with the extinguishing of evil spirits. *Although,* every now and then I am tempted to give some very strategic and tactical assistance — particularly when those energies come around me and those whom I love.

> *The problem of racism will not be solved by ignoring the fact. Rather, it will be solved when the U.S. acknowledges its wrongs and begins to talk about race in a sincere and substantive forum.*
>
> —**Dr. Bing P. Howell,** *The Ideology of Racism*

> *Put bluntly, the nation will ultimately arrive at the bizarre point whereby it becomes so completely dehumanized and desensitized that the offender becomes the offended, and the hunter becomes the hunted. Today the nation of descendants of slaveholders are themselves the victims of senseless incivility and inhumanity.*
>
> —**Dr. Bing P. Howell,** *The Ideology of Racism*

One of the truly treasured memories I have of Daddy is riding shotgun *(yes, pun intended)* with him in some of those early years in Sacramento. The first car I remember of his was that sky-blue Monte Carlo — he was actually old school in his love of American cars. I still remember the feeling of immense rage that would populate my heart when he was pulled over by police and harassed. *I didn't even know what it was I was feeling at the time but I felt it.* I also remember when we would pull over and watch others who were pulled over by the police — to stand *vigilant* and provide a witness to a Black soul being harassed and potentially terminated by the system.

More often than not, Daddy would listen to cassette tapes of his favorite Caribbean calypsonians — Lord Kitchecher, The Explainer, Lord Baron, The Mighty Sparrow and Crazy, who he went to high school with. But sometimes he would ask us what we were listening to and I'd share one of my all-time favorite artists, *Prince*.

In the '80s, Prince blew up the entire infrastructure of what could and could not happen in art and on planet Earth with *Sign of the Times*, arguably the greatest album of all time. Nearly fifty years after its original release I listen to that album with the same awe and creative fervor as I did the first time. Music aficionados compare it to the Beatles' *Sgt. Pepper's Lonely Hearts Club Band* and it's often recognized as a counterpoint to Quincy Jones and Michael Jakcson's chart topping *Thriller*.

One day Daddy asked me to pop in what I was listening to on my Walkman, and I played the title song to Prince's opus: "Sign of the Times."

It's silly, no?
When a rocket ship explodes and everybody still wants to fly
But some say a man ain't happy unless a man truly dies
Oh why?
Time

Time
Baby, make a speech, Star Wars fly
Neighbors just shine it on
But if a night falls and a bomb falls
Will anybody see the dawn?

The syncopated pattern of the rhythm has nothing to do with anything in that frame of music, which was often driven by pop melodies, keyboards and full band sets. It's funky. *It's krunk.* Coy. Cocky and humble. It's smart without being preachy: *man ain't happy unless a man truly dies.* That song dealt with a lot of the anxieties of the day — Reaganism, the Cold War, the culture wars, the War on Drugs and tied it up in a neat little funky ode with heart and soul and purple Prince paisley panache. And it could be an anthem for our current moment — "Sign of the Times" *is timeless*. Anxieties play around Israel/Palestine, the War in Ukraine, the first criminally convicted felon-president, climate change, the rise of authoritarianism, age old demons, the emergence of artificial intelligence as a defining planetary force and all of the uncertainties pregnant in our current zeitgeist.

"Patrick, play that for me again." Daddy asked, curious, and we would listen on repeat all the way home. We live in those times, and this book and its sweet reminiscences, balanced observations and militant diatribes are a sign of these times. *Getting Deals Done* is *my* sign of these times.

It took Germany fifty years to apologize to the Jews for the Nazi atrocities committed against them. In a show of their remorse for the wrongs committed, Germany made a monetary compensation of $60 billion. It took America approximately the same time to apologize to the Japanese for sending them to concentration camps, and consequently compensation from the American government *to Japanese Americans who suffered through the odyssey was forthcoming. It's been two and a half centuries and America still seems unable to apologize to African Americans for the atrocities perpetrated against their ancestors and the racism vested upon them as a people. Why? Isn't it time? And what should consequently follow? Some monetary or material compensation is most certainly justified.*

—**Dr. Bing P. Howell**, The Ideology of Racism

Daddy's kids all see him so differently, and we all enjoyed a different relationship with him spiritually and relationally. I've often used his relationship to us to contemplate all the different religions — Christianity, Islam, Judaism, Buddhism, Hinduism, Taoism, New Ageism — and our different relationships to the Spirit Force. Daddy is, as he would surmise about himself, a honeycomb enigma wrapped in a riddle for which there is no solution other than your Spirit and its discernment. *Accept the mysteries as well as the known.*

My brothers, sisters and I
Are like the eight fingers on our father's hand —
When we flex
His blood flows,
Spirit dreams realize and His Power in this world
Manifests,
For we are everything he made.

Between all of these faiths and practitioners is *the Spirit Force* that travels and exists between, providing a relational basis of humanity. Similar to the Holy Spirit in the Christian faith, the Spirit Force travels amongst all of the Love energies. When he was working on publishing

The Ideology of Racism in 1997, I was living in New York City, working at RR Donnelley Financial at 75 Park Place. Charles Baker, a brilliant African American headhunter was a referral I had won working as an administrative assistant for the COO of the Wells Fargo Bank, who fell under the employ of Dennis J. Mooradian, the CEO. Charles took me to lunch at Bryant Park, which, as I noted earlier, would become another full circle with my mentor and rich dad, Gary E. Bryant.

"You're going to write about me, aren't you?" Daddy asked. I never really thought about it. But I guess I was going to — "Father's Face in June" was a piece of narrative poetry about his spirit and how the spirit travels outside of constants of time and space to manifest divine will.

"Yeah. I guess I will." I said nonchalantly when he was teaching at Roger Williams University and we were at his office. I told him he was already on Google. He was shocked to find information about himself there and he asked me in his litigious mode, "Who put that there? And who runs Google, Patrick?" *Ha!* I ignored the latter question with the easy answer of Eric Schmidt. He would have gone after Google and its CEO, *and won* a multi-million-dollar settlement for invasion of privacy and violation of a constitutional amendment or two.

"*It's okay, baby. I understand.*" he ended up conceding. I'm not sure about that now — whether he understood me, the rebellious and often decidedly independently minded eldest son of Dr. Bing P. Howell. Or if he understood that he, a Shakespearean character in the flesh, and a rejoinder to my spirit, was too rich a subject, so taboo, it would be an unforgivable crime of literary and humanitarian dimensions to pass up. *Cheers!*

> *We are involved in something "BIG" that's happening — the shift to an entirely new economy… a new age… and a vastly different approach is needed. If we are going to survive, attitudes must change.*
>
> *We can no longer hide behind the rationalizations that were used to justify slavery and the entrenched racism and discrimination found in the very "soul" of our American environment, debasing us all, and we, as a nation, will not survive if we continue to practice it.*
>
> —**Dr. Bing P. Howell,** *The Ideology of Racism*

The global economy has evolved from industrial to information to now digital and the age of artificial intelligence — race and racism are being codified within programming and machine learning, but you know what — that's *fine.* Nazi Germany Third Reich salutes are given at US presidential elections! Cambridge University and Kenyan Nairobi leader Wavinya Makai has expertly extended Daddy's concept in her creative non-fiction treatise *Capital Violence: The Economic War on African Dignity*. For centuries we have suffered from the exploits capital extraction.

We — both our tribes as well as greater humanity — however, are experts at spiritual IQ and as I said, in the end, ***Love wins.*** So, we practice our love and become part of something much bigger than ourselves, practitioners of a mastermind Spiritual IQ. Compared to what our ancestors endured? *This is the cake;* and as rich as the cake is, as sweet, wholesome and *yummy as it is? It's not quite as yummy as Patti Labelle's Good Life Peach Cobbler.* Ha! We are all part of something much larger than ourselves. We are all part of the body of a *Global I Am.*

The United States of America is the ultimate global initiation and the ultimate test of all the nations coming together in a singular identity to move collectively together *as a human race.* Sure, President Woodrow Wilson initiated the United Nations for peacekeeping initiatives (more diplomacy and politicking by me). But America is a place where every nation has roots within its rich and diverse tapestry and history. *Can we do it? Will we come together to become our best? The best.* America should be the shining city on top of the hill, but these days seems a place of deplorable raging idiots who refuse to reconcile their past… as well as the positioning of spiritual excellence for peace, abundance and joy at the nexus of the culture and *our* capital.

Near the end of *The Ideology of Racism* is the chapter "How to Promote Racial Healing: A National Therapeutic Solution," divided into seven sections: "Acknowledgement vs. Denial," "Knowledge vs. Ignorance," "Allowing vs. Controlling," "Understanding vs. Insensitivity," "Listening vs. Sounding Off," "Openness vs. Intolerance" and "Respect vs. Incivility." The epilogue to the solution plaguing our nation ends in a quote from Thomas Jefferson from 1780 to 1781 from his *Notes on the State of Virginia,* that the Institution of slavery is "*this blot in our country*":

> *Indeed, I tremble for my country when I reflect that God is just; that his justice cannot sleep forever; that considering numbers, nature and natural means only, a revolution of the wheel of fortune, an exchange of situation, is among possible events; that it may become probable by supernatural interference! The Almighty has no attribute which can take sides with us in such a context.*

Personal Didactic Dissonant Dado Daddy Disclaimer:

Now, I'm sorry if I've portrayed myself as noble, ethereal and majestic. And yes, my people are that. And so am I. So this is a humble entreaty.

And I do pray I am that to my son, Christian — noble, ethereal and majestic, as my father was before me. Greater than any acknowledgment or Nobel Prize for Literature, Academy Award, National Book Award, Golden Globe or Pulitzer, that's the greatest height I could aspire to. I am also an incredibly complex soul who — if my branches reach out to the heavens — has roots that reach deep down into hell and the mud, as do many of us who inhabit this earthly realm.

I've thought of Daddy as a spirit giant and I remember him thinking about his father that way too. I come from tribes of spiritual giants, the descendants of several tribes including the Carib and the Arawak. We were agriculturalists who farmed cassava, sugar and sweet potatoes along with yautia. Our traditional Igbo and Yoruba cultures are also there, emphasizing community, family and respect for elders, incorporating polytheistic beliefs, agrarian practices and art forms; casting bronze plaques, sculptures, ivory carvings and royal regalia. We would later become blue-collar laborers who packed our labor with the ambitions of our ancestors and carried forward the trust in our progeny, just as our parents before us did.

Now, we are me.

Tens of millions of my indigenous people were systemically terrorized and murdered between 1492 and 1530 by the brutal Spanish, British and French oligarchs; that systematic terrorization and brutality continued by the royal families of Britain and France, so-called royals in the modern era. The Africans arriving in the West Indies came from the area comprising today's Senegal, Gambia, Guinea-Bissau and Mali — cousins, relatives and ex-compatriots of our kingdoms and empires; as well as west-central Africa, including Angola, Congo, the DRC and

Gabon. The spirit of those barbaric systems as well as our kingdoms carry through to the present.

Through the Transatlantic Middle Passage between 1517 and 1776 (so-called Declaration of Independence) to 1865 our tribesmen and women were laid low. From 1619 to 2019, we endured not only the Transatlantic Middle Passage but Jim Crow, Racism and Discrimination. We have been rebuilding in our current era of growth, prosperity, peace and joy in the twenty-first century.

It is true that when people have seen me with my son, they often see a father who dotes limitless attention and affections. Well, I know who we are. I talk about him in keynotes, business stories and anecdotal tales to other people one-on-one, and they are always intrigued by him. They hear the quality of my love and admiration, as you probably have, oozing from my spirit and voice. My love for him and pride in him are qualities that are truly great about me.

Considering the bigger picture of your life can change your path to action. This "ancestry in motion" — immersing and aligning yourself within the story of your ancestors — can be powerful in helping you create new emotions in tough seasons of your life, or elevate and find clarity when success is accomplished. Ancestry in motion is a living breathing line through the generations and the valleys and peaks from one to the next.

So many have felt that they met my son through me. Or commented that they wish they could meet him through me. Christian is greater than I have ever been or will ever be, and he's the only man I'd ever say that to and authentically lovingly say what I mean and mean what I say.

Remember, I am a proud American too.

Ancestry is a priceless asset, a foundation upon which we all stand. Each member of the Spirit Force is both heir and architect, vessels of the past while carriers of a future. Whether that future advances the next generations or not? Well, that is up to you. True vision, preparation and influence over a generation begins long before birth, as the actions of ancestors ripple through the continuum and through the lives of their progeny.

My recent forays and travels into my own ancestry have led me to the distinct possibility of Sir Ellis Clarke being kin. Sir Ellis Emmanuel Innocent Clarke was the first president of Trinidad and Tobago and the second and last Governor-General. He was one of the architects of Trinidad and Tobago's 1962 Independence constitution. If so? I'll keep up with the studies and tests, but somehow, I have a sense, like a little bird, and that is Ancestry in Motion. High station or laid low, we have always worked along the arc toward Justice, Freedom and Prosperity. If he is not? Even if my ancestors are from humble stations like my beloved Uncle Leroy, an electrician in NYC. The search is the exercise. Connecting is the reward.

Ancestry in Motion is our living compendium of inherited wisdom, identity, and purpose coursing through the generations like high voltage. Ancestry in Motion is not just central to the African but our spiritual systems as a humankind. We are shaped by the electric minds and radioactive spirits and brilliant visions of those who came before us, seeing with their eyes and knowing with their intellect, charged with the current of their beings on our own. Our solar beings are a derivative of their dreams and love; resetting the cast and breaking the wheels of their precarious holds on us in the present — their knowledge base is not just history or a jurisdiction of mores, customs and habits passed through DNA — it is an active spiritual force within us, guiding our choices and shaping our futures. This collective of our beings, a repository aligned with ancestral energies, makes up the spirit and body of the Spirit Force.

Well!

Ha!

All of this book is to say: Christian, baby, I love you. Continue to rise spirit… and fly. You are unequivocally the greatest "deal" your mother and I have ever accomplished, and we have gotten some pretty good ones done. Raising you as a son has been priceless — the transaction and adventure of our lives.

Your coming to this side of reality was another harbinger of my own manhood. Overall it's been a joy, but there have also been challenges to being the best man I can be so I can continue to communicate with you with my very life — just as my Daddy does with his brilliant example.

NOW, let's see what you've got! What will you stand for in your time? How will you and your generation move the needle? Yes! Ha!!! Forget that needle and ***launch*** *your greatest ambitions into the stratosphere.*

Always know that your greatest currencies, Peace and Joy, will cement helping others be their best into a real asset. King, develop your spiritual practices and pray for your Mom, Dad and the planet; develop your intimate relationship with the Spirit Force. To Thyself Be True King.

Thank you, son. Bless you, King.

— Daddy

We live in an era where America's moral authority in a global world order is significantly diminished; where "AI God" is touted rather than the power of what is right, the power of good and the power of Love. In the New World Translation of the Bible, Exodus 3:14, God told Moses to tell His people, his chosen ones, "I Will Become What I Choose to Become" when asked by Moses the name of who sent him. At this juncture in our history, shouldn't we all choose to become Love?

Isn't that the only thing that is permanent in this universe? Love Almighty?

Yes it is. This is who we are. We are Love.

Afterword: Our Superpowers for Good

By Devin Thorpe

As I reflect on the profound journey captured in *Getting Deals Done*, I am reminded of the powerful interplay between leadership, integrity and the ever-evolving landscape of capital markets. Patrick A. Howell's narrative is not just a personal memoir but a testament to the transformative power of holistic entrepreneurship and the role of regulated investment crowdfunding in fostering social good.

Patrick's life story is one of resilience, vision and unwavering commitment to integrity. He exemplifies the essence of true leadership — a leadership that transcends corporate boardrooms and extends into the very fabric of our communities. Through his work in capital formation, economic development and investment crowdfunding, particularly in supporting social entrepreneurs, diverse founders and community builders, Patrick has created a legacy of inspiration.

Over the years, I've had the privilege of collaborating with Patrick on SuperCrowd22, SuperCrowd23 and SuperCrowd24. These events have provided platforms for thought leaders, changemakers and innovators to converge, share their visions, and drive meaningful change.

The Power of Crowdfunding

Crowdfunding has been instrumental in democratizing access to capital, empowering startups and fostering social entrepreneurship. Patrick's advocacy for this financing model has emphasized its potential to be a powerful force for positive change. Crowdfunding not only provides essential funding but also creates a sense of community and shared purpose among investors and entrepreneurs alike.

In a world where ethical considerations are often overshadowed by the pursuit of profit, Patrick's example is a reminder of the importance of maintaining principles. His unwavering commitment to doing what is right — even when it's difficult — has inspired countless individuals in entrepreneurial communities. Crowdfunding, particularly, has the power to revolutionize how businesses raise capital, transforming millions of social media users into budding venture capitalists and allowing valuable ideas to come to life.

Today, the global crowdfunding market is valued at USD 19.86 billion, and it's projected to reach a staggering USD 500 billion. The market exhibits a compound annual growth rate (CAGR) of 16.1% during the forecast period from 2024 to 2032. This growth underscores the immense potential of crowdfunding to finance businesses and foster social impact.

Leadership and Integrity in Action

Patrick's leadership in capital market formation is more than just financial acumen; it's a visionary approach that is grounded in responsibility and a commitment to social good. His journey demonstrates how leadership can drive systemic change, creating environments where capital becomes not just a means to an end, but a catalyst for social impact. His work underscores the importance of democratizing access to resources and ensuring that entrepreneurs from diverse backgrounds have the opportunities they deserve.

Integrity, as Patrick exemplifies, is more than just honesty — it's about aligning actions with core values. His story serves as a powerful reminder that integrity can be the driving force behind both personal and professional success. Patrick encourages us to remain true to our principles, fostering trust and respect in everything we do.

A Call to Action

The challenges of our time — economic inequality, social injustice and environmental degradation — demand innovative solutions and bold leadership. Patrick's journey offers a blueprint for leveraging capital markets and crowdfunding to address these issues, contributing to a more sustainable and equitable world. His vision for a more inclusive economy isn't just aspirational; it's achievable. By championing integrity, leadership and social impact, we can create lasting change.

Getting Deals Done is more than a book; it's a call to action. It challenges us to rethink entrepreneurship, prioritize integrity and harness the power of capital markets for social good. Patrick's work embodies a vision of expanding the United States' economic fortunes in a way that moves beyond Diversity, Equity and Inclusion and brings us closer to the America of our dreams — an America of full potential.

As we move forward, let us carry these lessons with us, striving to create a world where every deal contributes to a more just society. Let us be inspired by Patrick A. Howell's example and commit to doing our part in *Getting Deals Done* for the greatest possible good.

Devin Thorpe, CEO and Founder,
The Super Crowd, Inc.

Appendix: **Superachievers, Apex-Capitalists, and Uber Capitalism**

"All of that art-for-art's-sake stuff is BS. What are these people talking about? Are you really telling me that Shakespeare and Aeschylus weren't writing about kings? All good art is political! There is none that isn't. And the ones that try hard not to be political are political by saying, 'We love the status quo.' We've just dirtied the word 'politics,' made it sound like it's unpatriotic or something."
—**Toni Morrison,** on Art and the Artist

On United Emirates business class to Dubai on our way from Ethiopia. We stayed at the Desalegn Hotel on Cape Verde Avenue in Addis Ababa and immediately I recognized the history of this street and its significance in my own journey. Ethiopia is the world headquarters for the African Union that was founded by Kwame Nkumera and Emperor Haile Selassie — these are our Founding Fathers.

The so-called "Golden Age" and its implications for African Americans is complicated and multi-layered. Just as my assessments of the Ronald Reagan era in which I grew up to its bookend in the Donald J. Trump presidency are nuanced, so is this "Golden Age." Historically, African Americans have always faced *insurmountable* if not brutally barbaric systemic barriers, but despite these, *our tribe… our* "community," *blessed and chosen*, has continuously transcended adversity to achieve *remarkable* successes across industries.

That idea, essentially *ujima*, a Swahili word meaning "collective work and responsibility," the third principle of Kwanzaa, emphasizes community collaboration and shared responsibility for the well-being of the collective in African traditions. This practice speaks directly to the resilience, creative brilliance and collective drive within the African American community, a direct descendent of the former and greatest of African and mankind's *original* kingdoms, from Benin to Songhai. Every generation has been presented with these seemingly insurmountable challenges, yet each one has not only survived *but found ways to thrive*, transforming *unimaginable* pain and scars into power, beauty and massive forward movement against some pretty harrowing ongoing circumstances *(another gross understatement of the young millennium)*.

We have created throughout our generations kingdoms of wealth and prosperity, over and over *and over* again. Again, *nothing is new under the sun.*

Our massive spirits of righteous aggression, resilience and generational hunger *drive* African American success and are palpable today, solar and radioactive, particularly in spaces where African Americans — *spiritual innovators* — are forging new paths in business, finance, media, technology, sports, politics and entertainment. Our creative business and entrepreneurial force is being harnessed around the world. *We are hungry.*

We are force multipliers *by our very being* — one well-placed African American, Caribbean or African at an executive level of leadership can ensure leadership, creativity, discipline, strength, verve and moxie, perseverance and resilience that will diffuse through the company's corporate culture, pro-forma and balance sheets. Think Frederick Douglass. Or, how about Thomas Jefferson's Sally Hemmings? What about Kofi Annan? My ancestor — George Westerman? What about any of the "nameless" heroes of our countless battles over the centuries — the ones we only know about in our closed circles, families or communities? Or, how about Oprah Winfrey and Stedman, the contemporary reincarnation of Madam CJ Walker and their school in South Africa? Or, how about our Founding Mothers — Harriet Tubman or Sojourner Truth? Janice Bryant Howroyd, Mellody Hobson, Sheila Johnson or Rihanna? Was George Washington Carver an agriculturalist, inventor or economist? How about Booker T. Washington and W.E.B. Du Bois: political scientists, philosophers, civil rights activists or economic architects? How about "The Black Ethiopian," Benjamin Banniker, designer of the so-called *White* House and the District of Columbia? Or, what about the West African kingdom builders? How about Jesse Jackson and his spiritual prodigy the Rev. Al Sharpton — cultural and social advocates, *spiritual bank* CEOs or religious leaders of the gospel of prosperity? And yeah, how about those *generations* of Black architects, carpenters, metal workers, wood workers, engineers and astronomers who built the District of Columbia? Who built the United States of America? *Oh, you thought those were slaves?* ***Ha!!!***

Two to ten of us inside of a deal? *That ensures generational brilliance.* How about Ariel Investments, run by founder, chairman and co-CEO John W. Rogers, Jr. with $13.8

billion assets under management (AUM)? Or *Shark Tank*'s Daymond John's FUBU, which has grossed more than $6 billion worldwide? Think Barack Obama, Eric Holder, Susan Rice, Michelle Obama and Valerie Jarret, and the true absolute contribution of Obama's administration to global economics. Or, how about the LA Lakers from Wilt to LeBron, *lol — seriously*. How about LeBron's Springhill Entertainment with Maverick Carter, Devon Johnson and counsel Endi Piper? Why do you think we have all been glued to the NBA versus NFL for decades? Better just to bounce a ball than take a knee and be outcast; then multiply each one of those harbingers by the 1.5 billion of us that are the body of the *Spirit Force.*

If one considers the continuity, sheer power and regenerative growth of the African American population and what it has been able to accomplish *from slavery to the US Presidency,* from 1619 to today? From the lowest of slaves to the most exceptional of "kings and queens" (or, presidents, community leaders and prime ministers). From less than human — 3/5ths of a person (1857 Dred Scott Supreme Court decision) to $2 trillion in consumer spending power. It becomes apparent that the USA's elixir is *us* — infinitely resourceful humans, resilient spirits and creative geniuses who harvest spiritual assets into material ones for whole communities, generations and the zeitgeist of global culture — just like it has been *since the beginning of our first civilizations.* I saw a statistic about Michael Jordan that showed how 12% of the US GDP in the '90s — NBA, Gatorade, Air Jordan — was created from his Black sweat. It's never been different *with any of us* — Jordan is universally admired for his excellence, but the components of that excellence are Black sweat, Black confidence, Black pride, Black excellence and that Black ambition!

It becomes apparent that our ventures are pregnant with the limitless potential that we have infused in all of our kingdoms and empires. *KKK America's Trump moment?* A very real and sobering reflection of America as well as a certain inflection point in America's history and people, as well as global markets and economies born through four centuries of social, economic and demonic engineering. From George Washington to Trump, *alpha to omega*, right? *Perhaps.* But what is certain? *We are in another moment of prosperity, resilience and abundance.* End of the world? No Democracy? No freedom? Tyranny and cruelty? Spiritual degradation? *Perfect.* Let's move forward.

We have been doing this — creating the *Wealth of Nations* — since well *before* even Atlas shrugged; since the *literal* beginning of time. *Self-interest* is the seed to Greed, ego, war, hostile takeovers, monopolies, MAGA, junk bonds, stagflation, recessions, oligarchies, Depressions, spiritual poverty, no-income/no-verification loans, systemic disease, imbalanced humans and chaos. And those demons give birth to rage, material poverty, laziness, excess, discontent, violence, cruelty, depression, anxiety and every industry — war, disease, scarcity of food and death — that profits from the conditions induced by living in the very surreal reality of the United States of America. *Collective well-being,* otherwise known as *Harmony and Peace* — not self-interest — creates prosperity. *We know* — that's how *we* have gotten to where we are. Adam Smith, the intellectual father of capitalism, is *dead* wrong.

Black Ambition

"True leadership is not about power or wealth; it is about lifting others, fostering unity, and leaving a legacy that inspires generations."

— **Emperor Mansa Musa**,
the wealthiest man in world history

Whether it's through basketball icons and American originals like *LeBron James*, slugger George Springer, Kevin Durant, Steph Curry, Venus and Serena Williams, Tiger Woods, Marhsall Lynch, Patrick Mahomes, Richard Sherman, Colin Kaepernick or the Ball Brothers, whose capitalist *and community* achievements have made them not only athletic legends or elite business moguls, but a very special class of community activists who have embraced and targeted excellence in athletics as well as communities and finances as the manner by which to raise our collective frequency. King LeBron caught his predecessors — our winning Magic Johnson and *His Airness* Michael Jordan — at their post-career endeavors — billionaire *community* leaders — long before ever hanging up the laces.

And by the way, *the competition* has always been at the service of reaching our collective zenith. That's what *Love of the Game* is all about. Other than by the hook or the crook? We'll also dribble and make that shot. *Swwwwwwwwwwwwwwwwwwwwiiiiish!* I mean, *splaaaaaaaash!*

"The question is whether you have a proper, a solid, and a sound blueprint. And I want to suggest some of the things that should be in your life's blueprint."

—**Martin Luther King,** "What is Your Life's Blueprint?"

All of King LeBron James' boyhood friends are either multi-millionaire or billionaire community leaders with their own endeavors in SpringHill Entertainment, Klutch Sports Group, I Promise and Fashion House Cleveland (to name a few of the more prominent). His community in Cleveland finally enjoys the financial and cultural injection of a national championship for their collective self-esteem and future economic growth in the Midwest. NBA and global basketball fans have been inspired to their highest purpose by our incredible golden journey man — *The Chosen One,* The King. And yes, the metaphor of his name is an abbreviation of Martin Luther King's — to the point, succinct and *totally in the black.*

The children of King James' "I Promise" elementary and junior high school have their college educations paid for as long as they meet the minimum GPA requirement; within the first year of the school's program, these children went from the lowest 25% of test scores within Akron Public schools to a remarkable improvement, with 90% exceeding individual growth goals in reading and math, outpacing peers in the district. The wife of LeBron's youth is — rather than a home-maker — *an empire architect,* responsible for raising three beautiful, self-assured children who will blossom into inheritors of James' legacy. That's why he is *King* James — *not* because of his basketball prowess, which will stand singularly when he finally hangs them up. I do believe the *true* GOAT Ali would concur. At the apex of their careers, their service was on *behalf of our communities.* That is playing the game of life the right way.

Then there are industry titans like *Master P, Snoop Dogg,* Beyonce, P-Diddy, *Ice Cube, Eminem, 50 Cent, Jay-Z, Kendrick Lamar* and *Dr. Dre*, who have leveraged their creativity into empire-building *and restoration. African Americans are exemplifying apex-capitalist Uber Capitalism success.* This success isn't simply about individual gains — it's rooted in the *community*, authenticity, and giving back, not unlike the reformed Germany that was the leader of the free world when Trump took over in 2016. These individuals are creating blueprints for hundreds of millions to follow, ensuring that our tribes thrive *together. Just like the blueprints left for us by Malcolm and Martin have created generations of so-called "influencers"* — we are harbingers of the New Age, begging to burst our current reality and to be born in stunning reality. Honestly, by the eye test, does this seem like *just* 14% of the US population or a community of exceptional exemplars?

And there are the less celebritized pioneers for emulation — Christopher Williams, Byron Allen, Melody Hobson, Janice Bryant Howroyd, David Stewart, Sheila Johnson, Robert Smith, Alexander Karp or Tope Awotona — who have their fingerprints on the blueprints of American as well as global capital formation. Can we all be billionaires and millionaires? *Trillionaires? How about beautiful amazing humans?* We are the direct progenitors of W.E.B. Du Bois and Booker T. Washington, Marcus Garvey and Madam C. J. Walker, Malcolm X and Martin Luther King, Jesse Jackson and Al Sharpton: We are *already* the wealthiest insofar as the metaphysics of spiritually are concerned, and we will continue to make the conversion to prosperity for a *collective* humanity. By the way, I believe W.E.B. Du Bois' central thesis of *The Talented Tenth* ought to be updated. His metaphysical *The Souls of Black Folk* was conjured in 1903, nearly 125 years ago. We *are* the dreams of our founding fathers and mothers.

And we *are* the *Blessed 100.*

Harnessing Tribulation into Collective Prosperity, Peace, and Security

In terms of networking, African Americans have a unique ability to leverage relationships — *and tribulation* — into a successful engagement in one-on-one interaction as well as in large transactions. We are endowed by the Spirit Force with centuries of brutally unimaginable circumstances and our resilience — in many cases a product of an immense Faith and through the institutions of our Black churches.

For many, this goes beyond business and touches on a deeper spiritual connection that empowers relational equity. It's about *truly* understanding people, loving life and/or people, being authentic as well as audacious in seeking out connections, and using those relationships as steppingstones to new possibilities. Those possibilities are sacred areas of energy and power — like bees in the spring that connect the plant world, daily harnessing pollen into a sweet library of combs filled with honey. You might call it *resourcefulness* — but it is a little more than that. The bee connects the world of plants and the best they have to offer, their sweet pollen, *to our world. These curious and brilliant creatures harness the sun.*

Melanated African Americans and our tribes around the globe connect the sweet marrow of the spirit world to this system — and we do it seemingly effortlessly financially every day in every transaction or we do it hip hopping, sprinting, jumping, jiving, moon walking, tomahawk dunking and rapping. But we also do it teaching, accounting, financing, laboring, accounting, calculating, creating, managing, leaning *forward and multiplying.* As with our ancestors in the kingdom of Benin, we are also capable of creating a worldwide community of millionaires and billionaires who are also incredible *ethical* humans. We are well on our way as we have *consistently* for the past four centuries.

This quality of *spiritual resilience* — sourced from fertile an unbound optimism and profoundly spirituality nature — has allowed African Americans to thrive in entrepreneurial ventures, especially in a country like the United States of America, where consumerism, racism and discrimination… and Slavery are not only rampant but coded, institutionalized, commodified and marketed chain by whips and click by clicks, millennium after millennium. *We have evolved* — and it is time to evolve from Spiritual Gangsterism to our mastermind collective form of *Spiritual IQ and its corresponding Prosperity and equivalency in Abundance.*

America is a place where hyper-consumerism, an acute elixir of economics and culture, reigns supreme; where people are encouraged to express themselves through what they buy, what they watch, and what they endorse. This system is a tough one—it's not designed for the very young, the very old, *or the meek. It is not designed for the principled or peaceful.* To survive in such an environment requires a near pathological *dog-eat-dog* grit (as well as a nearly *psychotic* competitive mindset) and African Americans, through centuries of experience, have honed this resilience, making it a core element of our entrepreneurial and cultural identity.

Podcast discussions like the one from the *Native Land Podcast* titled *What Do Tulsa, Evanston, and Fearless Fund Have in Common?* or Jabari Young's Forbe's BLK's These Are The Business Titans That Made The First Forbes BLK 50 List shed light on the successes, structural challenges and opportunities faced by African Americans as they continued the battles and struggles passed on by ancestors, creatively endeavoring with enterprising dreams in modern America. As it stands, the African American community continues to push forward, making a clear case that not only can they compete in America's *Golden Age of capitalism*, but they will continue to *lead* it — from the front, from behind, from under, from within and throughout. *The African American economy is the most powerful emerging growth economy on planet Earth.* This energy, momentum and focus on collective growth hold the promise of a future where African American prosperity is not the exception but a global normative.

Here are some definitions in the evolving international landscape:

Apex-Capitalist

The *apex-capitalist* refers to a master entrepreneur of the African American, Caribbean and African business communities who creates, occupies, innovates the highest levels of economic and corporate power. These individuals, often C-level executives, exceptional entrepreneurs and board members, are characterized by their ability to influence markets, drive significant financial growth and shape industry standards. This class is distinguished by their advanced education, elite mentorship, leadership in Fortune 500 companies, or the establishment of high-revenue ventures.

Apex-capitalists are pivotal in transforming not only their own industries but also contributing to the broader global community by promoting a sense of togetherness, shared prosperity (otherwise known as "community"), equity, diversity and wealth creation. Their role is critical in challenging historical economic barriers and paving the way for future generations of *American* leaders in business and governance.

Inversely, "apex-capitalist" can also refer to a powerful individual or group whose wealth accumulation, influence and control over markets and governments mirrors the behavior of the Gilded Age's robber barons. Like those wealthy industrialists, apex-capitalists use exploitative and questionable business practices to concentrate vast amounts of power and capital into the hands of a select few. This includes monopolistic practices, suppressing competition, exploiting labor and manipulating regulations to benefit themselves while stifling broader economic growth or fairness. Apex-capitalists, in this sense, embody a form of oligarchic dominance where financial elites dictate economic policy, often to the detriment of the larger population. Perhaps a better moniker for this sort of crass capitalist is *apex-beasts*?

This concept has been revitalized in the modern era, particularly through the rise of tech giants and billionaires who attended events such as presidential inaugurations, symbolizing the close ties between capital, systems and governance and the new tech or "AI God," as white supremacist technologist racist Elon Musk calls it! At these events — really rituals of arcane practices — the salute to Adolph Hitler and the white power first are pumped with pride, malice, violence and a disturbing lack of protest by the majority. *Sheer wickedness in stunning twenty-first-century color.*

Donald Trump's reference to a "Golden Age" at his inauguration can be interpreted — coming from him — as a huckster's cynical romanticized vision of unchecked parasitic capitalism. What does that mean? It means we inhabit a reality where individual rights and human freedoms are subordinate to selfish *self*-interest or, aggregately, the interests of the wealthiest or "most powerful" few. These apex-capitalists often resemble modern-day so-called oligarchs (in fact, closer to Richard Prior's Herman Smith, the anxious unhappy little man operating the Wiz), creating a distorted form of governance as well as culture and reality where their pursuit of extreme wealth overrides democratic principles, leading to a system that marginalizes the majority and causes severe injury to humanity and peace. In this environment, fascist tendencies can emerge as power becomes concentrated in the hands of a few, and the rights and voices of individuals or marginalized groups are increasingly silenced.

Superachievers

We are legion. The *Superachiever* represents a class of not only African American but pan-Africanist (Afrofuturists, pan-Africanists, Caribbeans, Africans et. al.) individuals who reach the pinnacle of success through exceptional leadership, education and influence across various sectors. Money, finance and investments may or may not be important to Superachievers — but what's important is excellence, prosperity and an egalitarian accomplishment and peace in endeavors.

The "Superachiever" term encapsulates those who have risen above systemic challenges to establish themselves as leaders in business, healing, biological and agricultural, technological, entertainment, academic and civic engagement. These individuals are not only successful in their careers but are also influential in shaping cultural narratives and creating pathways for future generations, metaphysically harnessing frequencies. By the way, many of us also enjoy designations as white, Asian, latino, Arab… hyphenated multi-nationals.

Superachievers may possess advanced degrees (particularly from the University of Hard Knocks), with many coming from elite educational backgrounds, whether Ivy League or HBCU or aforenoted Hard K.U. But many, such as influential icon and Superachiever Rachel Cargle, completely shun formal education, instead founding their own movements as "The Great Unlearn." The Great Unlearn is the name of both a podcast and concept emphasizing the importance of questioning and unlearning ingrained beliefs, ideas and behaviors to find a more authentic and fulfilling way of being.

Nearly 30% of African Americans aged 25-29 have obtained at least a bachelor's degree, reflecting the increasing academic achievement within the community. They hold key positions in Fortune 500 companies, serve on boards, and lead entrepreneurial ventures that significantly guide, contribute and enhance the $1.6 trillion spending power of African American consumers.

Beyond financial success, Superachievers are dedicated to community uplift, often engaging in mentorship, philanthropy and advocacy. We play critical roles in promoting diversity and inclusion within corporate structures and use their influence to drive social change. Our achievements inspire and motivate, serving as beacons of possibility and success for the African American community while also setting new standards for excellence and leadership across all industries.

This is our way — ever since our *first* civilizations.

Uber Capitalism

Uber Capitalism refers to a super-enhanced form of free-market capitalism that emphasizes paranormal economic growth, free enterprising innovation and wealth creation, paralleling the economic boom and prosperity often idealized by proponents of Donald J. Trump's "Golden Age" and MAGAnomics.

"Uber Capitalism" envisions a future where deregulation, lower taxes and robust private enterprise drive unprecedented levels of financial success for individuals and businesses. In contrast with the current administration's MAGA blueprint in Project 2025, *Uber Capitalism* focuses on interlacing and accelerating business-friendly policies with creating opportunities for wealth generation across all sectors and demographics. Uber Capitalism imagines *truly* the greatest economic prosperity for *all*, a concept aligned with Governor Arnold Schwarzenegger's or Robert Reich's ideas of free-market capitalism.

Nomenclature like "uber," Reich, Schwarzenegger, "super" and "apex" all has decidedly Germanic and English roots, further signifying that our movement towards our highest collective good includes *all* frequencies of the rainbow, including white. In color theory, just beyond Michael Jackson and Paul McCartney's "Ebony and Ivory," white and black are often considered opposites. In this case, black represents the presence of all colors and white represents the translucence of light or high-frequency color, whereas each presence accentuates the other. The only color we don't mess with? *Orange*, Ha!!!

For African Americans, *Uber Capitalism* represents a positive shift toward economic empowerment and inclusion within the broader wealth-creation framework initially drafted by Marcus Garvey, oftentimes considered a prophet and the father of the Rastafari Movement. By leveraging entrepreneurial spirit, Harmony, Faith, Hope, light, access to capital and emerging markets, African American business leaders, professionals and investors can harness this system to close wealth gaps and establish themselves as key players in the national and global economies. The African American business class, including C-level executives, board members and Superachievers, is central to shaping this vision of *Uber Capitalism* by fostering innovation, building generational wealth, expanding opportunities within their communities and raising the tide of humanity.

Uber Capitalism also incorporates African ideas and practices, but not at the exclusion of other cultures unless diametrically opposed — such as Neo Nazism, symbolized by the new global Nazi white supremacist alliance of Trump-Putin-Musk(Vance). Sankofa, for example, from the Ghanaian Akan means, *"go back and go get it"* and if transcendental meditation requires the practice of "*being present*" or the Tao practice of "*mindful breathing,*" the action of the moment takes precedence. Continuity, gestalt and Balance are all important cornerstones of Uber Capitalism.

This future portends African Americans thriving as owners, investors and innovators in key industries such as technology, finance, real estate and entertainment, ultimately creating a stronger, more inclusive economic foundation for future generations. *Uber Capitalism* for African Americans focuses on removing barriers, ensuring fair access to economic opportunities and encouraging participation in a thriving capitalist system, where entrepreneurial success drives collective uplift and shared prosperity, irrespective of ideology, race or sex.

Man, am I proud to be a twenty-first-century holistic entrepreneur! Just minding my own business, *getting deals done — Ha!!!*

Global Emerging Markets with the Greatest Upside Potential

The International Monetary Fund (IMF) identifies key African nations such as Nigeria, Ghana, Rwanda and South Africa as emerging growth economies, bolstered by expanding industries in natural resources, technology and infrastructure development. These nations are also benefiting from increased investment by global powers, including Russia, China and the United States, which are all vying for influence and access to Africa's vast markets and resources. China, in particular, has been a major player in Africa through its "Belt and Road Initiative," funding infrastructure projects in exchange for trade and strategic partnerships. The United States, meanwhile, focuses on partnerships promoting democracy and trade, as seen through initiatives like Prosper Africa. Similarly, non-profits and world organizations have recognized Africa's potential, supporting sustainable development, education and entrepreneurship programs to harness the continent's vast human capital.

In the Caribbean, islands such as Barbados, Jamaica and the Bahamas are emerging as significant players due to once-in-a-generation powerful leadership and revenue drivers in sectors like tourism, financial services, energy (Guyana) and renewable energy. These islands are increasingly becoming attractive for foreign direct investment (FDI) from Fortune 500 and Fortune 100 companies, as well as venture capital from global firms. With tax incentives and business-friendly environments, many companies are setting up bases in the region to tap into its strategic location between North and South America. The Caribbean and Africa are at the heart of a global shift towards emerging growth markets, with global corporations and investment funds capitalizing on their untapped potential. These regions are crucial for diversifying portfolios and exploring new frontiers in economic development.

For the past decade, we have been getting our house… *our tribes* in order and really, it's not broadcast on CNN, MSNBC, *The Washington Post* or *The New York Times* with the same fervor and zealotry as the first-world Banana-Republic exploits of Donald Trump and a Republican party beyond all rationale, stuck in its seedy terrorist past of white supremacy, white so-called superiority and all of the damage their spiritual sickness has done to *all lives* and souls on the planet… *for centuries.*

Our tribes know that we come from a legacy of kings, kingdoms and palaces and the ancestors are pushing us to return to those centers of commerce, trade and finance as we speak. Look around planet Earth and you will find that the International Monetary Fund has designated Colombia, Guyana, South Africa and Rwanda among the top emerging growth economies globally. *Visual Capitalist* has designated the following countries as the world's fastest growing economies in 2024: Guyana, Niger, Senegal, Libya, Rwanda, Côte d-Ivoire, Burkina Faso and Benin.

From the outside in, CARICOM (the Caribbean equivalency of the European Union or the global United Nations) has designed policy and organized the Caribbean region via a range of functional institutions with critical mandates including education executed through the University of the West Indies and the Caribbean Examinations Council; the Caribbean Agricultural Development Institute (CARDI); health via the Caribbean Public Health Agency (CARPHA); disaster preparedness and response via the Caribbean Disaster and Emergency Agency (CDEMA); security through the Caricom

Implementation Agency for Crime and Security (IMPACS); and many more that are overlooked until a crisis hits and their niche area of expertise is catapulted to the forefront.

Now, from the inside out, hip-hop *planned, blocked and strategized* a generation into its own army of aspirational entrepreneurs and super megaton bomb intellectuals, movers and shakers. The same tribes that made the Transatlantic trip from Africa to the Americas are the same ones that now have become a new breed of Superachievers in the Caribbean and America... across the diaspora. Hip-hop, it turns out, is our constitution and CARICOM our organization, marshaling the wills and destiny of a struggle, a people and a legacy. It is the new *esprit de corps* of our people, humankind and our ancestors coursing through this world in a different form... *again*.

REPEATER BOOKS

is dedicated to the creation of a new reality. The landscape of twenty-first-century arts and letters is faded and inert, riven by fashionable cynicism, egotistical self-reference and a nostalgia for the recent past. Repeater intends to add its voice to those movements that wish to enter history and assert control over its currents, gathering together scattered and isolated voices with those who have already called for an escape from Capitalist Realism. Our desire is to publish in every sphere and genre, combining vigorous dissent and a pragmatic willingness to succeed where messianic abstraction and quiescent co-option have stalled: abstention is not an option: we are alive and we don't agree.